CONFLICT IN CENTRAL AMERICA

CONFLICT IN CENTRAL AMERICA

Approaches to Peace and Security

EDITED BY
JACK CHILD

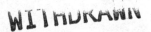

Published for the International Peace Academy by
ST. MARTIN'S PRESS, NEW YORK

Library of Congress Cataloging-in-Publication Data

Main entry under title:

Conflict in Latin America.

   Includes index.
   1. Central America--Politics and government--
1979-   --Addresses, essays, lectures. 2. Central
America--Foreign relations--1979-   --Addresses,
essays, lectures. 3. Revolutions--Central America--
History--20th century--Addresses, essays, lectures.
4. Peace--Addresses, essays, lectures. I. Child, Jack.
F1439.5.C65 1986   327.1'7'09728   85-27916
ISBN 0-312-16230-8

FOREWORD AND ACKNOWLEDGEMENTS

This book represents the culmination of two years of effort by the International Peace Academy and a substantial number of collaborators, to address the major issues of conflict, peace and security in Central America.

In the period between May 1983 and February 1985 the International Peace Academy held a series of four off-the-record workshops to discuss these issues: at Bridgetown, Barbados, in May 1983; at Cancún, Mexico, in October 1983; at Ixtapa, Mexico, in March 1984; and in Panama City, Panama, in February 1985. These four workshops brought together an extraordinary group of well over 100 academics, government officials, international organisation representatives, businessmen, private individuals and other interested parties concerned with the explosive situation in this critical region. Over thirty countries were represented; these included all the regional states, many of the Hemisphere nations, and a number of European countries.

The general purpose of the workshops was to bring together this distinguished group in an informal atmosphere which would permit a free-wheeling exchange of ideas in a non-attribution environment. Although some of the participants felt obliged to state their national positions on certain matters, little time was spent on formal posturing, and the workshops quickly turned to an active, frank and spirited discussion of key issues. The format for the workshops included prepared papers (distributed ahead of the meetings) which provided the starting point for the discussions; these papers also form the core of this volume. The appointed rapporteur prepared (and the Academy has published) reports on the workshops, but these do not attribute specific comments to any individual. The workshops also produced brief press releases and (in the case of the last two) a series of recommendations which were made public.

Specific agenda items included:
— the roots and nature of the Central American conflict environment;
— the Contadora process as the principal peace initiative;
— the role of the superpowers in the crisis and its resolution;
— the contribution that development efforts can make toward peaceful resolution of conflicts in the area;
— the contribution that conflict resolution techniques developed in other situations could make to Central America. These included considerations of peacekeeping, peace-observing, peacemaking, confidence-building measures, and the role of technology in this process;
— the mechanics of defusing the 'detonators' (i.e. those critical

situations which might spark a wider conflict).

This book brings together the results of these two years of effort.

The Academy's two-year project was a unique attempt to blend ideas and experiences in conflict resolution gained in other areas of the world with the specific needs of the region as presented by the opinions and experiences of experts on the area (to include a good number of representatives from the countries themselves). This attempt at blending outside experiences with indigenous knowledge is evidence of the deep concern felt by outside observers over Central American developments; it also symbolises the respect that these outside observers have for the Central Americans and their immediate neighbours themselves, and the fact that ultimately it will be up to them to find a uniquely Latin American way out of the crisis.

Acknowledgements

This book, and the workshops which provided the ideas and papers that fill its pages, would not have been possible without the enthusiastic support of the numerous participants in the process, and I would like to acknowledge the special contribution of the academics and officials who prepared the papers which formed the basis for the ensuing discussions. Among them were the three co-directors of the workshops, Dr Richard Millett, Licenciada Helen McEachrane, and Dr Jack Child (who also served as rapporteur, and editor of the four workshop reports and of this book).

Although many individuals contributed generously of their time and efforts to make this project possible, I would be remiss if I did not mention the special roles of Carl L. Ince and Richard P. Brown at the Barbados workshop; of Licenciado Pedro Joaquín Coldwell, Governor of the State of Quintana Roo, at the Cancún workshop; of Licenciado Alejandro C. Delgado, Governor of the State of Guerrero, and Licenciado Manuel Barros Nock at the Ixtapa workshop; and of Panamanian National Assemblyman Dr Guillermo Cochez at the Panama workshop.

The members of the IPA staff were, of course, intimately involved in the details of the workshops and the reports. I should like to acknowledge the splendid efforts of IPA vice president Peter C. Harvey, of Anne Denvir, Richard D. McDonnell, Lauranne Pazhoor, and Bosco Nedelcovic, as well as IPA interns Jessica Byron and Patricia Millett.

New York,   INDAR JIT RIKHYE
November 1985   *Major General (ret.)*
                              President, International Peace Academy

CONTENTS

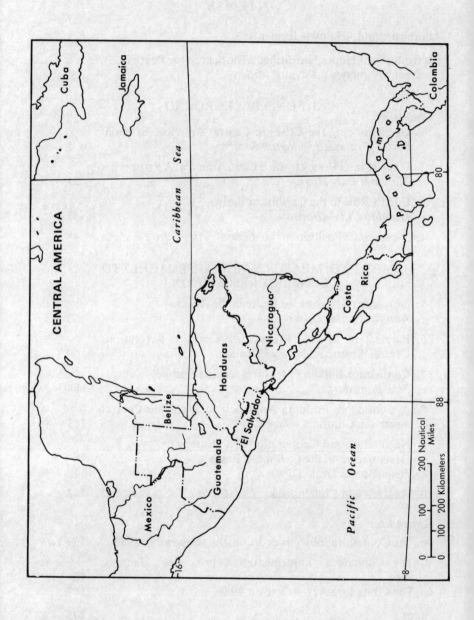

CENTRAL AMERICA

Cuba

Jamaica

Caribbean Sea

Colombia

Panama

Mexico

Belize

Guatemala

Honduras

El Salvador

Nicaragua

Costa Rica

Pacific Ocean

| 0 | 100 | 200 Nautical Miles |
| 0 | 100 | 200 Kilometers |

INTRODUCTION

HOPES UNFULFILLED: THE SEARCH FOR PEACE IN CENTRAL AMERICA

Richard Millett

In Central America and the Caribbean, 1984 and early 1985 were times of both unfulfilled hopes and unrealised fears, with only limited visible change. Hence the region continues to face most of·the same problems that prevailed then. In presenting a brief summary of the events of this period, this chapter will not approach developments from a chronological perspective, simply listing events in the order of their occurrence, nor will it endeavour to cover all the major developments in this time-frame. Instead an attempt will be made to examine possible trends, to look for areas where progress towards peace may be made, to locate major obstacles to such progress, and to suggest tentatively some areas which might provide profitable material.

It could be argued that during 1984–5 what occurred in Central America was less important than what did *not* occur. At least five of these non-events are worth noting. First, despite frequent alarms, there was no invasion of Nicaragua, nor was there any introduction of foreign combat units into El Salvador. Also, no advanced combat aircraft were introduced into the region. These two non-events contributed directly to the third: there was no international conflict, no regional war, no spread of existing civil conflicts.

The final two non-events relate to the search for peace. Despite serious problems and tensions, there was no collapse of the Contadora* process, no failure of the central process in the effort to restore peace to Central America. At the same time, however, there was no agreement on a formal treaty, no clear progress toward ending regional conflict. Paradoxically, 1984–5 brought Contadora closer both to success and to collapse, with a clearly heightened probability that events in the succeeding few months would be decisive in determining in which of these directions the process would ultimately go.

There were, of course, some events in the region which influenced the search for peace and stability in an important way. The most important of these dealt with internal political developments within the region, or in nations deeply involved in the regional situation.

---

* The countries making up the Contadora Group are Mexico, Venezuela, Colombia and Panama. Contadora is the island in Panama where the Group came into being in January 1983.

There were national elections in El Salvador, Panama, Nicaragua and the United States. The first two elections produced new leadership, while the others confirmed existing leaders in power. There was also a Constituent Assembly election in Guatemala designed to be the first step in restoring civilian government there.

A final factor to be noted is the change in the leadership of the Honduran military. Most observers believe that this change has both reduced tensions within Honduras and improved the prospects for an ultimate accord between Honduras and Nicaragua, although the extent of the improvement in each area is still a subject of considerable debate.

Another major characteristic of 1984–5 was how often hopes were raised but not fullfilled. One example, of course, was the continued failure to reach an accord through the Contadora process. In addition, there were at least five other areas apart from Contadora where hopeful beginnings failed, at least for the time being, to produce concrete progress. The first of these was the contact between the government of President José Napoleón Duarte and the leadership of El Salvador's armed opposition represented by the FDR and FMLN. The first meeting at La Palma raised hopes that a negotiated solution to that country's civil conflict might be possible, although few doubted that the process would be long and difficult. But the second meeting of the two sides served apparently only to widen the distance separating them, and plans for further meetings have so far failed to materialise.

Three of the areas where results were generally disappointing involved Nicaragua. The most publicised of these was the series of joint meetings between the United States and Nicaragua, arranged with Mexican assistance in the city of Manzanillo. Although representatives of the two countries met several times, little concrete progress was made, and in January 1985 the United States suspended the meeting. While the official US position was that this suspension was not necessarily permanent, there was little reason to expect that similar bilateral talks would be resumed in the near future.

The other two areas of unfulfilled promise involved meetings between the Nicaraguan government and domestic opposition groups. The first of these was the effort at a national dialogue following the November 1984 elections. This broke up quickly when those participating were unable to agree on an agenda for their discussions. The other area involves discussions between the Nicaraguan government and the leader of one faction of the Miskito, Sumu and Rama (Misurasata) Indians in armed opposition to the Nicaraguan government. That leader, Brooklyn Rivera, travelled to Managua for talks with the leadership of the FSLN, then visited several Indian communities. Talks appeared to be making some progress, but then Rivera was wounded in an attack and broke off further talks, refusing to attend a proposed meeting in Colombia. Prospects for future negotiations of this type are clouded, but contacts have been maintained and both sides continue to express hope for an ultimate agreement. Deep divisions among the Miskito's leadership are an additional complicating factor.

The final event which might be labelled as an unfulfilled hope or possibility was the proposal of the Costa Rican government to make permanent neutrality a part of that country's Constitution. This project met considerable domestic opposition and has been withdrawn for the time being from consideration by the Costa Rican Congress.

Along with the unfulfilled hopes and high tensions of this period there were also some potentially encouraging developments. On at least two occasions the countries of Central America, despite the deep divisions between them, demonstrated a capacity to work together. The first was at the joint meeting of Central American and European foreign ministers held in September 1984 in Costa Rica, and the other, less publicised but perhaps more significant, was the signing in January 1985 of a new Central American Tariffs and Customs Agreements. Negotiations on this agreement began in 1975, but languished until 1984. El Salvador, Costa Rica, Guatemala and Nicaragua signed the agreement, which helps to preserve the possibility of a reactivation of Central America's Common Market, and increases incentives for regional trade. The fact that it was possible to reach this agreement (which Honduras has not yet signed) shows that cooperation in some areas remains not only desirable but possible, and that negotiations long deadlocked can ultimately be resolved when the political will is present.

There have also been some encouraging signs in international relations. Despite the frustrations of the actual negotiations, the meetings between the government of El Salvador and its armed opposition and between the government of Nicaragua and Brooklyn Rivera established the principle that such meetings are possible and produced added pressures for peace. In Guatemala the decision of the Social Democratic Party (PSD) to resume public activities, with some of its leaders returning from exile, must indicate at least the possibility of a broadening of the political spectrum which could lead to a political solution of the conflicts there.

Despite the problems which the Contadora process had encountered, world support for this effort continues to be strong. The countries of the European Economic Community gave it their full endorsement during their meeting at San José with the Central

American foreign ministers. It has been supported by both the United Nations and the Organization of American States. The United States Congress, in House Concurrent Resolution 261 of the 98th Congress, declared that it 'strongly supports the initiatives taken by the Contadora Nations and the resulting Document of Objectives and Principles for Implementation', and added that 'the United States should support the effort to translate the agreed Principles into practical and concrete arrangements.' The Socialist bloc, including Cuba, has also expressed its support. Thus Contadora has received as broad a measure of international support as has ever been expressed for an international peace-making effort.

Finally, it should be noted that in one of the Contadora countries there was notable progress in 1985 in an effort to arrive at a peaceful solution to civil conflict. In Colombia, the government reached an agreement on halting hostilities with the major insurgent groups and began reincorporating the guerrillas into the national political process. While many problems remain to be resolved, this progress towards ending a civil conflict in Latin America through negotiation has provided a hopeful example for Central America.

Although there were some encouraging signs in 1984–5, very serious problems must still be overcome before significant progress can be made in resolving regional conflicts. Levels of confidence between the countries of the region are often low, and communications are hampered by the high levels of emotional rhetoric and accusations which frequently characterise public statements. Serious problems of this type exist between Honduras and both El Salvador and Nicaragua, but at the time of writing this problem is probably most serious in relations between Nicaragua and Costa Rica. The dispute in 1985 between those two countries over Nicaragua's alleged violation of the right of diplomatic asylum graphically illustrates the tensions and sensitivity in this area. The case involved a Nicaraguan citizen who sought refuge in the Costa Rican embassy in Managua but was later arrested by the Nicaraguan authorities, tried, and convicted of desertion for refusing to accept compulsory military service. Costa Rica refused to attend Contadora meetings until the case was resolved, a position which forced the cancellation of a meeting of the Central American and Contadora foreign ministers scheduled for February 1985. The Contadora countries, the OAS and even West Germany all attempted or offered to help resolve the situation, but with little success. Meanwhile, the issue became involved in Costa Ríca's domestic political debate, leading to further complications. Continued stalemate on this point could have doomed the Contadora process. Even the ultimate resolution of this crisis did not provide renewed momentum towards regional peace because the tension and rhetoric it had produced both exemplified and further exacerbated the prevailing climate of fear and suspicion between the two countries concerned.

The number of countries and organisations that became involved in the efforts to resolve the dispute between Costa Rica and Nicaragua illustrates another important development in Central America. There has been a proliferation of dialogues outside the Contadora framework. While generally positive in and of themselves, these efforts do have a potentially negative aspect. The meetings at Las Palmas and Manzanillo, the proposal for Papal mediation (rejected by the Vatican), the unilateral proposals for peace advanced by the Nicaraguan opposition and the Reagan administration in the United States, and various other international or domestic efforts to deal with the ongoing crisis may be useful, and even necessary, but they carry with them the danger of fragmenting the peace effort and of communicating the impression that hopes for the success of Contadora are diminishing.

Costa Rica, El Salvador and Honduras have all raised specific objections to some aspects of the Contadora Group's draft of a regional peace act. Some of the objections involve the timing of the implementation of the act's provisions, others concern issues of verification. Apparently some progress has been made in dealing with these objections, but problems remain, especially in the area of verification. Nicaragua has resisted efforts to alter the existing document, and the possibility of a deadlock remains.

In a discussion of the Contadora process, several issues raised during 1984–5 must receive attention. There is the danger that failure to achieve significant progress in the near future will cause the process to lose credibility and lead to a proliferation of other efforts outside Contadora. Indeed it may be necessary to consider whether the Contadora process has a time-limit. It may also be useful to consider what is implied by the problems which efforts at internal dialogue in Nicaragua and El Salvador have encountered, and the reasons why the bilateral meetings between the United States and Nicaragua were suspended. Can and should the international community attempt to reanimate these efforts? What steps might be taken in these areas, and how would such actions effect the Contadora process? What are the implications for the region if no further progress is made? All these questions demand serious attention.

The Colombian peace process may offer some lessons which can be applied to Central America, and therefore some attention to developments in Colombia could prove valuable: special attention might be given to the obstacles which arose during the negotiations between the Colombian government and the insurgents and how these obstacles were overcome. Obviously, the Colombian experience can also provide examples of the process of confidence-building.

Finally there is the question of what further steps would follow the signing of a Contadora agreement. The signing of an agreement would constitute major progress in restoring peace to the area, but it would by no means be the end of the process. What problems would remain unresolved? What role can the international community play in ensuring that progress towards peace continues after a Contadora agreement has been signed?

The record of 1984–5 provides, at the same time, reasons for hope and excuses for despair in the search for peace and stability in Central America. The object of this book is to seek ways to tilt the balance somewhat more in the direction of hope.

October 1985

PART ONE

BACKGROUND

1

UNDERSTANDING THE CRISIS IN CENTRAL AMERICA

Francisco Villagrán Kramer

Since the downfall in 1979 of what was commonly known as the 'Somoza dynasty' and the collapse of the Nicaraguan National Guard, Central America has been in turmoil and facing what seems to be a recycling crisis. The triumph of the Frente Sandinista de Liberación Nacional not only introduced a new socialist-oriented ideological element in the region, but was soon followed by armed insurrection in El Salvador and Guatemala, although the internal processes that led to that insurrection were already taking shape, as in Nicaragua, in the early 1970s. Since 1982 the new Nicaraguan government has also faced insurrection, this time in the form of a counter-revolution by forces based in its border zones with Honduras and Costa Rica. Two different factions of Nicaraguan insurgents — the 'Contras', identified by President Reagan as 'freedom fighters' for the purpose of gaining public support, and the Alianza Revolucionaria Democrática (ARDE) led by Edén Pastora (Comandante Cero) — have brought about internal dissension in Honduras as well as disputes and conflicts between the governments of Nicaragua, Honduras and Costa Rica. The existence of a revolutionary and socialist Nicaragua has created not only the above-mentioned conflicts but also a steady flow of refugees to neighbouring countries, while the armed conflicts in El Salvador and Guatemala have generated their own refugee flows to Mexico and the United States.

In this context the United States government, along with providing military and economic assistance to the governments of El Salvador and Honduras, and support to the 'Contras', has carried out frequent military exercises in Honduras. The US Navy makes its presence felt in the Caribbean and off the Pacific coasts of Central America. One US agency — the CIA — sponsored the mining of Nicaraguan ports, and when Nicaragua filed a complaint before the International Court of Justice, the US government challenged the Court's jurisdiction.[1] For their part the Soviet Union and Cuba have

1

ensured a regular supply of economic assistance and military hardware to Nicaragua, thereby raising strong apprehension and debate in US government circles. The crisis in Central America is therefore not only internal to the region, but it is also external, spilling over to areas beyond its geographical and geopolitical importance, confounding Central Americans in the process. Two introductory approaches to understanding the crisis are advanced in this chapter.

Central America in an East-West context

In the words of the Former United States Ambassador to the United Nations, Mrs Jeane Kirkpatrick, 'The United States is by no means a new participant in Central America's politics, having played an important if intermittent role in its political struggles throughout much of the century. The United States has been important as a source of aid and also has exercised a veto power over governments. Therefore, the objective economic and political dependency of nations in the area has been reinforced by a widespread sense of psychological dependency'.[2] Hegemony and dependence, then, are relevant factors that cannot be overlooked.

Thus when conflicts emerged in the region and guerrilla warfare spread, 'psychological dependence' also began to change, inducing General Alexander Haig, then US Secretary of State, to express the need for the US government to draw the line in El Salvador against the expansion of communism in Central America. By 1982 President Reagan considered it important to emphasise before the Organization of American States that, in the absence of prompt action, 'new Cubas' would emerge out of guerrilla conflicts in the region. Other US government officials likewise expressed the concern that Nicaragua was already sliding into the communist camp; they claimed that further leftist successes in Central America would endanger the Panama Canal, the oil fields of Mexico, and the strategic Caribbean sea-lanes, vital to the United States, thereby recalling the 'domino theory' espoused in Vietnam — and in Central America in the 1960s during the first stages of the Cuban revolution.

Since then, Central America has been placed in a context of vital interest to the United States, and Nicaragua has displaced El Salvador as its main cause of concern. According to US government spokesmen, this is due to Nicaragua having become the centre from which regional struggle has radiated, and the primary exporter of revolution and political turmoil to the rest of the region. This activity, maintain the spokesmen, has been motivated by the predominantly leftist ideology of Nicaragua's government and its acceptance of Soviet and Cuban military support and economic assistance. The US government has therefore made Central America an East-West issue, and as a result has created a new strategic border along which East-West tensions now zig-zag through the Caribbean and the Central America isthmus. Hence turmoil and civil wars have not only aggravated relations between governments, dislocated societies and brought enormous hardships upon the peoples of the region but have also drawn into the area the active presence of the United States and the Soviet Union. Instead of evolution and economic growth, involution is occurring, aggravated by external economic, financial and trade factors.

A Central American approach

Prolonged periods of oppression and repression and a lack of political cal space, along with the preservation of rigid structures that obstruct not only economic growth and development but modernisation, and a framework of subordination in which US hegemony placed Central America — these give way in the long run to conflict and social upheavals. Therefore, in order to place the issues and events in a clearer perspective, a distinction must be made between, on the one hand, local armed conflicts (Guatemala, El Salvador, Nicaragua) and, on the other, the necessary adjustments in national political and socio-economic systems by open political process. The latter, often lost sight of in the news media's coverage of Central America, still exists to some degree in Honduras, and much more so in Costa Rica, Panama and newly-independent, bilingual Belize.

Attention must also be focused on the efforts undertaken by the governments of the region to resolve the region's problems. In so doing another distinction must be made between the purely political actions on a regional level and the other efforts and sacrifices discreetly but persistently made by the same governments in order to preserve the Central American Common Market, together with its economic, financial and commercial relations. The actions on those two broad fronts show a clear functional dislocation.

The dynamics of conflict

Due to conflicting situations and processes, major events have occurred. First, in January 1984 the National Bipartisan Commission on Central America was created in 1983 by the US President and presided over by former Secretary of State Dr Henry Kissinger. Its report, published in January 1984, advances useful guidelines for the interpretation of the crisis and also for US policies for the region.[3] Secondly, the formation by Mexico, Venezuela, Colombia and Panama of the 'Contadora Group' has in turn played an important role in setting up a framework for interregional negotiations on the political level and supporting economic integration. However, its role has been and is complicated by the fact that fundamental issues cannot be dealt with effectively and exclusively by the governments themselves, but must also take into account revolutionary and counter-revolutionary demands and expectations. It entails compromises between the interests of contending forces, and between oppressors and oppressed. Likewise, the particular geopolitical and geostrategic interests in the region of the United States and, however limited, of the Soviet Union and Cuba cannot realistically be overlooked. The third important event has been the initiative taken by President Napoleón Duarte of El Salvador to open negotiations with Salvadoran guerrillas. Likewise, political proposals have been advanced in April 1985 by Nicaraguan opposition leaders to the Sandinista government — proposals that, when realistically clarified and demystified, should give way to an agenda for negotiations.[4]

Thus violence, intimidating language and a search for consensus run parallel courses in Central America.

1. *Asynchronism in revolution, counter-revolution and open political processes*

The vulnerability of the societies to revolutionary processes can best be appreciated by evaluating in which country pre-revolutionary conditions exist, in which country revolutionary conditions exist, and in which country these are already past, and therefore a revolutionary process is being forged. This method clarifies the role played by the endogenous and exogenous factors. It leads also to an understanding of the role which each society designates to the social, economic and political forces in order to preserve a system either established by consensus or imposed and maintained by public security forces.

Using this methodology, it becomes clear that Costa Rica, for example, is far from having revolutionary processes erupt and that this is due to its social and power structures being flexible enough to adapt to new situations. In spite of this, social and political tensions arise and are aggravated by recent financial strains.

Honduras, by contrast, is involved in conflicts with the government of Nicaragua and revolutionary movements in El Salvador. There is a concern, then, over the security measures the government is forced to adopt, which hinder the freedom of its political and social forces and which cause internal friction. We are thus led to the focal point of why Honduras suffers more than Costa Rica from the spill-over effects of events occurring within its neighbours. The intensity and depth of the revolutionary struggles in Guatemala and El Salvador are themselves evidence of the varied degrees of a single phenomenon. In addition, if an objective approach is made, it becomes clear that the revolutionary process of El Salvador has matured into one which has affected not only the power structure in that country but the social and economic structures as well. Although this had not occurred in Guatemala, the possibility cannot be ruled out.

Not only can this phenomenon be considered in a regional context but it is also present at the international level, and reverberations are felt from the actions of the governments from outside the sub-region. The United States, for example, does not ignore the impact that the uprising has had on El Salvador, and therefore promotes agrarian and legal measures, while it is disinclined to pursue similar political action in Guatemala with the same vigour. A 'double standard' can be theoretically argued were we to employ the parameters used by Mrs Jeane Kirkpatrick.[5]

Nicaragua, then, is the only Central American country where in the recent past a revolutionary process has emerged triumphant. At present it is undergoing a revolutionary process with a strong ideological flavour, while at the same time the Sandinista government is confronting counter-revolutionary processes of various ideological tendencies and with varied degrees of support from outside.

Armed conflict is, therefore, a phenomenon common to three countries — Guatemala, El Salvador and Nicaragua — with varied degrees of intensity and depth. This has not, however, led to an active and dynamic interrelationship either between all the revolutionary movements in the three countries or the governments. The asynchronism, then, is not only one of timing but also one of ideologies. It is the far left that is revolutionary in El Salvador and in Guatemala; in Nicaragua it is the far right. The Leftist Centre in El Salvador is part of the revolution, while in Guatemala it is undergoing a period of pondering its strategy. The ideological interrelationship of ARDE with the 'Contras' is weak or practically nil, and their objectives are dissimilar.[6]

These phenomena have been and are continuously being analysed by international ideological movements: the Socialist International, the Christian Democratic International, the III International (Communist), the Conservative International, and the actual governments in which members of these Internationals are present.

These same ideological tendencies exist in Central America, and several Central American parties and movements are members or observers of the Internationals.

Thus there is no single common 'Central American crisis' but rather a combination of situations within the heart of each country. At the same time, power is disputed between two or more countries and between their opposing ideological sectors.

2. *Actions at the sub-regional level: a functional dislocation*

In the last four years the five Central American governments have been making a series of efforts to build inter-Central American forums aimed at seeking solutions to the difficult problems that beset the sub-region as a whole. They have also been using the still existing mechanisms of the Program for Central American Economic Integration and testing solutions to the commercial, fiscal, industrial and monetary problems that affect the functioning of the economic integration scheme. Two distinct models exist, therefore, to plan actions at the sub-regional level — one strictly political and the other economic and financial.

2.1 *Political relations*

Prominent among the first of these plans of action was the creation of the Central American Democratic Community, initially consisting of Costa Rica, Honduras and El Salvador. The exclusion of Guatemala and Nicaragua emphasized the difficulty of (*a*) making the interests of the five countries compatible and (*b*) defining, without an ideological ingredient, the parameters of democracy as the common denominator of such a scheme. On the other hand, the US government apparently found in that Community the embryo of a political scheme that would allow actions based on the difference between totalitarian and authoritarian systems. For their part, some of the Latin American governments favoured the creation and expansion of the Community in order to stress democratic flexibility as its common denominator. In the mean time, others cold-shouldered it because of the exclusion of Nicaragua.

Another pattern of action being tested is that of meetings of Foreign Ministers and of Heads of State. In both cases there have been problems and obstacles. On the one hand, the Foreign Ministers have not agreed either on their agendas or on what could be the common denominator. On some occasions, ideological factors have obstructed the interaction, especially between the governments of El Salvador and Nicaragua which at the ideological level are obviously disparate and antagonistic. In other cases the interrelationship between some

Central American governments and others in the hemisphere have compelled them to act with caution (Guatemala). The meetings of Heads of State have not come to pass precisely because of the same factors that have minimised the potential of the Foreign Ministers' meetings. Thus the bilateral meetings — short in duration and with limited agendas — have been the only ones of any significance.

2.2 Economic relations

The dislocation that is evident at the political level is not however, present in the economic, financial and monetary areas. Here several mechanisms established by means of inter-Central American treaties and pacts since 1958 play an important role — among them the Central American Bank for Economic Integration, the Central American Monetary Council and the meetings at the level of Economic Ministers and vice Ministers (senior permanent officials).

It is certain that not all problems at the sub-regional level, or the financial problems such as those related to intraregional payments can be solved in these forums. However, it is also true that these institutional mechanisms continue to operate, and through them ideological problems seem to be diluted.

A valid assumption can be made: an intensive and growing economic interrelationship between these countries and between the various economic and social groups, which has so far continued for twenty-five years, has created links which are not affected by ideological problems stemming either from the left or from the right.

3. Ideological Pluralism

The previous analysis, related to asynchronism and functional dislocation in Central America, leads us on to focus on a phenomenon which is new in Central America: ideological pluralism. The 1970s revealed another phenomenon: military governments or governments run *de facto* by the military in four countries — Guatemala, El Salvador, Honduras and Nicaragua. The 1980s has revealed the other side of the coin: a heterogeneity not only at the level of governments but even in their makeup and their ideological trends. What, fundamentally, caused the introduction of this qualitative change in the region?

It is not necessary to detail the internal process of each country in order to determine the cause and effect of the change that occurred and is occurring, since it has been sufficiently explained elsewhere.[10] However, it is useful to mention certain facts common to all the countries of the region: the evident increase of population and its concentration in urban centres; the growing gulf between urban development and the rural stagnation; the continuous addition of youths to the job market and the reduced capacity of the economic systems to absorb them; and the growing income disparity between the countryside and urban centres and along with that between low and middle-income sectors and the middle and upper classes. These and other factors which have been the object of many analyses are framed within rigid social structures if we compare them to other Latin American countries which have progressed towards a capitalist development.

Thus the phenomenon of ideological disparity among governments and revolutionary groups demonstrates that plurality is a fact today and that the countries of the region do not agree on either the model of pure capitalist development or that of centralised economics.

Revolution has brought obvious changes in each of the countries involved, in the methods and strategies used to combat it. The maxim of one of the guerrilla groups in Guatemala — 'every fighter must know how to use his weapons: the rifle and political science' — clearly illustrates that the object is not a revolution *per se* or a simple takeover of power to establish a political system, but rather processes that will bring about change in the economic, social, political and cultural systems. And what one must not lose sight of is that the revolutionary processes take place within systems characterised by their ideological rigidity, and a reluctance to compromise.

Ideological plurality is also strengthened by interrelationships and communication between the various ideological groups in each country and their foreign counterparts, especially outside Central America. The role played by the 'internationals' cannot be overlooked since the Socialist International and the Christian Democratic International lean towards the establishment of flexible systems in which structural changes are promoted within the framework of capitalism in order to modernise societies. The III International — the Communist International — leans towards a substantial modification of the national systems without the ingredient of an open political participation, based on models of planned and centralised economics. The so-called 'Anticommunist International' leans towards the preservation of the pre-capitalist systems with cosmetic changes in order to satisfy formal demands and foreign financial requirements.

It is opportune in this context to bring into play the concept upheld by the political leadership in the United States to prevent a second Cuba in Latin America ('no second Cuba').

In this same context, one must add the national security considerations seen in an economic, social and political perspective, which are also present in other Latin America countries whose governments manage the above-mentioned parameters realistically. However, as opposed to the United States, it is evident that they differentiate between ideological considerations and their own security.

4. *Causes and dimension of the Central American crises*

Since the beginning of the 1980s conflicts in Central American countries have been the object of increased attention, concern and action on the part of other countries whose governments have ideological, economic or political interests in the region. For some governments, then, Central America became of interest in an East-West context or because it is a sensitive area within the Caribbean Basin. The second of these considerations has not excluded the East-West complications that gradually arise.

Without excluding the very real interest of the Soviet Union, the countries with borders on the Caribbean have the right to show or demonstrate their interests and concern for the solution of the problems that beset the region today, aggravated by economic and financial realities. Without giving an inventory of the problems affecting the sub-region and each of its countries individually, we can identify several relevant elements.

4.1. *Ideological solidarity*

A Christian Democratic government has to demonstrate its solidarity towards another government with the same ideology in Central America (i.e. Venezuela and El Salvador during the Duarte regime) and a Social Democratic party or government does the same. Conservative and Marxist-Leninist governments are linked to each other by ideology and accordingly show mutual solidarity; in either case ideology further permeates foreign policy. Although this is a relatively new phenomenon in inter-Central American relations, the truth is that today it cannot be avoided, especially if it is a question of seeking options to find some type of solution to critical situations.

Thus the component of expectation for the respect of the individual and his fundamental rights, which has gradually been incorporated into the foreign policy of several countries and is even becoming its foundation, cannot be overlooked. Several Central American governments and armies cannot understand that a democratic government respects the rights of the governed, particularly at home, and thereby considers it important that a similar standard be followed in other countries with which it has relations. In support of this position, we find compliance with international commitments and the right of those to whom a country is linked by virtue of such covenants to demand or expect that they comply, for their part, with the letter and spirit of those agreements.

It would be unreasonable, then, to separate ideologies from the fundamental rights of human beings. Certainly, the regimes with substantial democratic leanings, aside from the ideology prevalent in their governments, keep the component of fundamental rights very much in mind. Other political systems, in which economic and political democracy is not a basic concern, insist on the assurance of certain basic rights although the stress is not placed on the rights of a political nature — i.e. political freedom — but rather on those which are basically economic and social. In the former case, government consents to the exercise of certain rights and prerogatives, and, in the latter case, the government fixes the scope of the rights of the governed. Thus we have the paradox of governments subjected to the demands of democratic governments because of violations of human rights of their own governed. These, for their part, believe strongly in the equation 'human rights equals communism' or 'human rights equals intervention'.[8]

4.2. *The trend towards a militarization of the state*

It is necessary to place this point in its correct perspective and to differentiate between military governments on the one hand and militarised states on the other. In the former the armed forces take over executive power generally in a hierarchical manner while the other functions of the state are adjusted to the format of civilian governments. Judicial power is to a certain extent subjected to the persuasions of the executive; but in general the state apparatus is not affected, although freedom and social justice are. Decision-making is shared between civilian and military leaders. This model is, therefore, identified by a military president, a military chief of state, or a military government.

The militarisation of the state, on the contrary, implies a different model because all state functions remain under the control of the military apparatus. The *raison d'état* acquires a different dimension. All citizens remain, to a greater or lesser extent, subject to the control of the national security forces; the control of the population and the exercise of their rights are within the concept of national security. This model lends itself to the exercise of various types of ideologies excepting those of a democratic hue. Fascism — not in a pejorative sense but as a model known to political science and theory — can be introduced, as can a model of Peronist socialism. Whether fascism falls into an 'authoritarian' or 'totalitarian' category is a matter of opinion or circumstances.

Within this theoretical framework the Central American countries (except Costa Rica) have experienced the model of military governments. Other societies that experienced the phenomenon of revolution and ideological guerrilla movements (i.e. Colombia, Mexico and Venezuela) persevered on the democratic and civilian path. But because of the degree of turmoil affecting them, the Central American regimes have followed a different course. Their citizens have not had the option to contribute to any different course. The polarisation has been and is so glaring that it has obstructed the road. It has even let to the identification of 'armies of the poor' and 'armies of the rich' (Guatcmala).

What role is to be played by the armed forces in future? This matter cannot be ignored since it has very sensitive implications; also, it is linked to increased public expenditure on security in all the countries of the sub-region. None of these countries has been able to avoid increased military and security expenditure which in several cases has reached extremes, with more being spent on military installations than on education or public health. The magnitude of the fiscal and balance of payments deficits has not yet slowed down the increase in national security expenditures.

Although each society must confront this problem, none of them (except Costa Rica) has the internal flexibility or conditions to reach favourable understandings and definitions for economic development and democracy. However, third-party countries can play an important role in this area, especially those that have experienced similar situations. The question cannot be ignored, since factors of external and internal origin come into play and must be dealt with each within its own context.

4.3. *Economic interrelationships*
The programme for Central American integration propelled internal growth at the national and sub-regional levels, by seeking to create and to divert trade in and towards that scheme. Whether the results were satisfactory or not is less important than the effect of the growing interrelationships among the countries themselves. In this same measure, the countries of the sub-region sought more or less diligently to correct the deterioration of their terms of trade by broadening their economic and trade relations with other countries, among them Mexico, Venezuela and Panama. The energy component (oil) thus acquired greater relevance, demonstrating that the balance of trade and payments of Central American countries with

the Contadora Group countries does not take place in an economic vacuum. Neither Mexico nor Venezuela has used that factor as a lever for its foreign policy towards Central America, but a situation of relative and involuntary dependence has nonetheless been generated, which stems from countries outside the sub-region with which the balance of payments is chronically negative. What must be stressed is that the member-countries of the Contadora Group — and the United States — are interested in dislocating sub-regional economic integration. Similarly, any risk of economic expansion by Mexico, Colombia and Venezuela, with political results, is counteracted by the financial problems of the modern world. The economic factor is, therefore, one that allows for a compatibility of interests and actions.

5. *An interpretation of the US perception*

We can illustrate the nature or type of the existing relations between the United States and Central American governments as follows:

> Guatemala: tense.
> El Salvador: supportive and protective.
> Nicaragua: hostile.
> Honduras: supportive and protective.
> Costa Rica: cordial and by consensus.

This method can be used to make a correlation with other Latin American governments. But it must be noted that this classification in itself is fluid and reflects only a situation subject to modification in the light of ponderous factors. It is preferable instead to use the parameters of foreign policy as identified by officials knowledgeable on the subject.

President Reagan has encountered opposition to the policies and actions of his government in Central America. Since 1984 he has therefore taken upon himself the weight of what has been perceived as a personal crusade. The extraordinary number of formal and informal statements he has made reveal that the issues of the region, principally those in Nicaragua, are very much upon his mind, thus giving the erroncous impression that he is obsessed with the subject. All this creates major difficulties for Central American analysts of US policies in the sense of being able to distinguish between the strong rhetoric used by the President, the Secretary of State, senior members of the National Security Council and other spokesmen for the government, rhetoric that can be considered simply as intimidating language, and those signals which are basic and substantial and therefore should be taken as clear indications of policy and future actions, or ingredients of a broader policy. Official pronouncements and written statements must therefore be checked, when possible, with international documents that the US open political system allows to be 'leaked' to the press, and further examined in the context of the powers that the President enjoys under the Constitution as opposed to those functions and powers that correspond to Congress. Viewed within the framework of the United States as a highly developed democratic and capitalist society, the appropriations process for government expenditure plays an important role in the formulation and execution of foreign policy and it is in this area that an objective foreign analyst can best understand the factual and legal limits of the language that is being employed. It is in this process that Central America has become not only an external issue — one of foreign policy — but also an internal matter for the United States between political forces that at times compel the Executive either to campaign for its causes in an attempt to bring public pressure on Congress or seek a compromise.

In any event, the agenda of grief for Central Americans continues to grow. What was originally viewed as a 'manageable crisis' to be resolved by 'going to the source' (ex-Secretary of State Alexander Haig) gave way in the course of two years to an escalation of internal and bilateral conflicts, with the potential for an inter-regional war and increasing participation by countries from outside the sub-region. Those who manage the science and conduct of war go even further; Lt. Gen. Wallace H. Nutting, former Commander in Chief, US Southern Command, Panama, stated: 'Central America is already at war and my country — the United States — is already involved in the Central American war.'[12] Certainly the narrow vision of a military commander with well-defined responsibilities is not shared by those in the United States and in Central America who believe that the situation has not reached that point and that it is feasible to find solutions which would prevent a war involving the United States. Yet, we cannot ignore the well-known principle of military science: that technically a war begins when one begins to think about it.

This is why each element and component of US strategy must be carefully studied, analysed and scrutinised by the governments of the Contadora Group and to some extent by all the Central American governments. There is, therefore, no mystery to unveil because it is the US government which is concerned about it and the beneficiaries and victims will be those at whom the strategy is directed. In this sense there is a notable difference from what occurred during the 1950s and 1960s, when issues were not discussed publicly and 'leaks' were infrequent.

6. *The Principles and Denominators of the Contadora Group*

The Latin American governments who are members of the Contadora Group have outlined the common denominators of the group and the principles they share and which they also propose to the Central American countries, without regard to governments or insurgent and revolutionary groups. In the text of the declaration issued on May 13, 1983, in Panama, they stated, on the one hand, that the original and essential purpose which brought about the Group's creation 'consists of fulfilling a diplomatic function aimed at seeking, through a political route, the solution of the conflicts and counting, in order to accomplish this, on the collaboration of the involved parties'. On the other hand, they urged the Central American countries to contribute to the peace efforts and in this way to pledge their political determination to the search for avenues leading to a dialogue and understanding in order to settle their present differences. This call was aimed not only at the governments but at their peoples as well.

All the Contadora principles are part of the international juridical order and based on the inter-American system. This is why it would have been consistent for the suggestion to have been included that foreign military forces and advisers withdraw from Central America, agreeing thus with the position stated by the United States. The functions of the Group, then, involve sensitive negotiations that could include Cuba and the Soviet Union. The mechanisms have to be designed. But there is an additional positive element in play: Panama's participation in the Contadora Group. Panama has shown an interest in the Isthmus since the time of the government of General Omar Torrijos, as well as an active presence which is not only commercial and financial, but is also fundamentally political. The relationship of the Central American governments with the Panamanian government is one of trust. The attitude of the revolutionary groups towards the government of Panama is, certainly, not the same as towards the person of General Torrijos, but in any event it is one of trust and respect. Thus Panama plays a valuable role within the Group. On the one hand, it is an isthmus country with the characteristics which this condition implies; and it is part of Central America. On the other hand, Central America needs Panama to be actively involved in the sub-region for the purposes of making its future more feasible.

Similarly one must look at the role Belize can play. Certainly there would be limits placed on this because of the present controversy between Guatemala and Belize. However, this should not preclude a formula that would permit its participation, since the rest of the

Central Americans have no reservations regarding Belize and, at the same time, the revolutionary groups supported its independence. Even its participation in the Contadora Group, whether as a full member or an associate, would constitute a positive factor for the region as a whole. One cannot deny that nowadays Central America consists no longer of five countries, but rather of seven, and that this new geographic dimension contributes to the strengthening of pluralism and makes the sub-regional economic options more viable.

7. *The mandate of the UN Security Council*

The UN Security Council Resolution of May 19, 1983, was of considerable significance. Citing the same principles which created the Contadora Group and reaffirming the right of Nicaragua and of all the countries of the area to live in peace and security, free from foreign intervention, the Council on the one hand *urgently appealed* to the interested States to cooperate with the Contadora Group via a frank and constructive dialogue for the purposes of settling their differences. Further, the Council *urged* the Contadora Group to find solutions to the problems of the region and to report the results to the Council.

Although the Contadora Group is not a regional mechanism as defined by the United Nations Charter, and although its creation does not divest the OAS of its competence, it is certain that the member-countries of the Group have received a broad, specific and clear mandate from the UN Security Council. It is broad in the sense that it includes five countries of the sub-region geographically and without restricting the efforts of the governments confronting similar problems or conflicts with other governments, while, at the same time, it includes the conflicts in each of the countries. It is specific because the Group must strive to find solutions to the problems of the region within the framework of the principles stated in the text of the Resolution; and clear because it must pursue a frank and constructive dialogue.

The experience that the governments in the Group have acquired in their dealings with the governments of the area has certainly been positive. But one cannot overlook the difficulty involved in discussing the problems of peace and co-existence with groups that have been radicalised by prolonged struggles. In addition, one cannot ignore the legitimate concerns of other governments, among them the United States.

Geopolitics stresses the fact that the Contadora Group has in its grasp the conditions suitable for action. Its members are in open communication with the government of Cuba and, consequently, with the Soviet Union. The Central American countries that for a long time have been inhibited from taking part in this type of communication now have a valid spokesman. The Group can, therefore, 'go to the source' from which some believe the problems originate.

While the Contadora process gained momentum and Central American governments were able to submit their respective proposals, the main core of the agreements on security matters and verification began to be openly questioned, interestingly enough not in Central America but in the United States. Thus reactions to Nicaragua's proposals to Contadora in 1983, as expressed by Dr Constantine Menges (Senior Director for Latin American Affairs in the National Security Council) on November 28, 1983, were adverse, given the fact that they were 'wholly inadequate in proposing verification monitoring by virtually the same countries that were implicit guarantors of the July 1979 negotiated settlement which brought the Sandinistas and their democratic allies to power, based on democratic promises, the same countries that had failed to in any way bring about an effort to get compliance'.[13] This type of reaction, despite the fact that the countries were the same but their governments were not, allowed the Group to become aware of the importance the United States assigned to security agreements and verification and the degree of resistance that existed over the composition of the Group. Thus negotiations became truly multilateral, in the sense that while negotiations were being carried out between the Central American governments themselves, and with the members of Contadora, one or more of the former also negotiated with the US government, forcing 'Contadora' to consult with the United States before a draft could be submitted to the Central American governments.

The need to accelerate the presentation of a draft text was soon felt in order to have a basic document that could be the focus of concrete negotiations. Hence by June 1984 the Group was able to present a formal draft of an '*Acta*' for Peace and Cooperation in Central America, outlining the main points needing agreement: namely internal measures to be taken to restore peace, a proposal for the adherence or ratification by Central American states to different international treaties, the strengthening of economic integration in the region, and reciprocal security measures and methods for verification.

Contadora has substantial documentation at its disposal, and has therefore reactivated negotiations. These are being supported by distinguished members of the US Congress,[14] by different Latin American statesmen, and by other countries of the hemisphere, among then Argentina, Brazil, Ecuador, Uruguay and Cuba. The problem is that time is running out. Negotiations within the OAS Rio Treaty would not necessarily be incompatible with the mandate of the Security Council. The Council, in all events, retains its jurisdiction.

8. *Central American positions*

No statesman can deny the difficulty that every government faces in acknowledging the existence of an uprising on its soil, because this eventually leads to the recognition by other countries of a state of insurrection or civil war. The juridical-political effects of this, nationally and in third-party countries, are diverse. Therefore it is believed that such a recognition or acknowledgement would offer an avenue to the rebels at the international level. However, it also subjects them to regimes that are established precisely to take care of those eventualities. It is a double-edged sword. However, such a problem does not arise in conflicts (situations or controversies) where two or more states are involved.

When confronted with revolutions and counter-revolutions, governments are reluctant to grant them a status different from that of 'terrorists' or 'subversives'. These terms, however, include those who are and those who are not. The common denominator is the reluctance of each government to acknowledge a situation that differs from its public manifestations and which calls for a scheme of negotiations based on facts and not appearances.

Each national situation is different, as are also the ideological trends and the objectives of the various revolutionary movements. The strengths or weaknesses of each group rest on their willingness — favourable or unfavourable — to seek and accept solutions that differ fundamentally from those gained after a military victory. It must also be noted that the crises involving violence in some countries are not exclusively limited to their governments and armed fighters. Other sectors in each country advocate their own proposals and invoke their full right not to be forcibly represented by one or another.

The gamut of conflicts affecting the countries of the sub-region has deep roots in economic and social inequalities and violence. It means that these countries did not open up political space or create the mechanisms for popular participation which might have overcome — by means of evolution or peaceful avenues — the serious problems besetting them. People are reacting with violence to the closed models of society and systems of subjugation. Fortunately for some and unfortunately for others, these situations cannot be resolved with cosmetic solutions. Democracy is not just form but also substance for the peoples of Central America; and so is voting in elections, and their greater participation in the decision-making processes. The right to self-determination has gained greater dimensions than in the past. Therefore, the expectation of elections as the main ingredient of a solution, however valuable the elections may be in themselves, cannot resolve the series of questions which have become the agenda for the day. An ensured freedom of organisation at the economic, social and political levels is also imperative. The armed forces will, therefore, not be able to attempt to direct the participatory process; they must rather become a part of it. The results of the 1979 struggle in Nicaragua generated an entire spectrum of fresh expectations in other countries of the sub-region. A new ideological ingredient disturbed the political relationships between governments — though not economic and financial relations. No statesman can ignore the law of the pendulum or the effect it has on a country if its swing is abruptly stopped. If the external pressures by the US government are softened, it is more feasible that those who govern and those who are governed in Nicaragua will study the political and economic model they wish to establish, as well as the framework of the fundamental rights for one and the other.

It is within this spectrum of realities and expectations, therefore, that each country sees current development. This explains the reservations, resistance and conditions imposed by the governments confronting conflicts from within and without. To promote authentic openings of the political systems would lead to national agreements and consensus. Statements of diplomats reveal how difficult the road to peace is. The reaction of several governments to the appointment of Ambassador Stone illustrated the resistance to the idea that third-party countries — who also lend economic and military support — might be exploring the avenues of an understanding between the governing and the governed and between the governments of the region.

The government of Costa Rica has shown that it is possible to explore solutions to sensitive problems with Nicaragua. Hence the role that the political parties of democratic ideologies can play in other countries must be recognised. For instance, the Liberal Party — in government — and its democratic opposition in Honduras might agree on the suitability of reaching understandings with Nicaragua for a return to the flexible road and away from an external confrontation. This possibility would contribute to the relaxation of the tensions rapidly growing between Honduras and Nicaragua. Central Americans do not forget that the peace between

El Salvador and Honduras took more than a decade to be consolidated after the hostilities ceased. The relations between those countries were derailed for many years and the scheme for economic integration had to learn to live with an 'institutionalised crisis'. This should be kept in mind.

Guatemala and El Salvador basically need broad national agreements which they could reach via the cooperation of the Contadora Group. Strangely enough, the problems of Central America also demand certain reflections and consensus within the United States, among them those of an international order which is accepted by the national system. However, it is certainly up to the leaders and thinkers of that country to wrestle with this topic.

NOTES

1. The issue of the World Court's jurisdiction is being discussed not only in academic and political but also in legal circles, among them, the American Society of International Law, which publishes a quarterly Journal.
2. 'US Security in Latin America', *Commentary*, Jan. 1981.
3. Report of the National Bipartisan Commission on Central America, Washington DC, January, 1984.
4. See Arturo Cruz Sr. and Arturo Cruz Jr., 'A Peace Plan for Nicaragua', *The New Republic*, March 1985. Ambassador Carlos Tunnermann (Nicaraguan Ambassador to the United States) wrote a letter to *The Washington Post*, published on March 30, 1985, explaining his government's reasons for not negotiating with the 'Contras'. President Reagan submitted formal proposals for negotiation on April 4, 1985, at the same time that President Betancur of Colombia was visiting Washington. President Reagan also wrote to Pope John Paul II explaining his proposal.
5. The reference is to 'Dictatorship and Double Standards'. It can also be applied to the discussion whether the 'Contras' should be entitled to share power in Nicaragua while the left in El Salvador is not.
6. In his letter of March 22, 1985, to President Reagan (*Diario Las Americas*, Miami, Fla., of April 5, 1985) Edén Pastora expressed full agreement with the US government support, and although he mentions discrepancies with other groups, he stated that his movement shared 'the common goal'. In Nicaraguan opposition circles, it was an important turn-about.
7. Among other recent publications, see Thomas P.Anderson, *Politics in Central America — Guatemala, El Salvador, Honduras and Nicaragua*, New York, Praeger, 1982; Martin Diskin (ed.), *'Trouble in our backyard' — Central America and the United States in the Eighties*, New York, Pantheon, 1983; Stanford Central America Action Network, *Revolution in Central America*, Boulder, Colo., Westview Press, 1983; Howard J.Wiarda (ed.), *Rift and Revolution: The Central American Imbroglio*, Washington, American Enterprise Institute for Public Policy Research, 1984: Richard Fagan and Olga Pellicer, *The Future of Central America*, Stanford University Press, 1983; Robert S.Leiken (ed.), *Central America — Anatomy of Conflict*, Pergamon Press, 1984. The Kissinger Report also contains important interpretations.
8. A good example of the equation in Guatemala is the exhortation made to members of the civil patrols by their instructors, as shown in a TV series, 'Are you for

Guatemala or are you with human rights?' In El Salvador and Guatemala, some government officials and members of the press have linked the issue of human rights to foreign intervention, when it is brought up by visiting foreign parliamentarians.

9. The Junta de Reconstrucción Nacional of Nicaragua sent, on July 12, 1979, a telex outlining their objectives, which in turn was circulated to all delegations. The US Department of State, in a statement made then, referred to the new government of Nicaragua as having pledged 'to avoid reprisals, to provide sanctuary to those in fear, to begin immediately the immense task of national reconstruction and to respect human rights and hold elections'.

10. Stephan Kinsen and Stephen Schlessinger, *Bitter Fruit: The untold story of the American intervention in Guatemala*, New York, Doubleday, 1982.

11. The Origins of the Crisis in Central America, *Rift and Revolution*, pp.18-19.

12. *The Washington Post*, May 22, 1984.

13. See Roy Gutman, 'America's Diplomatic Charade', *Foreign Policy*, no.56, Fall 1984, p.19. Mr Gutman reviews the Contadora process from a US perspective.

14. E.g. see Congressmen Alexander and Panetta, *Congressional Record*, House of Representatives, Feb. 28, 1985; Senators Edward Kennedy and Christopher Dodd have likewise openly supported Contadora's efforts.

2
UNDERSTANDING UNITED STATES POLICY TOWARDS LATIN AMERICA AND THE CENTRAL AMERICAN CRISIS

Margaret Daly Hayes

Introduction

To craft a policy toward Latin America, it is first necessary to understand United States interests in Latin America. To understand US policies toward Latin America, it is necessary to know the constraints of the policy making process. Too many administrations, academicians and amateur policy-makers have had a policy first, and then have tried to match US and Latin American interests in the region to it. It is not surprising that the policies have failed or fallen short of expectations.

To complicate the process, there is a reluctance among scholars and the public to confront the notion of a US interest in Latin America, or in other world regions, or in specific sets of events. The US public is often more comfortable *reacting* to world events than in working to *shape* world events. Henry Kissinger wrote in 1967, in his essay 'An Inquiry into the American National Interest':

Americans have historically shied away from addressing the essence of our national interest and the premises of our foreign policy . . . A mature conception of our interests in the world . . . takes into account widespread interest in the 'need' for stability and peaceful change. It would deal with two fundamental questions: 'What is it in our interest to prevent?' and 'What would we seek to accomplish?' (Kissinger 1973)

This Chapter is an effort to explore the requirements of a more goal-oriented policy in Latin America (what we might seek to accomplish) and to explain the limits and constraints on the choices inherent in that policy (what we might seek to prevent). Although the proposed policy framework is applicable to the whole hemisphere, the specific focus of discussion is Central America. We seek first to define US interests in Latin America; secondly, to discuss current policies and their relations to the US interests identified; and, finally, to discuss US attitudes and actions related to the Contadora peace process in Central America.

A definition of US interests in Latin America

Elsewhere I have sought to develop a formulation of the US interests in Latin America that encompassed the broader concept of national interest that Kissinger describes. A definition of those interests must encompass political, economic and security considerations — in addition to the narrower concept of military security usually adopted (see Hayes 1983; 1984). The formulation is intended to capture what US policy might be; the values it might reflect, and what it must be, given the constraints of the US political process. It is a definition of US interests defined from a US point of view, not of policies that others might want to elicit from the United States. I believe that it describes fairly accurately the fundamental components of interest that fuel US Latin American policy:

It is in the United States' national interest that there exist in the Western Hemisphere friendly, prosperous states with stable responsible governments that permit the free movement of goods and services throughout the region; that respect the political intergrity of their neighbors; and that offer no support to the United States' global political rivals. (See Hayes, 1982; 1983; 1984.)

Of course, not all policy flows from these premises. The policy process is not deductive. Nevertheless, when put to empirical test, I believe the basic elements of the definition are upheld. Below we examine the formulation point by point.

US interest in government responsibility and system stability

It is in the US national interest that the countries of the hemisphere have stable political systems and responsible governments. US government attentions focus principally on East-West issues, on our relations with our allies in Europe and Japan, and on major problem areas like the Middle East. Frequently in the past, and less so but nevertheless still in the present, Latin America receives high-level attention only when rent by crisis. Although regional specialists inside and outside the government would like to see greater and more sophisticated attention paid to routine Western Hemisphere issues, this is not likely to come about in the foreseeable future. This is a lamentable fact that many would like to correct. Its consequence is that US-Latin American relations in general are managed with limited resources and certain constraints on the government's policy flexibility.

Political instability anywhere in the world is of concern to the United States for a variety of reasons. Because of the country's global commitments, instability in the regions close to the US borders, particularly when it has ideological overtones, is especially worrisome to the US government; it has a direct impact in the United States. For example, recent instability in the hemisphere has resulted in massive migrations of Latin American populations to the United States, which are difficult to manage and to absorb. In addition, they drain some of the best human resources from developing countries, thus compromising the future growth prospects of those countries. Finally, managing crisis and instability in this hemisphere requires a great deal of decision-maker time in the United States, and only a limited amount of high-level decision-maker time is devoted to the Western Hemisphere at present, or is likely to be in the future.[1] For all these reasons it is in the US interest that Latin American countries be able to conduct their own affairs and cope with and accommodate change so that the United States is not called upon to deal with regional events on a crisis basis. Countries that can cope with and accommodate change are likely to be more politically stable and more responsible in their dealings with their domestic political problems.

In the past — partly because of the limited interest in the region — the United States has focused almost exclusively on the stability of regional governments, forgetting that stability may only be temporary if governments do not serve the needs of their societies in some minimal way. It is recognized increasingly that governments must be judged by what they accomplish for their societies. They must be responsible and responsive to those societies. Responsible government in this sense means a government that respects human rights, plans for the political and economic wellbeing of the population, and responds to the demands of a variety of groups. Many Latin American governments can be found wanting in this essential attention to the needs and desires of their populations. Increasingly, political thinking in the United States recognizes that these failures of government responsibility have contributed to the region's endemic political instability.

'Stability', as we use the word here, does not mean *status quo* right-wing dictatorships. It means, rather, effective, efficient responsive governments that are able to cope with the demands of their own populations. It also means political systems that can conduct elections and absorb changes of political leadership through constitutional means and not just by coup or revolution. It means political systems and practices that serve to incorporate all elements of society into the political process. It means, in effect, 'good government'.

[1]This idea is developed in greater detail in Hayes 1982.

US interest in friendly relations in the Americas

It is in the US national interest that relations among the nations of the hemisphere, and between them and the United States, be friendly, i.e. relations that facilitate the accomplishment of mutual goals. They presume a level of confidence and trust among leaders. Having friendly relations does not mean that there are no differences between countries. Too often it is assumed that the United States demands of its Latin American neighbors acquiescence in US desires. This is not the case, nor should it be. The United States has friendly relations with its allies in Europe and with Japan and yet has important differences with those countries as well. Having friendly relations means keeping differences in perspective.

Friendly relations need have nothing to do with alignment or non-alignment. Factors other than mere labels define the quality of relations between nations. Having friendly relations does mean avoiding name-calling. It means using normal diplomatic channels to accomplish the business of the bilateral relationship. It means avoiding purposely irritating uses of high rhetoric. High rhetoric characterizes the poor relationships that exist between the United States and Cuba, Nicaragua and, from time to time, other countries of the region. Latin American politicians sometimes fail to appreciate how their own use of rhetoric asserting their national independence from the dominant regional power complicates the quality of US-Latin American relations.

US interest in regional economic prosperity

It is in the United States national interest that countries of the Western Hemisphere be prosperous. Though barely conscious of it, the American public generally wishes prosperity and well-being for its neighbors. US assistance programs are supported in the Congress because of lawmakers' sense of responsibility for assisting the poor of other nations.

Increasingly it is recognized that regional economic prosperity is a key interest of the United States. Clearly the region's poverty, deprivation and income inequality are a shocking human tragedy that cannot be ignored; indeed they have direct consequences for the United States.

While the United States often benefits from the presence of migrant entrants to the US labor market, large-scale, uncontrolled migrations from Central America and the Caribbean region (see Pastor 1985 for a review of Caribbean migration to the United

States) are increasingly difficult for the United States to deal with. From time to time taxpayer backlash threatens such illegal migrants. The political factors that cause migrations complicate US domestic and foreign policy.

The economic consequences of Latin America's poverty are also direct. Latin America's economic recession of the early 1980s resulted in hundreds of thousands of lost income dollars and employment in the United States as purchases from Mexico, Brazil and other large-market countries were cut back. More urgently, regional poverty and income inequality have created fertile ground for the development of political instability, for exploitation by hostile ideologues, and for the emergence of militant opposition groups. In this regard, it is useful to remind ourselves that bad governments generally are bad at solving economic problems. Thus the question of economic prosperity goes hand in hand with the question of political stability and responsible government. The less responsible the government in a developing country, the greater the prospects for political instability, and less will be done to ameliorate economic problems. A vicious cycle ensues.

It should be stressed that prosperity does not mean economic activity dominated by US multinational corporations. Latin American governments long ago learned to regulate and control foreign investors for their own purposes.[2] Nor does economic prosperity merely mean growth measured by an expanding gross domestic product. It also means distribution of the benefits of growth across the populations and the involvement of that population in the development process. Stable economic growth requires not only access to external markets and sources of hard currency, but also broad-based domestic consumption.

We now recognize that fundamental changes in the domestic economic policies of our neighbors must be undertaken in order to end the cyclical and structural causes of the severe economic problems that they face. In the past the United States has regarded issues of economic management to be the responsibility and concern of national governments. Because of the direct effects that Latin America's economic management and mismanagement have on the US economy, the US government is now pressing aggressively for economic reform and adjustment.

In seeking to stimulate greater prosperity in Latin America, policy-makers have become much more conscious of (1) the limits of

---

[2]Latin American governments have been so successful in regulating the activities of multinationals that the region has ceased to be an especially desirable place for investment (see Council of the Americas, 1984).

foreign assistance; (2) the regional requirements for investment capital to fuel the engine of economic growth; (3) the roles of governments and multilateral institutions in providing complementary funding; and (4) the need to coordinate development programs across institutions. These recognitions come in the United States at a time when Latin American countries and mainstream economists in those countries and in the multilateral lending institutions have also recognized the limits of import-substituting industrialization. All have now begun to look for ways to develop export markets and to encourage foreign capital investment in their economies.

The world economic situation in the mid-1980s does not promise an easy flow of new capital to the developing world. The policy community is concerned that neither the multilateral lending institutions, the private commercial banks, nor private entrepreneurs have the capital needed to restart growth in Latin America.[3] Moreover, a very large share of the domestic capital of the region is languishing in European and North American bank accounts. These Latin American funds must be recaptured and channelled to productive use at home.

US interest in the free movement of goods and services

In describing US security interests in the Caribbean Basin, US government spokesmen and academics like to exhibit a large map of the region with fat arrows pointing out US strategic military and commercial sea lines of communication (SLOCs). These sea-lanes are vital to the United States in the event of global conflict and must be defended. However, even the most pessimistic of future conflict scenarios grants low probability to sustained global conflict.

A much more immediate requirement for US security in the regional is regional prosperity and growth. Prosperity must be associated with increased commerce throughout the hemisphere. The economies of the Caribbean Basin countries and of many of the South American countries are too small to support diversity of economic activity necessary to achieve prosperity and competitiveness in the world. Even the larger economies — Mexico, Brazil, Argentina — must export today as an integral part of efforts to recover economic development momentum.

The United States itself is more export-oriented today than ever

[3]The InterAmerican Development Bank estimates that Latin America will require approximately $47 billion in new money before the end of the 1980s if it is to achieve a sustainable recovery and a growth rate of 5% per year (see InterAmerican Development Bank, 1984).

before. We are beginning to understand what it means to be in an interdependent world. Our own ability to export depends on the prosperity of our neighbors' economies. Their ability to import from us depends on their ability to sell to us.

United States goods will move through the Caribbean to our major markets in Europe, Japan and elsewhere despite changes in the world economic environment. It is more difficult to assure the commerce of the other small and less developed nations of the region. The key is enhanced trade relations.

The United States supports an open market even when there are strong pressures for protection in some industries. But more important, in the Hemisphere, and especially in Central America and the Caribbean Basin, open markets and a division of productive labor are needed if the countries of the region are to realize economies of scale on which to create viable industries. In Central America, the Contadora countries recognize that the economic integration that occurred during the heyday of the Central American Common Market must be rewarded. The eastern Caribbean countries are becoming much more conscious of the need for an integrated and common economic policy in their region. US programs like the Caribbean Basin intiative, with its one-way duty free entry policy, and the Kissinger Commission's recommendations for stimulating private sector initiative and economic growth are all intended to increase regional productivity. The Central American and Caribbean economies are reacting positively to the incentives. Hopefully this will contribute to prosperity and political stability.

US interest in respect for the political integrity of borders

On a more political dimension, it is in the United States national interest that the countries of the region respect each others' sovereignty and the political integrity of each other's borders. For the most part, Latin American countries have managed disagreements over border definitions and other classic international disputes well and peacefully. The record for managing subversion is less clear.

The Latin American tradition is one of non-intervention in the affairs of neighbors. On the one hand, interfering in the domestic affairs of one's neighbors is simply not respectable national behaviour. On the other, in more practical terms interference by one nation in the affairs of another creates instability and uncertainty. It fosters a sense of threat and lack of confidence in the predictability and reliability of the words and behavior of those neighbors. When governments and political institutions are threatened, all other efforts to pursue desirable social and economic goals are undercut, and only efforts to survive remain. Moreover, fragile political institutions are not well equipped to manage such interference. Repression, political and economic instability, and policy failure are a few of the consequences of hostile interference across borders.

From the US perspective, Latin America's broad tolerance for cross-border movements of political organizers of the left is sometimes viewed as excessive. US concerns are justified to the extent that regional instability affects US domestic and foreign affairs. The effects are often quite direct. When there is instability in the region, the United States is called upon to take sides. The example of El Salvador is illustrative. At the height of the recent Salvadorean crisis, representatives of the center, the right and the left all came to the United States, particularly to the Congress; but also to universities, churches and towns seeking to establish and exploit constituencies. The US public was ineluctably drawn into and made part of the domestic conflict in El Salvador. That country's domestic political contest and US foreign policy became intertwined and confused in the minds of the public and the policy-maker alike. Activists on all sides of the political spectrum failed to comprehend the very real limits of US policy — both what the United States would support and what it would tolerate.

It does not suit the US political system to have these foreign political disputes fought out in the United States on the floor of the Congress or in university classrooms, church pulpits or town meetings. There is very little that we as a nation can do to resolve the domestic political problems of other countries. As Henry Kissinger argued in the essay cited above:

The United States is no longer in a position to operate programs globally; it has to encourage them. It can no longer impose its preferred solution; it must seek to evoke it. . . . our role is to contribute to a structure that will foster the initiative of others . . . to encourage and not stifle a sense of local responsibility (Kissinger 1973).

The political problems of Latin American countries must be resolved by the people of those countries themselves. Nevertheless the United States is drawn into the political instability of the region. It is drawn into the conflict between countries when the political institutions of those countries are threatened. For these reasons it is in the US interest and in the interest of every country of the region that those institutions be strengthened.

US interest in the political alignment of its neighbors

Finally, it is in the US national interest that the countries of the region do not provide support for or align themselves with the global political rivals of the United States. This, of course, is the key to the current US problems in the hemisphere with Cuba and Nicaragua. The United States is a global power and the global power balance is of vital interest to it. In this sense, it supports the world *status quo*. I use that term as it was used by political realists like Hans J. Morgenthau, for whom the *status quo* referred to the distribution of power among nations at any given moment in time. However, I hasten to add — as Morgenthau himself added — that the *status quo* does not refer to the distribution of power within nations; that is to say that the political make-up of individual nations, other things being equal, does not need to concern us (see Morgenthau 1973). But the political support and alliances that countries may establish with our major rivals, especially those with a hostile complexion, is vitally important.

In the context of the global power balance, and from the US perspective, Latin America is a part of East-West competition. A cornerstone of US policy toward the hemisphere has always been that the ideological balance in the hemisphere should not shift against it and, in recent times, against the Western Bloc generally. It is useful to reflect on John F. Kennedy's pronouncements in this regard after the 1962 missile crisis. The public record states that Kennedy's understanding of the 'agreement' reached with the Soviet Union was that the Soviet Union would withdraw its missiles from Cuba in exchange for a US commitment not to threaten Cuba. The United States in turn would understand that Cuba would not interfere in the politics of the countries of the region. That is, Cuba would not seek to export its revolution or to aid 'brothers in revolution' in the Western Hemisphere.

Of course, most of these understandings were not joined by either the Soviets or the Cubans. Neither was eager to limit its future options in that way. Nevertheless, the principles established in Kennedy's statements — US acceptance of a Marxist Cuba and Cuban non-intervention outside its borders — have remained a cornerstone of US policy toward the region. Most critics of recent policy in Central America have failed to appreciate the singularity and consistency with which those principles have persisted over time and have guided the formulation of attitudes at the highest levels of US government and in the public at large.

A second anecdote of the Kennedy period underscores this posture, and illustrates the dilemma the United States confronts in dealing with ideology in the hemisphere. The anecdote concerns Kennedy's reflection on the possible US policy position following the death of the dictator Trujillo in the Dominican Republic. Arthur M.Schlesinger Jr. reports in his book on the Kennedy period (*A Thousand Days*, 1968) the Kennedy inner staff's discussions of what might emerge in the untested political system of the Dominican Republic following Trujillo's death. Kennedy noted: 'There are three possibilities . . . in descending order of preference: a decent democratic regime, a continuation of the Trujillo regime, or a Castro regime. We ought to aim at the first, but we really can't renounce the second until we are sure that we can avoid the third.'

The issue here is above all one of alignment in foreign policy. Internal political dynamics are secondary for the United States in its assessment of countries' attitudes towards its own global political rivals. A country's foreign policy is the element on which it is judged most strictly. In this respect it is conceivable that a Spanish (social democratic) or even a Yugoslav (independent communist) model might prevail in the hemisphere. However, it is difficult to envisage any Communist government that does not have an aggressive and pro-Soviet foreign policy. Certainly past experience provides little encouragement for such expectations. The current situation in Central America and the Caribbean is instructive. The Reagan administration argues that the Nicaraguan government has supported guerrillas in El Salvador and that Cuban and Soviet advisers in turn are supporting the Nicaraguan government. In Grenada, Maurice Bishop desired a warming of relations with the United States, but colleagues of his were uncomfortable with the proposition and ultimately disposed of him in order to have their way. Yet even while Bishop was asking for more leniency from the United States, Grenada was voting in the United Nations in support of the Soviet invasion of Afghanistan, an issue on which only the hardest-line Soviet Bloc countries cast their votes with the Soviet Union. Papers of the Bishop government now show that Bishop was also committed to a Marxist-Leninist regime for Grenada (see Grenada Documents, 1984, and Valenta and Valenta, 1984). In 1979 the United States and many other countries wished the Nicaraguan Sandinistas well in their efforts to bring a better quality of life in Nicaragua. But as Sandinistas moved more and more purposively toward Cuba, the Soviet Union and its Eastern Bloc allies, US government policy and US public opinion have turned increasingly strongly against the Nicaraguan regime.

Policies supporting US interests in Central America[4]

Current US foreign policy toward Central America responds to the interests set out above. The region's political experience has been one of turmoil, external support to armed oppositions and an economic crisis rooted in both domestic and international circumstances. Fragile civilian democratic governments that emerged to preside over the transformation of Central America's politically obsolescent political systems are constantly threatened by domestic instability and a hostile external environment that pays them little heed. The US government's policy prescription for dealing with this complex crisis has been (1) to increase the degree of commitment to the region; (2) to promote democratic institution-building; (3) to increase military assistance sufficiently to enable local forces to counter external aid to guerrilla factions; and (4) to promote a positive negotiating strategy in the region.

Economic assistance. In keeping with the recognition that regional economic prosperity serves the US national interest, there is a recognition that a shot in the arm is necessary to stimulate the Central American economies. This shot in the arm must respond not only to the worldwide economic recession, but also to the inadequacy of the domestic infrastructure, the errors of past policy, and the ongoing political crisis that has caused massive capital flight from the region. One political response, the Caribbean Basin Initiative (CBI), was an idea conceived during the Carter Administration and supported vigorously by the World Bank. As carried out under the Reagan Administration, the CBI is a program for a special aid and trade relationship with the region, with emphasis on trade as the component most likely to build a firm foundation for future, independent and sustained growth. The CBI also has a component of direct assistance — rapid-disbursing balance-of-payments support to the economies that had been hurt by a glut of their primary export commodities on the world markets and low international market prices. The CBI program is intended to bridge an economic gap so that the countries can begin new, non-traditional production for which they would receive preferential access to the US market under the trade provisions of the CBI.

The National Bipartisan Commission on Central America, the

---

[4]This discussion of current US foreign policy toward Central America borrows from a speech to the Latin American Program of the Smithsonian Institution's Woodrow Wilson Center by Ambassador Stephen W.Bosworth, formerly Deputy Assistant Secretary for Latin American Affairs and then Director of the State Department's Policy Planning Staff.

Kissinger Commission, also had this idea. The Commission was born in a period of discussions about a Marshall Plan for Central America, just as the Caribbean Basin Initiative had been born amid discussion of a 'mini-Marshall plan' for the Caribbean. The Kissinger Commission correctly recognized that 'only one country is ever going to commit the dollars to the region to accomplish the massive development, because we think development is in our own and the region's interest' (National Bipartisan Commission, 1984). The Kissinger Commission easily arrived at a consensus on the need for aid to develop the countries of the region and on the need for policy reforms at the local level. The questions frequently raised by the Congress in approving the Commission's recommendations were whether the countries of Central America could and would use the money wisely. Critics denounced corruption and incompetence as proof that so much money could not be used effectively. They often pointed to a seeming lack of political will to correct those problems. The Congress continues to ask 'Why give them money when it is just going to be wasted through corruption, skimming, or by ending up in Miami banks?' There is not much confidence in the commitment of many of the leaders of the region to their own political development.

With the prevailing levels of skepticism, there will be no 'bail out' of Central American countries by the United States. Continuing large-scale assistance to Central America will have to be fought for. The proof of its merits and of the effectiveness of current policy lies with Central American leaders and society. North American policymakers expect Latin Americans to contribute considerably more of their own personal and organizational energy to the institution-building task.

Promoting democratic institutions. The United States and most Latin American countries were born in a period of flowering of democratic political philosophies. For a variety of reasons Latin America has not been very successful in realizing the democratic dream, but that does not mean that the people of the region do not continue to aspire to it.

There are many models of democratic institutions. Those in the hemisphere do not need to be carbon copies of US institutions. Indeed, it is likely that in Central America political institutions will emerge looking like those of Venezuela, Spain, France, Germany or other such countries and not like the Anglo-Saxon system of the United States.[5] US policy is to work with the institutions and human resources within these political systems in order to promote more

[5]Mexico is often mentioned as another model for Central America, but the Mexican political system is as unique in the hemispheric context as are the North American

effective performance by their institutions. It is recognized that Latin American government responses in creating a more honest and efficient political climate will facilitate both economic and political development and stability. These more effective systems will contribute positively to national and regional political security.

In this regard, the US government has begun to encourage programs of legal reform, respect for human rights, and more distributive economic programs. It has also begun to try to assist the transfer of the institutional and organizational aspects of the democratic political experience to countries that claim to desire democracy but for a variety of reasons have been unsuccessful in institutionalizing it on their own. One of the most far-sighted projects of the current administration is judicial and legal reform. Laws are on the books in all the Central American countries that should provide for a well-functioning legal system; however, the human resources and the commitment to make those institutions work within the framework established by law have been lacking. Efforts are being made to generate a critical mass of support for legal reform and to stir a consciousness of the need for an independent, autonomous and effective judicial system. On the Latin American side, there is a serious need for Latin Americans, or Central Americans, to demonstrate the political will to create and maintain responsive political party systems that will, in turn, support responsible legal systems. Although political institutions are perhaps more viable in the Eastern Caribbean where there has been a greater tradition of parliamentary democracy, they are very fragile even there, as events in Grenada demonstrated. One cannot, or should not, take political stability or responsibility for granted.

Military assistance. The United States does not intend to use military force to resolve current difficulties in Central America. Military assistance will be used to support other, parallel efforts to create or restore a political and economic climate that is conducive to national development.[6] The United States will provide enough assistance to friendly Central American countries to permit local forces to prevail in their individual struggles. The Congress correctly insists that security assistance must be conditioned on a parallel commitment to responsible human rights behavior and demonstrable implementation of those goals.

---

systems. This author feels that a powerful single party like the PRI is unlikely to emerge in the conflictive atmosphere of Central America.

[6]US military assistance programs reflect the lessons of Vietnam more than many recognize. Chief among those lessons were that the political and military environments are linked and that local governments must implement policy.

Administration officials have frequently insisted that the use of US force in Central America is 'unnecessary and unwise'. General Paul F. Gorman, former Commander of US Southern Command in Panama, has said that the use of US troops in Central America would be 'catastrophic'. Moreover, he and others have argued that US military force is simply not the appropriate tool for dealing with the kind of situation one finds in Central America. At the same time, the United States will not, and should not, deny itself the option of using military force. No sovereign country denies itself the use of the full range of policy options open to it, especially in a situation as dynamic and fast-paced as that in the Central American region is today. That is simply standard bargaining tactics and a fact of political life. However, it is also important to look beyond the standard tactics to the intent behind policy. At the same time, it is also a natural response, and guerrilla doctrine and practice, to use against an opponent the tools to which he will not respond (see Summers, 1982, for a detailed analysis of this logic).

The purpose of US military assistance in Central America is to train and arm forces that can cope with terrorists and a guerrilla military challenge. In Costa Rica it is to prepare the local national guard to deal more effectively with unwanted military and paramilitary forces that operate over its borders and with subversive elements that operate internally. In Guatemala US military assistance had been prohibited since 1977, and current efforts to renew programs of military education and exchange are intended to forge new ties with a new generation of Guatemalan officers.

The controversy over military assistance to El Salvador revolved around 'how much' assistance was needed for fighting a guerrilla war. During the critical period of debate on military aid to El Salvador, the administration argued that 'how much' meant enough to overcome the stalemate. The figure was never precise because it was never known what new forces would be thrown against the Salvadoreans, or how readily the Salvadorean political and military leaders would adapt to the changed circumstances of their countries. From today's vantage-point, that criterion seems to have been adequate and successful. The Salvadorean military have been successful in extending control over larger and larger areas of the country. The guerrillas have been denied the freedom of the mountainous areas and have been forced to adopt tactics like forced draft and attacks on the economic infrastructure and on civilian political leaders to continue their domination in areas where they used to roam freely. A new political leadership is engaged in promoting political, social and economic change. Human rights are guarded more carefully by government, and the economy seems to be making a turnaround.

Carefully conditioned assistance seems to have worked in this one case.

Negotiating strategies. In negotiating, each party must be able to exercise leverage on certain dimensions of the bargain. There must be bargaining chips. Moreover, each side must see itself in a position of being able to gain something in order for the negotiations to be meaningful. Each side must want to negotiate to bring an end to an undesirable situation. Why else go to the table?

The United States and a number of Latin American countries have argued that without pressures — political, military, diplomatic and economic — none of these goals will be achieved in Central America. Some agree that pressure is needed, but dispute the amount and kind of pressures. Others argue that pressures are counterproductive and that it is unlikely that conditions would change with or without pressures.[7]

The negotiating strategies adopted by all sides in the recent Central American conflict have been to bring to bear maximum pressure so that there are maximum incentives and opportunities to achieve a desired outcome. In this respect, the US government has applied political, economic and security pressure; the Contadora countries have applied both political encouragement and pressure; the Nicaraguan 'Contras' have exerted military pressure. The Salvadorean guerrillas continue to threaten a military offensive that will put the Salvadorean military on the run, and have reverted to their 1970s tactic of political retaliation against civilian political leaders.

The United States has several desired outcomes in Central America. These reflect US interests in the region and US foreign policy goals. They include
— improved relations with Nicaragua;
— successful incorporation of the democratic left into the political process in El Salvador;
— incorporation of the democratic right into the political process in Nicaragua;

[7]Without pressure there is no motive for Nicaragua to change its behavior or for the Right or Left in El Salvador or Guatemala to change theirs. The United States argues that the community of nations, both in Central America and in the international community at large, has to keep pressures on all the Central American actors. The administration will also say that the United States is encouraged to keep pressures on by countries in the region. I can testify from personal experience that there are a good number of people within the region that believe that the positive steps from Nicaragua over the last several months have resulted from the difficult situation it finds itself in as a result of pressure from the United States and other countries.

— an end to support to guerrillas in other countries by nations within and outside the region;[8]
— the removal of all agents provocateurs from the region;
— the end to regional political and military tensions, and
— a return to a period of prolonged development.
The goals are entirely consistent with the objectives announced by the Contadora group in their 21 points of September 1983.

The United States and the Contadora peace process

The Contadora process is an important part of these pressures on Central America. The pressures that the Contadora countries bring on the Central American situation is the pressure of peers. The 21 Objectives adopted by the Central American countries and the Contadora arbiters in January 1983 and the Principles for Implementing the Objectives adopted in January 1984 are fully consistent with the US interest and goals in the region. The Contadora effort warrants strong US support. It has support from the vast majority of policy people concerned with the region.

The question that perplexes many observers is 'Why has Contadora taken so long?' To appreciate the long delays, it is necessary to understand clearly what Contadora is in fact promoting. It is not promoting the present *status quo*. The Principles for Implementing the Document of Objectives are quite clear on this. The Contadora process aims at more open, democratic processes in all the countries of the region. It does not look favourably on a military build-up by any country, and it recognizes that freedom from military and political threat is a key to regional security. Such outcomes serve the interests of all the countries involved in the region. If they are achieved — a big, and frustrating 'if' for all the nations involved — it will be a tremendous success for Latin American diplomacy. The success of Contadora will be measured not by the effort, however, but by the results.

Certainly, there was undeniably initial skepticism from the United States about the Contadora process, due in part to the spontaneous and informal origins of the process. In addition, there was already an ongoing and parallel San Jose process which the United

---

[8]President Duarte of El Salvador has observed that his government will not support the Nicaraguan Contras even though it welcomes the pressures that those forces put upon Nicaragua. El Salvador will not support the Contras because it does not want to be in a position of doing to Nicaragua exactly what Nicaragua is doing to El Salvador when it provides assistance, use of its territory and moral support to the Salvadorean guerrillas.

States had undertaken to stimulate and which was still alive. There was a reluctance to promote competing processes. There also was skepticism because of the profound suspicions among some in the United States about the Mexican role in the process, particularly during the Lopez Portillo administration. Mexico's more lenient approach and insistence on accommodating the Nicaraguan perspective became an excuse for those in the United States who did not want to see a successful compromise that left the Sandinistas in office.

In spite of early suspicions, it became increasingly accepted over time in the US government that the Contadora process was the only viable forum for regional peace negotiations. It became important that Contadora should succeed in an agreement that would assure the political, economic and security interests of the United States and its friends in the region. This shift occurred only after the Contadora countries themselves began to recognize the scope of the problems into which they had inserted themselves (see Hayes 1983).

When the Contadora countries initially undertook their effort in January 1983, they thought that they had a simple task ahead of them. That task was to bring about a reconciliation between countries in the region that would forestall and obviate what was then perceived to be a real possibility of a US military intervention in the region. The Contadora leaders soon learned, after multiple visits around the region, that they had opened a Pandora's box of regional and internal conflicts. Every country in the region had a different interest to defend, a different set of concerns, and a different posture *vis-à-vis* its neighors and *vis-à-vis* the United States. Reconciling all those differences was the difficult task that confronted Contadora and that still confronts it.

The United States was specifically asked not to be involved in or vocal about the Contadora process. Members of the Kissinger Commission reported that when they went to Colombia in the fall of 1983, they asked President Betancur whether the United States should get involved, and were given a negative answer. Betancur reportedly argued that if the United States were to embrace the process, given the political tensions existing between the United States and the Cubans, the Nicaraguans, the Mexicans and everybody else, it would be much more difficult for Latin American leaders to work out a reconciliation. Later, when the United States was asked by President de la Madrid of Mexico to engage in a dialogue at Manzanillo, Mexico, it did so. More recently, US patience with Nicaragua's government has worn thinner.

But why has Contadora been difficult? Ambassador Harry

Shlaudeman, US Special Envoy for Central America, has observed
that the Contadora talks are the most complex political negotiation
that Latin America has ever undertaken.[9] It has been undertaken by
four countries — Venezuela, Colombia, Panama and Mexico —
which, despite their geographic proximity to Central America, did
not know a lot about Central America when they began their effort,
and by five Central American countries that didn't like each other
very much, that didn't trust each other, and that had different views
of their regional problems, and different problems that have
stemmed from the regional and global economic crisis. Each
country's individual problems are exacerbated by regional political
difficulties.

   The process began in a period of very high political and military
tension in which there was a sense of loss of room to manoeuvre in
Guatemala; in which many were predicting the imminent fall of the
Salvadorean governments; in which there was a threat, real or imagined, of US military intervention; and in which there was a (hopefully imagined) fear of rapid escalation of the Soviet military presence. These tensions were so high that initially it was very difficult
for the Contadora countries to persuade the five Central American
countries to sit down in the same room with each other. There was
suspicion about the whole process and of one another. There were
suspicions about cross-border incursions, support for subversion,
support for guerrilla groups opposed to governments, and so forth.

   Suspicions were so pervasive in the region that it was almost
impossible to untangle them. Honduras feared that the political
instability in El Salvador might bring to power a leftist government
that would be hostile to Honduras' more conservative democratic
regime. Honduras also worried lest a well-trained and armed
Salvadorean military might be victorious against the guerrillas and
then turn its attention once more against its neighbor as it had in
1969. Hondurans also feared being drawn into the Salvodorean,
Guatemalan and Nicaraguan conflicts as a consequence of the
armed oppositions using its borders as sanctuaries. The
Nicaraguans were afraid that the United States would insert itself in
the Salvadorean conflict. The Salvadoreans, the Costa Ricans, and
the Hondurans all thought that the Nicaraguans were supporting
subversion across their borders. Hondurans and Mexicans thought
that the Guatemalan guerrillas were using their border territories as
safe havens. The story goes on.

   Contadora's success to date had been in sorting out and allaying
the tensions generated by those suspicions, and forestalling the out-

[9]Personal communication with the author.

break of regional conflict. We in the United States and others outside the region have been overly impatient about the Contadora process. We have looked for an immediate solution, a good fix, a signing of a document that we could put on the international law library shelf — an action that would permit us to go away to attend to other issues. Such an easy solution is not likely to be found in Central America today. Relations between the participants in the Contadora process is one of near-total lack of trust. Arriving at agreement on a piece of paper that commits a country's national prestige to certain behavior, especially if that behavior represents a compromise of principle and of national mode of behavior, is no mean feat. It is even more difficult and risky to arrive at an agreement when the parties fear that the others will cheat, or are negotiating in bad faith, or are committing themselves only part of the way.

The process that the Contadora countries have undertaken is comparable to trying to achieve a SALT agreement between the United States and the Soviet Union. Elsewhere in this book Dr Falk Bomsdorf observes that it is very difficult for parties on the opposing sides of the ideological divide to believe that the other side is sincere when it says it is going to do something. It is very difficult to agree to something that is not easily assured. In the Contadora process, verification of security commitments is one of the key commitments that must be assured before the negotiating parties will be willing to move ahead in the negotiations. But assurances against political aggression and subversion over time are perhaps even more important to regional peace, and a greater constraint on the negotiation process.[10]

Participants at the meeting of the International Peace Academy in February 1984 concluded that if the Contadora countries — the four and the five Central Americans — cannot solve the problem of internal oppositions committed to armed resistance and operating out of neighboring sovereign territory, and if they cannot resolve the problems of suspicions that are generated by seemingly antagonistic ideologies, Contadora is unlikely to be about to solve the regional problem. As long as there are ideologically antagonistic oppositions that belong to each of the countries in the region; that operate as

---

[10]A number of observers who have commented on the problems faced by Contadora mention the question of security against political-ideological threat and subversion explicitly. For the Contadora countries, verification of trans-border arms flows, while tremendously difficult, is a question of technology and funds. There are no mechanisms that can be put in place that can guarantee against infiltration, training and organizing of dissidents and other potential threats to the political stability of a political system. Thus the political ideological threat is by far the most serious of the problems that the regional countries face in trying to resolve the Central American problem.

armed forces out of other countries in the region; and that refuse or are denied the opportunity to compete internally, it is going to be almost impossible to resolve the political problems of Central America. It is not useful for the Central Americans to sign a document which says they can solve their problems if in fact the problems cannot be solved. Outside observers should not insist on the appearance of solutions when a solution is not in the offing.

This does not mean that Contadora has not achieved tremendous success in creating space for discussion on the very issues that still block its conclusion. In this regard, we must enthusiastically support its continuation. No one, including the US government, wants the Contadora process to fail. Even those who are convinced at the time of writing that the effort has failed do not want to admit as much in public. It is in the interests of the United States and of the Central American countries that Contadora continue successfully.

Conclusion

To be successful, US policies toward Latin America must build on, and be consistent with, US interests in the region. They must be feasible within the limits established by public interest and tolerance. A successful policy must also find a response in the societies toward which it is directed. It must recognize the interests, attitudes and aspirations of those societies and encourage responses that are commensurate with US interests and aspirations.

US policy toward Latin America has often been practised in an on-again off-again fashion. Sometimes it has been exercised on behalf of special interests, but more often it has reflected a too narrow set of political goals for the region that focussed on the absence of outside (extra-hemispheric) intervention. In the more complex world of the 1980s and beyond, US interests in and goals for Latin America must be broader. The goals must include economic and political security, respect for human rights, good government, and freedom from physical and ideological aggression. These are not inconsistent with the interest of all Latin American countries themselves. How effectively all work to achieve the goals is the key to the quality of the future relationship.

BIBLIOGRAPHY

Council of the Americas (1984), 'Debt, Economic Crisis and United States Corporations in Latin America' (mimeo).

Grenada documents (1983), *The Line of March of the Party by Comrade Maurice Bishop.*

Hayes, Margaret Daly (1982), 'United States Security Interests in Central America in Global Perspective' in Richard Feinberg (ed.), *Central America: the International Dimensions of the Crisis*, New York: Holmes and Meier.

—— (1983), 'Promoting U.S. Security Interests in Central America', Lead Consultant's presentation to the National Bipartisan Commission on Central America (September).

—— (1983), 'Regional Perspectives on the Situation in Central America', manuscript prepared for the Council on Foreign Relations Central America Study Group (November).

—— (1984), *Latin America and the U.S. National Interest: A Basis for U.S. Foreign Policy*, Boulder, Colo.: Westview Press.

Kissinger, Henry A. (1973), 'On the National Interest' in *American Foreign Policy* (expanded edn), New York: W.W. Norton.

Morgenthau, Hans J. (1973), *Politics Among Nations: The Struggle for Power and Peace*, 5th edn, New York: Alfred A. Knopf.

Report of the National Bipartisan Commission on Central America (1984), Washington, DC: US Government Printing Office.

Schlesinger, Arthur M. (1968), *A Thousand Days*, Boston: Houghton Mifflin.

Summers, Jr., Harry G. (1982), *On Strategy: A Critical Analysis of the Vietnam War*. New York: Dell Publishing Co.

US Senate, Committee on Foreign Relations (1984), *Hearings on the Report of the National Bipartisan Commission on Central America*. Washington, DC: US Government Printing Office.

Valenta, Jiri, with V.Valenta, 'Leninism in Grenada', *Problems of Communism*, July-Aug. 1984, pp. 1-23.

3

CUBA'S ROLE IN THE CARRIBBEAN BASIN

Haroldo Dilla Alfonso

It is a well-known fact that the triumph of the Cuban Revolution constituted a milestone in the history of the Hemisphere, inasmuch as the process that began on January 1, 1959, severed the ties of neocolonialist dependence and set down the bases for a new social system in the Hemisphere. At that time Cuba became a variable to be taken into account in the political game of the Hemisphere.

Cuba's influence was extended throughout the Hemishpere and was felt particularly in the region where it shares the most similarities and has the strongest historical ties: the Caribbean and Central America. For the countries to which we refer here as the Caribbean Basin, the Cuban Revolution held more than one attraction. First, the United States considers it a region unilaterally situated within its national security boundaries and as a area within its natural sphere of influence. As such the area has experienced, in the flesh, the rigours of a dependence plagued by imperialist interventions and aggressions. Thus the Cuban challenge to North American dominance showed the viability of national liberation to the Caribbean region.

On the other hand, these societies, saturated by social injustices and inequalities, had experienced economic growth and wealth for which they paid a high social price. For them, the success of the so-called Cuban model, which addressed the vital needs of the masses especially in the areas of education and health, marked the road towards social justice that many socio-political sectors in the region chose to follow.

However, if Cuba's struggle against dependence and under-development was regarded with hope by important sociopolitical sectors of the Hemisphere, the United States opted to interpret the Cuban Revolution simply as a challenge to its traditional geopolitical ambitions and against its principles of domination; as such it had to be crushed. Space does not permit us to explain here each one of the manifestations of this hostility. Cuba was isolated diplomatically and economically from its natural historical habitat: the Latin American Hemisphere (with the honourable exception of Mexico). It was forced to accelerate its process of internal changes

42

and carry out diverse defensive actions in order to preserve its socioeconomic and political victories. At the same time, Cuba accepted the generous offer of assistance from the socialist world, thanks to which its Revolution is a reality today and not a glorious memory of the holocaust of an entire nation in pursuit of a better tomorrow.

During the 1970s, significant changes took place in the situation described above. On the one hand, the rise to power in Latin America of more realistic political forces brought about a partial rapprochement of Cuba with the Hemisphere, whether by means of the establishment of diplomatic and commercial relations or simply through diverse contacts which, though informal, manifested the overcoming of political docility against imperialist mandates. It also marked the awakening of a strong Latin American awareness between the nations of the region. Further, the definitive fortification of the Cuban Revolution also has repercussions within North American political circles. They were now forced to adopt more flexible policies, even if they were still hostile, in order to confront the first socialist state in the Hemisphere.

However, in spite of several positive steps taken during the first stages of the Carter administration, the slackening of tensions between the two countries did not produce a substantial change in the hostile attitude of the United States, and in any case did not survive the test of the popular insurgencies in other parts of the Hemisphere — i.e. the popular victories in Nicaragua and Grenada in 1979. Suddenly a peculiar interpretation of popular movements in the area began to emerge as a result of the Cuban-Soviet involvement. This found its most outspoken voice in the official policy of the Republican administration headed by President Ronald Reagan. It is outside our task here to outline the contents of this policy, whose arrogant and over-simplified manifestations can be found in almost any official document or statement by North American government spokesmen. Instead we will show the Cuban position *vis-à-vis* the present conflicts — actual or potential — which characterise the convulsive region of the Caribbean Basin.

In the first place, the real causes of the Central American conflict and the visible deterioration in the Caribbean region are not due to East-West confrontation or to alleged Cuban-Soviet expansionism. Rather they are the result of the dependent capitalist development in the region, whose negative features (high concentration of income, alarming levels of unemployment and underemployment, weakening of social services, constant degradation of the cost-of-living indices) are accentuated by the heat of the world economic crisis and the plundering economic policies adopted by some developed capitalist countries, particularly the United States.

At the same time, the lack of democratic channels in Central America that would allow, through legal means, the interaction of interests of diverse sociopolitical groups, leave the democratic political forces with no other recourse but armed struggle in order to oppose the highly repressive military dictatorships which systematically violate the most basic human rights. Popular insurgency is therefore the direct product of the socio-economic and political conditions prevalent in Central America after decades of distorted and dependent capitalist growth.

Neither the Caribbean Basin Initiative, with its denationalising and politically conditioned incentives, nor the omnipresence of the recessionist prescriptions of the International Monetary Fund, nor the military build-up of the region, nor the interventionist formulas contained in the Kissinger Report — none of these will alleviate the present situation; rather they will aggravate it. At no time will they become substitutes for the only viable alternative to achieve a lasting peace in the Caribbean Basin: the implementation of socio-economic projects that will take into account popular interests and political forces interested in substantial social changes, democracy and a real national independence.

In the second place, the worsening of the conflict in the area is determined by the interventionist and militaristic policy of the United States, in cahoots with the local oligarchies and the most reactionary political circles. The Central American and Caribbean regions are experiencing today a North American military deployment unprecedented in its magnitude and comparable in its results to that of the early years of the century, when Teddy Roosevelt 'took' the Canal and imposed his big-stick diplomacy on the nations of the area. Huge increases in military assistance to the region, naval manoeuvres, reactivation and/or establishment of military bases, direct or indirect interventions against the popular movements, virtual occupation of the countries of the area by contingents of marines, and so on — all are manifestations of the aggressive North American will and of the creation of a scenario extremely dangerous to the survival of our countries.

The actions of Cuba in the Caribbean Basin are in keeping with the legacy of Bolívar and Martí and with the internationalist spirit and the solidarity which has sparked its historical evolution and was rooted institutionally in the Constitution of the Republic via a popular referendum. First of all, the Cuban effort is noted for its strengthening of cultural, commercial, diplomatic and other relations with the countries of the region, based on common goals and mutual respect for national self-determination. Cuba has hosted important regional events — such as 'Carifesta' or the Central American and Caribbean Games — and has participated actively in others. In addition, it has supported the positions of the Caribbean and Central American countries in global issues such as the struggle for a new international economic order, or in specific issues such as the demands of the people of Panama for their sovereignty over the Canal and of Belize for independence. In keeping with its anti-colonialist positions and because this constitutes its historic legacy, Cuba has been in the forefront in defending the independence of Puerto Rico — an issue which has become a permanent source of friction with the United States.

Because of its importance, Cuba's cooperation and collaboration with the other countries of the Caribbean Basin deserves specific analysis. Cuban economic cooperation, though modest, is not subjected to political or ideological pre-conditons, and has been implemented both in times of emergency, as when a country has suffered national disasters, and in more long-term plans always based on mutual respect and lack of vested interest. This collaboration has included thirteen economic and social areas and has been especially significant in the area of public health, where Cuban advances have been recognised worldwide.

A confirmation of the foregoing can be found in the experience of Cuban-Jamaican cooperation. After 1975, as under the social-democratic government of Michael Manley, Jamaica received Cuban aid in more than a dozen areas, which proved to be extremely useful for the recipient. This aid was continued after the coming to power of the labourite politician Edward Seaga, despite the fact that a good part of his election campaign consisted of anti-Cuban attacks, and particularly the accusation that Cuban assistance was a means of subversive infiltration and penetration. In maintaining these commitments Cuba held to its policy of humanitarian principles, taking into consideration the important role played by Cuban technicians there, especially the medical brigade. This assistance was interrupted only when — after the breaking of relations decided by Seaga in October 1981 — it was impossible to keep Cuban personnel in Jamaica because of the lack of minimal security guarantees.

We also stress the aid given by Cuba to the people of Nicaragua, especially in areas such as health, education, construction, agriculture and the provision of a small group of military advisers and professors requested by the Nicaraguan government, in full exercise of its sovereign powers, to strengthen its defences in the face of the most blatant aggression financed by the United States. US propaganda regarding Cuba's aid to Nicaragua tends to distort its real content, inflating its military component and ignoring the fact that this assistance is based simply on a Latin American tradition which predates the revolutionary victory — as when an earthquake destroyed the city of Managua. Similarly slanderous interpretations have been made regarding collaboration with other countries. One example of this led to worldwide discredit: the construction of the Point Salines airport in the tiny island of Grenada which, according to North American spokesmen, is a strategic military point for Cuban and Soviet operations in the area. As has been demonstrated, the construction of the Grenada airport has purely commercial and civilian objectives; planned by the government of Eric Gairy, it had been demanded by the country's private sector, and its technical implementation was carried out by a British company contracted by the government of Maurice Bishop. Paradoxically, the first to use the airport for purposes of military aggression were precisely the North Americans when they invaded that tiny Caribbean island.

With regard to the Central American conflict, the Cuban position has been clearly explained by the top political leaders of the country. From the early stages of the conflict, Cuba supported — as it continues to do — the principal initiatives in favour of a negotiated settlement, such as the French-Mexican Declaration and other proposals and negotiations from the government of Mexico, the Socialist International, COPPAL, and other organisations and governments. At present it supports the Contadora Group in its active and constructive role in the treatment of several issues of the conflict, as well as any other initiative dealing in the same vein. But at the same time the Cuban government has stressed the need to include the El Salvador problem in any negotiations, in particular the search for a solution that will take into account the interests of the people of that country as represented by the FMLN-FDR. Obviously, any possible negotiation attempting to solve the Central American conflict cannot exclude El Salvador.

Cuba does not consider itself as a party directly involved in the conflict, as the United States does. However, given its ties of solidarity with the popular movements in the area and particularly with the Sandinista government, Cuba has manifested its willingness to make commitments — just as all the other countries, including the United States, have made them.

In lending its full support to the search for avenues leading to a just and honourable solution to the Central American conflict, Cuba neither pursues national interests nor considers the nature of its relations with the United States as an essential issue in negotiations. Cuba has manifested its willingness to undertake mutual steps for the relaxation of bilateral tensions, including the possibility of a direct dialogue with top officials of that country, provided that such negotiations do not violate any basic political principles. However, the experience of the last 25 years indicates that any US willingness for dialogue with Cuba has been based only on positions of force unacceptable to a sovereign and independent nation. Relations with the socialist world, international compromises, solidarity in favour of Puerto Rico's independence, the irrevocable commitment to the construction of socialism — none of these can be issues for discussion with the United States. The possibilities of a dialogue appear further away today than ever, given the ideological focus of the present US administration's foreign policy and the emphasis of anti-Cuban hostility as an important part of that focus.

In any event, the years which have elapsed since 1959 have shown that relations with the United States are not needed in order to march triumphantly on the road to economic development, social progress and national liberation. US political circles must ponder seriously the irrevocable nature of the Cuban Revolution and the repeated failure of their policies towards Cuba. They must remember an accurate phrase of ex-Assistant Secretary of State, Viron Vaky: 'Our inability to link ourselves to democratic sectors has placed us on the wrong side of history.'

4

NICARAGUA'S POSITION IN THE REGION

Alejandro Bendaña

Recent developments in Central America are an outrage against regional peace and cooperation, and against the efforts to achieve peaceful solutions to the existing disputes through dialogue. The most recent sign of this was the boycott that certain Central American countries declared against the Contadora process.

At this point, hindrance of the negotiation channels is accompanied by an unprecedented concentration of US troops less than 12 km. from our northern border, and the presence of US warships, like the battleship *Iowa*, in Central American waters. All this is done under cover of military manoeuvres, which obviously constitute on-the-spot rehearsals for direct intervention which could be staged at the right moment. We cannot refer to the peace efforts without mentioning the existence of a warmongering determination that not only checks that effort but also exacts a price, in terms of the deaths of innocent civilians at the hands of those whom Reagan calls 'freedom fighters'. On the same day that Reagan compared his mercenaries with Bolívar, the so-called 'freedom fighters' ambushed two civilian vehicles and killed several construction workers as well as a father and his five-year-old son. For them and their relatives, as for thousands of other victims, peace and cooperation will arrive too late, and the advances made in the negotiating processes will have ceased to be a life-and-death matter. However, it does remain a life-and-death matter for the rest of our people and for all the people of Central America. This is why Nicaragua, in addition to giving its firm support to Contadora, is also intent on holding a dialogue with the United States in order to reach an understanding marked by mutual respect within the framework of International Law.

However, on 17 January 1985 the United States suddenly and unilaterally suspended the bilateral talks that had been taking place in the Mexican city of Manzanillo. This dealt a harsh blow to Nicaragua's negotiating effort to normalise the relations between the two states and, along that path, to help restore peace and friendly coexistence among the Central American nations. It was also a blow to Contadora, since only nine days earlier the foreign ministers of Contadora had exhorted 'the governments of the United

48

States and Nicaragua to intensify the dialogue they have been holding in Manzanillo in order to reach agreements that will favour the reactivation of their relations and regional détente.' One day after making this unilateral decision, to the detriment of previous agreements, the US administration took the unusual step of disqualifying the jurisdiction of the International Court of Justice and the proceedings initiated by Nicaragua — in which the United States had participated actively until that tribunal issued a ruling on 26 November 1984, declaring itself competent, and received Nicaragua's suit demanding a stop to that government's military and paramilitary activities against our people. This development, which by itself admits guilt and acknowledges the inability to defend the indefensible, also set a precedent in the history of that court, for it was the first time that a country withdrew from the proceedings on learning of the Tribunal's decision after having initially accepted its compulsory jurisdiction.

The path to a negotiated solution was again undermined in the wake of a decision by Washington and certain Central American governments to boycott the meeting called by Contadora on 14 and 15 February 1985 to advance toward the signing of the Contadora Document. It is undeniable that this new attempt makes the outlook for Central American peace appear even more sombre. But paradoxically this blow dealt at the goodwill of Latin America and the world as expressed through Contadora, and at the peaceful negotiation promoted by Nicaragua, results from the foiled US effort to subject our country through pressure and blackmail. The same escalation of aggressive actions on the part of the United States on all fronts leads to a further endorsement of the policies of the Nicaraguan Revolution. These policies seek negotiated solutions and reject actions which threaten sovereignty by force.

Throughout the entire difficult and lengthy process of Contadora, the whole world has been able to witness Nicaragua's stand as well as the specific contributions that our government has made to strengthen that process and guarantee its successful culmination. Immediately after the Contadora Declaration of 9 January 1983 establishing the Contadora Group, Nicaragua gave it unrestricted support, and requested the same from the delegates of those countries which were then being represented in Managua, at an Extraordinary Ministerial Meeting of the Nonaligned Countries Movement's Coordinating Bureau. Also in 1983, Nicaragua introduced a draft resolution at the UN Security Council in support of the Contadora Group initiative. That Resolution (530) reasserts Nicaragua's right, as well as that of all the other countries of the region, to live in peace, free from foreign interference. After the Contadora Group presented its Document of Objectives in September 1984, Nicaragua was the only country to fulfill a request by the Contadora foreign ministers that the Central American countries should present specific proposals on ways that the agreements included in the Document of Objectives could be fulfilled. Specific proposals were presented on 15 October 1984, covering the entire Document of Objectives. This was in contrast to other Central American countries which did not show willingness to co-operate with the Contadora effort.

Contadora later adopted a new approach, conducting intense consultations and exchanges of views with all the Central American governments. This culminated in the presentation of a draft document for peace and cooperation in Central America on 7 September 1984 which, according to Contadora itself, 'reflects the observations and comments that the five Central American governments made about the plan'. The Contadora foreign ministers, therefore, announced at the meetings held on 6 and 7 September 1984 that the commission and the Technical Group had concluded their work. The note sent to the heads of state also says that 'it is now up to the political determination of the Central American governments to give legal scope to the commitments made during the process . . . The signing of the Contadora Document for peace and cooperation in Central America must lead to the establishment of a framework of security and mutual respect, which is essential in order to guarantee the political and economic stability that the peoples in the area aspire to achieve.'

After carefully studying the proposal officially presented by Contadora on 7 September, and in response to Contadora's urgent appeal that the document be signed as soon as possible, Nicaragua announced on 21 September its willingness to sign it. It was not an easy decision, since Nicaragua is not a member of any military pact; we are not part of either the Warsaw Treaty or, much less, NATO. Our security rested on international moral support, especially that of Latin America, which might serve as an argument in the event of an aggression. The security of other Central American countries, if they accepted the Document, would always be safeguarded through the military support of the United States. Nonetheless, we trusted then and still trust the word given by those countries that might sign that document. We agree with the Contadora foreign ministers, who stated in their note that 'to negotiate entails partly giving in, in order to obtain an ultimate goal deemed essential.' For Nicaragua that ultimate goal is peace in Central America, the peace that our peoples demand as an essential condition before they can undertake the tasks inherent to our political, social, and economic development.

For the sake of peace, Nicaragua chose not even to suggest adding further finishing touches to the foreign ministers' statements, feeling that this might be used to raise objections to the signing of the Document through useless discussions that would have no effect on the substantial aspects of the proposal since, as the Contadora foreign ministers have themselves stated, the substantial aspects of their proposal could no longer be negotiated.

The announcement that Nicaragua had decided to sign the document elicited an immediate reaction from the US government, which forced the governments of Honduras, El Salvador and Costa Rica to withdraw their initial acceptance and support for the draft document. This was fully demonstrated with the publication of an official document of the US National Security Council on 30 October 1984, which asserts that 'after intense consultations by the US government with El Salvador, Honduras and Costa Rica, those Central American countries introduced a counterproposal before Contadora on 20 October 1984. It reflects many of our concerns if Contadora's direction is changed toward a document consistent, in general terms, with the interests of the United States.' This assertion allows the US government to rejoice in its victory by stating in the same document that 'we have effectively blocked the Contadora Group's efforts to impose its draft revised document.' At one point Nicaragua stated that the interventionist US policy against Contadora had not only foiled the signing of the document for peace and cooperation in Central America, but had dealt a blow from which, in our view, the Contadora negotiating process would be hard put to recover. In line with its policy 'effectively blocking' Contadora, the US government has resorted to the Costa Rican media, which it has been using to foment warmongering stances in the region and to discredit the Contadora process through a campaign which, because of its violence, could have only been orchestrated by the CIA. The goal of this campaign was to pressure the Costa Rican government into making its future participation in the Contadora process conditional on Nicaragua's acceptance of arbitrary demands for resolving a non-existent violation of the Right of Asylum, unconnected to the foreseen mechanisms for solution.

We can only regret that the suspension of the Contadora meeting of 14 February 1985 was deliberately provoked under the pretext of an incident which is totally out of proportion with such a stand. To resort to a case of that nature in order to block an international action of such importance is to fly in the face of common sense and the cause of peace. The principle of the Right of Asylum* is a serious one, and

---

*The right of asylum has a long history in Latin America, and is embodied in a number of bilateral and multilateral agreements. It is generally respected by all countries of

Nicaragua is anxious to discuss it thoroughly in all its ramifications and expressions, since we have seen that the most flagrant and systematic violations of its norms and principles occur in the neighbouring countries. This violation takes the form of overt propaganda and even of military activity by alleged Nicaraguan exiles in those countries.

If it were a matter of using bilateral conflicts as excuses for not attending a meeting, or to set conditions on the entire Contadora process, Nicaragua could adopt such a position with greater reason, if one considers the violations of our territorial integrity and the almost daily killing of our citizens as a result of attacks launched from neighbouring countries. In fact, since the Contadora process began, there have been bilateral conflicts as grave or even more serious than this one, which have been resolved thanks to Contadora's mediation and the political determination to overcome the problems. Can it be that some have harboured the illusion that Nicaragua could be pressured and blackmailed because it was under attack? As several high-ranking Central American officials have said, Nicaragua is the party most interested in signing a peace agreement. This manoeuvre, which led to the suspension of the meeting called by Contadora on 14 and 15 February 1985, to which a Nicaraguan delegation was sent, shows that the US government is determined not only to block Contadora but is literally preventing a process that requires from all the countries involved the capacity to make their own decisions on the basis of their own national interests without intervention or impositions from third states. Nicaragua firmly believes that the conflicts among the Central American nations are artificial because they respond to foreign intervention.

There is no doubt that the United States is defending its own interest, and that to this end it has taken on itself the task of blocking the ratification of the Contadora Document and its modifications. It is using pressure to impose its will on Central America. The positions held are clear and the key issue is the eradication of the foreign military presence in Central America. We are witnessing a historical moment in which Latin America has proposed a Latin American solution to a Latin American problem. That solution — the Contadora Document — is in total contradiction to the Monroe Doctrine. Let the United States answer: Will the military manoeuvres be banned, as Contadora proposes or will they not be banned, as the United States demands? Will the foreign military advisers leave, as Contadora proposes, or will they stay, as the United States

---

the region when the reasons for seeking asylum are political and when the individual in question is not involved in violent or criminal activities.

demands? Will the military bases be banned, as Contadora proposes, or will they not be banned, as the United States proposes? Will the US military presence be legitimised or will it not?

President Reagan's strong attacks on Nicaragua and his request to Congress to renew the financial aid for the counter-revolutionaries confirm that the White House is behind the failure of the Contadora meeting. Only a few hours before the suspension of the meeting, Reagan delivered what the *New York Times* described as the most virulent attack against the Sandinista government, and expressed most open support for the counter-revolutionaries, whom he called 'our brothers' and shamelessly compared to Simón Bolívar. The position adopted by the United States and its Central American allies had thrown the area into a new and more serious crisis, as the possible acceptance of the alternative presented by Contadora is called into question. Still, we cannot weaken in the search for a negotiated political solution.

An important way to prevent the bogging down of Contadora would be for the United States to accept the resumption of its bilateral dialogue with Nicaragua in Manzanillo as soon as possible. Secondly, it must heed the protective measures ordered by the International Court of Justice in order to lay the groundwork for a negotiation leading to a normalisation of the relations between our two countries. Thirdly, the resumption of the Reagan administration's financial aid for the mercenaries must be prevented. The approval of funds might destroy the last chance to reach regional understanding. In addition, a universal appeal should be made for strict adherence to the rules of international coexistence and peaceful solution established in the UN Charter. We must speak clearly and firmly. Central America is not anyone's private game reserve. We have the right to ask Washington to modify its dangerous and absurd position, and not to hinder the Contadora process. Thus we will also safeguard the legitimate interests of the US people.

PART TWO

MEASURES AND APPROACHES TO CONFLICT RESOLUTION

5

OBSTACLES TO DIALOGUE AND A NEGOTIATED SOLUTION IN LATIN AMERICA

Adolfo Aguilar Zinzer

The purpose of this Chapter is to identify the principal obstacles which impede the search for a negotiated peace in Central America. It is written from a Latin American perspective. Since 1979 the political and social crisis in the region has become a source of concern for the international community. Numerous governments, political movements and personalities from different countries, and with different viewpoints, have attempted repeatedly to bring the protagonists in the conflict together to discuss their differences; the expectations have been that they would be able to establish a just and acceptable framework, based on democratic and peaceful participation, in order to resolve the tremendous challenges posed by the social changes needed in the region. Up till now all these attempts have failed. However, the experience they have provided has strengthened demands for a peaceful and negotiated solution of a problem that, despite its limited regional dimensions, is a threat to international peace and security.

The dimensions of the conflict and the players

Any definition of the nature of the Central American conflict must start from a global hypothesis that explains its nature, origins and factors and their relationship to the violent conflict. There are two major alternative propositions: one that places the conflict within the general framework of the East-West confrontation, and the other that presents it as an historic consequence of that framework: the backwardness, political intransigence and discriminatory repression experienced by Central America since independence.

If, as a point of departure, we acknowledge that the causes of the crisis are socio-economic and manifest themselves in the profound and violent destruction of the old order, it is also possible to discover that this essentially involves a generalised struggle for power. The whole crisis for power makes us confront a violent and acute derailment from the traditional political track. At the same time, it also radically changes the face of regional politics, and almost inevitably places all the political and social forces in the region in either of two major sectors in the struggle. These are, first, simply defined as a desire for power — armed, strong, tangible and capable of conquering. It is a force born outside the traditional game of politics and with ample popular legitimacy. The second sector is counter-revolution, an area in which all sectors, groups and forces who directly or indirectly defend the prevailing system are bunched together regardless of their convictions.

Revolution and counter-revolution have fatally become the fundamental expressions of the struggle for power in Central America, and are therefore the two main protagonists in the conflict. The struggle, in its forms and manifestations, emanates directly from the political history of the area. Therefore, it must be recognised that the players involved in the action are conglomerates and entities that are political and social, national and regional, independent and autonomous; each seeks, by itself and for itself, the acquisition or preservation of power. To question the established power or to preserve it are not exclusive postures of each group. The counter-revolution defends the deep-rooted power, but it also attempts to restore a vital and lost space in Nicaragua. Consequently, the revolution not only seeks to seize power from the old regimes in El Salvador and Guatemala, but it also defends it in the Sandinista state. Because of this dichotomy, the ideologues of the conflict confuse and distort the true identity of the players.

Although it might be viewed as rigidly categorical, the admission that the conflict ultimately involves a power struggle, in accordance with a specific historical/social reality, constitutes the indispensable, analytical basis to explain the problem of peace and a negotiated solution. In fact, it is essential to locate the exact hub of the conflict, and to find the players who must sit at the negotiating table without ambiguities or equivocation. To speak of a dialogue, or struggle for confidence, or to hope for any kind of transaction is useless unless these basic definitions are taken into account.

It was right after Somoza's fall in Nicaragua that the basic social and political conflict in Central America became a regional one. However, this phenomenon was not due to a revolutionary epidemic or to an exported revolution — long before the Sandinista upsurge, Central America was already suffering from the ills of a revolution

— but rather to the fear, irritation and sudden awakening of the traditional powers. The counter-revolutionary leap was felt even in moderate circles, because in the political history of Central America — from colonial times to the present — no organised and well-defined force had succeeded so violently and determinedly in overthrowing a regime. In Nicaragua, power was changed so radically that even the new state conscripted its own army from the ranks of the stampede within the ranks of the old. In the rest of Central America, this brand-new revolution had to be regarded as a possible disaster and as a real alternative. Thus all the beneficiary groups and parties, or those aspiring to power under the old guard, regarded Nicaragua as a new, suspicious and even threatening embryo. Since then they have tried, urgently and implacably, to abort the birth of this 'three-headed monster'. The fundamental historical factor was, however, that the Sandinista movement tried to bring to Nicaragua a new model of power based on a radically different consensus. This model was not new; for decades the groups in power had feared and condemned it as an intolerable possibility. Revolution, in itself a nationalist, anti-oligarchic and anti-dictatorial demand, was always regarded obsessively as a threat. With the victory of the Sandinista movement this historical conviction — of being members of an often maligned regime — caused the defenders of the *status quo* to sound the alarm among their close national alliances. Regionalisation as a mechanism for the defence of specific political and economic interests is not a recent phenomenon in Central America; on the contrary, the major events in Central American history have always been regional and the present event could not be an exception. This also means that the opponents in the social battle identify fully with history, fear each other, and are willing to fight each other irreconcilably. Thus none of the groups can be accused of lacking basic autonomy; their own interests and objectives give identity to their respective struggles. None of them, then, would be motivated to obey the mandates of a foreign power, no matter how intimate or subordinate the relationship that each group maintains with any of the metropolitan capitals.

Regarding the latter point, the sole mention of foreign powers in the context of this analysis immediately poses various questions which must be explicitly addressed: are the two superpowers, the United States and the Soviet Union, really intervening in the conflict? Is the struggle for regional power a matter of special concern to the bipolar geopolitical balance? Do the two superpowers have, in essence, anything to lose or gain in Central America? To answer any of these queries would involve the prior unravelling of concepts which have become very diffused in contemporary political language, such

as *intervention, political balance and national security*. For the
benefit of our analysis we can, however, take a short cut: let us only
ask ourselves which of the superpowers has the purpose, motivation
and real capability to change, in one way or another, the balance of
power between the local regional opponents. The respective roles of
the two superpowers in the Isthmus can scarcely be compared. The
Soviet Union, for its part, lacks the cultural and political historical
ties that would allow it easily to make capital from the revolutionary
uprisings in that area. The distance of Central America from Soviet
borders makes it an area of costly risks and unattractive limitations,
as Cuba's case has already shown. In fact, no victory would com-
pensate for the difficulties and the political and economic costs. On
the other hand, the Central American revolutionaries, alleged
accomplices in the Soviet expansion strategy, are national forces —
regardless of any sympathies or dogma — who are struggling with
indisputable conviction for such pressing values as self-determination
and redistribution of economic power. No matter how much they
would demand solidarity from a foreign force or power, including
Cuba, they would do so in order to strengthen their own struggle and
not transfer or export it. The same can be said of the counter-
revolutionary forces, diverse as they are since each is struggling on
behalf of its own interests.

Conceptually, then, the problem consists of recognising that, no
matter how great the volume or density of the Soviet or Cuban
presence in Central America, it does not influence the actions of the
revolutionaries decisively, nor does it have any correlation to the
forces in the battlefields. Therefore, the role of Cuba and the Soviet
Union must be regarded as real but in all cases marginal. Thus if the
Central American revolutionaries seize the reins of power, that
power would not automatically belong to the Soviet Union or be
managed from Cuba. And if the guerrillas were eventually defeated,
the Kremlin would not mark it as a loss on its own strategic score-
board.

For the United States, on the other hand, Central America is
indeed an issue that involves its power. Whether or not the Soviet
Union is the cause of the conflict, the results would be the same. The
overthrow or restructuring of regimes allied to it in favour of greater
political autonomy and new economic and social forms in those
countries, would be a real threat to the traditional forms of the US
hegemony in the region. Therefore, it is logical to expect the United
States to do everything in its power to prevent the emergence of new
poles of local power in Central America and to impede demands for
regional autonomy. The United States has its own reasons for considering the social conflict in the Isthmus as its own, which do not
stem from its defence of lucrative commerce or its protection of

access to reserves of scarce resources. Hence, it appears odd that, on this occasion, the Washington politicians have opted for a military presence in Central America, but not in response to the anguished cries of a banana firm or an industrial or commercial financial consortium in the United States. The promoters of the war in Central America are the strategists, politicians, soldiers and ideologues of the conservative wing. They are the few friends the dictators still have. The real economic interests of US capital are not threatened by Central America, but rather by the staggering debts of countries like Mexico, Brazil, Venezuela and Argentina.

Up till now, we have dealt with what appears to be a clear argument on the nature, characteristics and dimensions of the conflict as described above. The first and original one consists of a savage struggle for power based on the historical events of the region: the social/historical dimension. The second is the regional dimension which involves the shift of the original conflict to the regional level and which, among other manifestations, appears in the form of confrontations and disputes among states. Finally, we recognise a geopolitical dimension emanating from the commitments and strategic projects Washington has proposed for the region.

Using these definitions and analytical elements, it is possible to deal with the obstacles impeding a negotiated solution. As a point of departure, it is necessary to acknowledge that, based on the course followed by the confrontations themselves, the principal obstacle is the lack of interest, purpose and will of the United States to negotiate its participation in the conflict. Without a US presence, no initiative for a dialogue would be productive; but US power is what is needed to open up the political and diplomatic channels which are blocked today by its military presence.

One of the major impediments to dialogue and negotiations is the US persistence in regarding the Central American conflict as an East-West scenario. This decreases, and even nullifies, the political importance of the Latin American protagonists. On the one hand, the perceived national security threat, which justifies the US intervention, does not originate or proceed from the Latin Americans, but rather from Moscow. The Central American revolutionaries, from Cuba to Guatemala, are but agents subjected to the interests of Soviet expansionism — which deprives them of their own identity and excludes them from dialogue or negotiations with the superpower. But, even worse and based on the same logic, the other countries or political protagonists in the region — such as Mexico and Venezuela, which made impartial proposals for a negotiated solution — are similarly ignored. The regional peace initiatives, especially those of the Contadora Group, are to an extent regarded by US leaders as goodwill exercises that are flawed by naivete, irresponsibility and even malice because they exclude the premise of a Soviet strategy in the area. US policy is not designed for Latin America and does not take the Latin American people into account. Its principle is to contain the Soviet Union, not to establish a framework for relations of mutual respect in the hemisphere. In the Washington logic, there are only two possible categories of Latin Americans: discreet and obliging observers of a struggle that is ultimately in their favour or dissidents and members of one faction or another.

The premises of the so-called Kissinger Report are an eloquent example of this. This was a bipartisan commission appointed to gather a consensus from among the various internal points of view on what US policy in the region should consist of, and not a consultation with Latin Americans to learn their aspirations and expectations with regard to Washington policies. Furthermore, the fundamental premise on which the Kissinger Report based its recommendations is that a material and tangible threat against US national security, backed by Soviet intervention, is evident in Central America. Based on this, the recommendations relative to economic development, which could have served as a basis for a better understanding of the United States in the region, have been subordinated to the need for a strategic defence — the main objective of the US presence.

The geopolitical dimension

Any rigorous and objective analysis of the Central American conflict must establish clearly that, among the various international players cited as active protagonists, only the United States plays a truly important role. Regardless of what the real Soviet or Cuban involvement may be, their actions would in no way alter the basic premises of the social conflict. Nor would they modify perceptibly the correlation of national and regional forces. On the contrary, any variations in US policy, however slight, would indeed result in visible and measurable effects; thus Washington's actions can affect the geopolitical dimension of the conflict. In principle, the national security concepts in the Kissinger Report would also lead to the assumption that negotiations with Washington are feasible — those most interested in reaching a frank understanding with the hemispheric superpower clearly being the revolutionary movements and the Sandinista regime in Nicaragua, which are at present under siege by the counter-revolution, with the support of the Reagan administration. The objective of this negotiation would be to assuage US concerns over national security, to favour a dismantling of the hegemonial military efforts, and to break the US alliance with the forces opposed to social change. This would allow a historical transition towards new forms of political organisation in countries such as El Salvador and eventually Guatemala, the restoration of sovereignty and democratic perspectives in Honduras, and the further strengthening of democracy and neutrality in Costa Rica. In the specific case of El Salvador, a North American withdrawal could be implemented within the framework of a negotiation to form a new government that would reflect the true correlation of that country's political forces. In Guatemala, it would simply accomplish the isolation of the military dictatorship there as one of the most anti-democratic and repressive regimes in Latin America. Taking into consideration the concern expressed by the Kissinger Report regarding the possibility of an intolerable threat to US national security, a substantive negotiation would be within reach. Nicaragua, as well as eventually the revolutionary forces in El Salvador and Guatemala, would be willing and able to offer Washington all kinds of guarantees regarding the non-installation of Soviet military bases, the non-acquisition of offensive military equipment and a genuine non-alignment. The Contadora Group could well be the mediating force and, even further, the instrument to put into practice any type of safeguard or verification that the United States might demand.

The United States would have ample means of ensuring that Nicaragua, and eventually the Salvadorean FMLN-FDR and URNG, observed the treaty to the letter. Mexico, Venezuela, Colombia and Panama would do whatever is appropriate, not only as mediators but also motivated by their own undeniable interests, to keep Soviet military strategy out of the region. Why therefore has the United States not even attempted to explore this option? The answer is found in the other national security elements set forth by the Kissinger Commission.

The truth is that US regional interests, as understood in the White House, are not limited to the prevention of a Soviet threat to their southern borders or even to maintaining Central America within the sphere of US hegemony, and it is precisely this which the revolution questions. The struggle for sovereignty and self-determination is an irreplaceable element of political and social change, not as a platform for threatening US security for the benefit of Soviet interests but rather for the exercise of internal political power. The myth of Marxism-Leninism as an intolerable threat and cause of instability, repression and disorder is only an ideological label to justify the reaffirmation of that hegemony. In practice, any nationalist regime which might overthrow the present armies and oligarchies is equally intolerable and equally open to the suspicion of being communist. The heart of US policy is eloquently stated in the fourth premise of the Kissinger document: prestige and credibility. These items, by definition, cannot be negotiated if they would be put at risk by the recognition in Washington of the independence and autonomy of countries hitherto governed by regimes which identify their national sovereignty with the preservation of power and privileges for a few.

At present the obstacles to a negotiated solution seem practically insurmountable. For this situation to change, we would need to see: (1) re-definition by the United States of its national security premises, divorcing it from hegemonial interest. In other words the gap between the historical objectives of political discourse for domestic consumption and the true, though disguised, objectives of the exercise of power would have to be closed. Thus, to negotiate the full guarantees of non-aggression and absolute respect of national security, in exchange for the renunciation of a conditional hegemony. (2) recognition of the personalities of the players who are committed to change, and agreement to a dialogue based on the awareness of autonomous wills capable of conciliation. As long as the US government insists on regarding the Central American revolutionaries as Soviets or Cubans in disguise even dialogue will be impossible. (3) a substantial modification of its policy of alliances and support in the region, even at the expense of a confrontation with the forces opposed to change. In any event, the present alliances and clientele will tend in future to become more and more costly in terms of economic and military resources and even political prestige and credibility. In the medium term, the military regimes of El Salvador and Guatemala could be defeated by their respective opponents and revolutionaries, and the United States would have to confront the inescapable dilemma of replacing them with their own military forces or taking responsibility for the failure of its present policies.

The regional dimension

We have proposed that the regional dimension of the conflict is based on two complementary phenomena: (1) the need for alliances among the opposed parties dictated by the social confrontation itself and (2) the political-military alignment of the region favoured by the United States in order to contain the revolutionary movements. The most visible and violent aspect of this regional dimension has been manifested in the border incidents between Nicaragua and its neighbours. Without reviewing the nature and origin of these disputes in depth, we must acknowledge that the determining, although not exclusive, factor has been the activity of the anti-Sandinista groups on Nicaragua's various borders. At the same time, San Jose as well as Tegucigalpa allege an offensive and expansionist purpose on the part of the Nicaraguan Sandinistas. These circumstances brought about the birth of the Contadora group. Although the concerns felt by the countries of the group over political and military instability and the dangers both of a regional struggle and of direct foreign intervention are not limited to the border disputes between Nicaragua, Honduras and Costa Rica, this has been the immediate issue on which most of their efforts have been focused. Therefore, in defining the scope and limitations of the Contadora Group, we must, above all, keep in mind its basic political premises:

(1) From a global perspective, and despite the differences between them, the countries of the Group have characterised the conflict as an issue truly divorced from any East-West conceptions. Each of the very different governments of the four countries sees the crisis as the inevitable result of the profound economic and political underdevelopment of the area, but also as arising from an existing social and political struggle to achieve the transformation of old structures. The most important and distinctive feature of the Contadora Group — and its most singular contribution to the discussions of the Central American problems — is that, for the first time, four influential countries of the region are proposing a genuine Latin American solution to these problems. This explains the huge support given to the Contadora Group by the international community.

(2) The Contadora Group bases its negotiations on the supposition that all the regional players in the conflict are, in principle, autonomous entities acting for their own interests and objectives, and not mere instruments of external strategy and designs. This prerequisite for a negotiated solution, according to the vision of the Contadora Group, embraces all the revolutionary forces and their opponents equally.

(3) As a mediating effort of these governments, the first commitment of this Group has been to seek the agreement of the governments of the area to resolve their disputes around the negotiating table and abstain from aggression against the sovereignty of others. Furthermore, the establishment of mutual criteria for collective security entails the responsibility and commitment not only of the states directly involved in the border disputes, but of all those countries in the area who are accumulating military equipment or receiving assistance or advice from foreign armies. The search by Contadora for concrete non-aggression agreements and its strivings for disarmament and détente constitute a truce that could prevent

the war from escalating. In fact, the Contadora Group has not included in its agenda even a specific effort to mediate the internal conflicts bearing on the regional confrontation. Despite this, the truce seems necessary at all costs in order to contain the dynamics of the regional factor.

Given the self-imposed limits of Contadora, the principal obstacle it faces is the lack of willingness on the part of several states to commit themselves to this truce proposed by Contadora, and the antipathy of the various social forces that regard the truce as preventing them from continuing their counter-revolutionary offensive; indeed the truce would clearly impair their offensive stance. Several spokesmen of the Central American right even believe that the signing of a Contadora pact would only benefit the revolutionary forces and the Sandinista regime in Nicaragua, who, according to them, receive most of their weapons clandestinely and would therefore not be subjected to the verification processes outlined by the Contadora Group. The strongest opposition rests, in any case, on the determination not to interrupt the counter-revolutionary war which is aimed at the modernisation of military installations, an increase in military equipment and the receipt of all possible foreign military and technical aid. The agenda of the United States and its allies obviously precludes a negotiated solution.

Thus it is clear that as long as the forces against insurgency and aligned with the United States do not regard the Contadora Group's efforts as promising specific advantages to their cause, they will not commit themselves sincerely to its overtures. Rather, they will continue to impede its progress by means of all types of dilatory tactics which will not unmask them unequivocally as adversaries of peace.

It is fair to say that President Reagan has not shown any enthusiasm for Contadora's efforts. The establishment of the Group in itself presented serious difficulties for the application of his policies in the area. On the one hand, the fact that four Latin American countries offered themselves to the world as mediators impedes the implementation of a policy that does not respond to Central American demands and turns a deaf ear to American concerns. On the other hand, the diplomatic support earned by the Contadora Group reinforces the opposition to the Reagan policies in the US Congress, and thus limits the Chief Executive's freedom to continue his military programmes in the Isthmus.

It is no coincidence that the Reagan administration has, at the same time, also had to manifest rhetorical support for the Contadora Group. Not to do this would have had a serious effect, internally and externally, on the credibility of his position. Although scorn for the Latin American voice is inherent in his treatment of the conflict, to manifest this scorn openly would be difficult.

Despite these difficulties and obstacles, the Contadora Group continues to be the best instrument to bring about a truly significant process of détente. If its present efforts culminate in a formal pact or a substantial commitment, there would be a legal and internationally recognised frame of reference in which the role of the various actors in the conflict can be assessed. At the same time, the Latin American multilateral example would lend it prestige and allow it to attempt negotiated efforts in the area of social conflict, particularly in El Salvador and at the geopolitical level. To date, the efforts of the Contadora Group are moving painfully through their initial stages and, although there are still many difficulties, the road travelled so far constitutes a degree of progress not to be disdained.

Social-historical dimension

To understand the perspectives of a negotiated solution within the scenario of the Central American conflict, we must acknowledge that only on rare occasions are revolutionary processes resolved by a sudden agreement between the opposing forces. In principle, the parties involved in the armed revolutionary conflict have reached that point precisely because all roads to dialogue and conciliation have already been blocked off. The political economic and military élite in power are, in all cases, the most uncompromising when it comes to negotiations; it is this that makes them targets for subversion. The experience of Zimbabwe, so often cited as an example for Central America, demonstrates that a negotiated political solution comes about only when that option has been firmly supported by foreign protagonists who have the capability and strength to influence the governments that are confronting armed opposition forces.

The case of El Salvador presents characteristics of its own which merit the search for a negotiated solution. The historical conflict in El Salvador, unlike that in Nicaragua, cannot be resolved by the mere correlation of internal forces. Although the failure of the reformist military coup of 1979 and the political events that ensued showed a clear and dramatic change in the correlation of the internal political forces, the US government, still headed by Carter in 1980, decided to lend all its support to the government forces in order to modify this change quantitatively and contain the advances of the armed opposition. In 1981, with Ronald Reagan in the White House, the United States became the principal protagonist in the conflict. As its State Department has acknowledged on numerous occasions, the FMLN would very likely be in power now if the United States were not giving military support to the Salvadorean army. This means that the resolution of the historical conflict has been delayed by an artificial and external modification in the correlation of the internal forces. The possibility of a negotiated solution rests on this although the United States would become an inseparable part of such a solution. Without it, the political conflict could very well be prolonged indefinitely with an enormous cost in lives and resources; or, on the other hand, the FMLN-FDR could, despite US support for the government, defeat the army and thus risk the possibility of direct intervention by US troops with a disastrous effect on El Salvador and the entire area. Under these conditions, it could be to everyone's advantage to meet around the negotiating table. According to the various initiatives presented by the FMLN-FDR, there would have to be substantial and significant participation by the government opposition in such negotiations, thus assuring the certain and effective implementation of the democratic mechanisms in the competition for power. For its part, the United States would have the opportunity to bring about a political restructuring with the participation of moderate sectors compatible with its strategic concerns and interests. In any event, it would prevent the opposition forces from reconstructing the state much more radically. A negotiated solution could thus be really achieved between the United States, as the principal source of military power in El Salvador, and the insurgents grouped under the FMLN-FDR. Within this context, the forces opposed to a negotiated solution would remain outside the spectrum, thus constituting a discussion point for negotiations with the FMLN-FDR.

Our analysis may make such a negotiated solution seem logical and attainable, but it is in fact not so, due to two irreconcilable circumstances:

(1) The objectives of US policy in El Salvador appear to be, above all, to defeat the insurgency and the armed revolutionary movement. So it is not a question of reconstructing the established order, but rather of preserving and modifying it under suppositions that exclude the opposition forces, who are mistakenly identified with Soviet leanings. In other words, a minimal restructuring based on the criteria of exclusion rather than incorporation.

(2) The historical conflict is so profound and autonomous that the mere negotiating intiative exacerbates the internal confrontations within the government and makes it impossible even for the United States to outline an orderly and peaceful process of transition at the negotiating table. If the United States were to support a true negoti-

ated solution in El Salvador, it would have to oppose, even with force, the sectors with whom it has hitherto been aligned in one way or another. Therefore, without a substantial change in US policy towards El Salvador, a negotiated solution seems impossible. Such a change would assume, among other things:

(a) The recognition of the legitimate and autonomous political character of the FMLN-FDR, which the Reagan administration has systematically refused to recognise. The interpretation continues to be that the armed opposition in El Salvador lacks any popular support and that it derives its strength from external military support, and that its political profile is nothing more than the strategic designs of the Soviet Union and Cuba.

(b) Washington would have to acknowledge its vital part in the negotiations. In spite of arguing that its presence in El Salvador is based solely on the call for help from a sovereign state, the United States has feigned absence from the conflict and presents itself as subjected to the demands of the Salvadorean government in power and conditioned by the political premises under which the latter operates.

(c) The United States must realise that negotiations do not assume the restructuring of the government with the participation of the FMLN-FDR before any mutually agreed elections until now, the negotiating position of the United States in El Salvador has been limited to a proposal for an immediate ceasefire, the surrender of arms by the FMLN-FDR, and its participation in elections organised under premises that do not even guarantee the lives of the rebels.

The context of the negotiations in El Salvador becomes even more complicated if we introduce the assumption that similar negotiations must be conducted in Nicaragua where, it is alleged, opposing rebel forces are also fighting against the established regime. Here the possibility of a negotiated solution is practically nil because:

(a) The conflict in Nicaragua definitely has irreconcilable characteristics. A counter-revolutionary movement, evidently representing a minority, advocates a process of change that has already occurred.

(b) In terms of the real correlation of forces, the anti-Sandinista guerrillas lack the necessary support to demand a seat at the negotiating table. Accordingly, even under international law, the fact that their principal bases of operations are outside Nicaraguan territory disqualifies them from the right to demand recognition under the terms of the Geneva Convention relative to the treatment of insurgents. Even presuming that Edén Pastora and his forces are already operating inside Nicaraguan territory, it would be in an uninhabited zone with no real political significance. Therefore, negotiations in El Salvador can not be linked to a political factor which is allegedly similar to Nicaragua's.

Conclusion

The Central American crisis is, above all, one of power caused by the erosion of the old forms of amassing riches and political control. The opponents in this struggle define their position of relative force in two ways. The first and most important is that power or the real possibility of obtaining power emanates from social support achieved through a consensus and not simply by means of international assistance and backing. The second is that, despite its genuinely national and regional nature, the struggle also poses a geopolitical question. However, in the Central American conflict, only one geopolitical player has demonstrated capabilities as well as a determination to correlate the emerging forces with a local, historical dimension. Therefore, the presence of this player — the United States — at the negotiating table is indispensable if the dialogue is to have any meaning. There must be a consensus consisting, first, of a formula for those shifts in power, profound and in some cases radical, demanded by history, and the geopolitical imperative of preventing the Isthmus from becoming the military and strategic preserve of any foreign power. Central America must not be, in effect, the game piece lost or gained by one metropolis in favour, or to the detriment, of another. It is equally intolerable for this region to continue to be treated exclusively in strategic terms, without the sovereignty and self-determination of its component states being recognised. Secondly, a negotiated solution is necessary to contain the military regional factors in the conflict. This will allow social conflicts to re-assume their original national dimensions, so that the struggle for power can be resolved or negotiated on the basis of the political game of each country. Until power is re-defined in accordance with the historical characteristics and needs of each country and ceases to be considered in a regional perspective, instability and violence will inevitably continue. No power can arbitrarily change this fact.

6

THE PARAMETERS OF THE PROCESS OF CONFLICT RESOLUTION IN CENTRAL AMERICA

Henry Wiseman

In October 1983 the Secretary-General of the United Nations reported that 'the five governments of Central America have assured me on a number of occasions of their firm commitment to contribute in good faith to the search for peaceful solutions.'[1] There can be no doubt, however, that the contradictory and very strongly held views and objectives of these governments, of the various other parties to the conflicts and disputes in Central America, and of interested governments overseas, make the passage toward a peaceful solution extremely difficult. The Contadora Group, through dedicated and consistent diplomatic work, has nonetheless produced a body of principles to navigate this passage in good faith. The passage, to be successful, must move the parties (for the sake of convenience all governments and factions are designated as parties) from the stage of confrontation and open hostilities to meaningful negotiation, from there to terms of agreement, and finally to the process of the medium of implementation.

In the volatile situation that prevails, no one can doubt the vast and grave impediments in the way. Should the current hostilities and the ever-present danger of escalation continue, the cost of failure will be measured in inestimable human carnage, economic devastation and aggravated regional strategic instability. The parties will, as a matter of course, make their own assessments of these human, economic and strategic costs against the advantages of the projected subjugation of their antagonists and the assumed achievement of their objectives. Actors not directly involved in the conflicts, but deeply concerned, hold the view that the passage toward peaceful solutions through negotiation and accommodation will limit the human and economic damage and strategic instability, and is therefore the preferred outcome. Such actors are often referred to as third parties. They can be more specifically defined as a recognised state, group of states, regional or international organisation, which acts as a neutral independent agent to assist in the resolution of conflict. They perform one or more of the functions of fact-finding, arbitrating, negotiation, peacekeeping and election supervision in conformity with international principles for the peaceful resolution of conflict as found in international law or the Charters of the United Nations or the Organization of American States. Which type of third party may be suitable to any particular situation will depend on the nature of the situation and the policy attitudes of the concerned parties. Third parties require the requisite independence, legitimacy, authority and acceptance by all concerned parties to perform their functions with credibility and effectiveness.

Yet parties in conflict will understandably have less faith and interest in the objectives of third parties than they do in their own. But they are not asked, in our context, to deny in any way the validity of their own objectives. They are, nevertheless, asked to consider that third parties can facilitate the process as long as the parties themselves hold a 'firm commitment to contribute in good faith to the search for peaceful solutions'.

It is important to distinguish between government third parties directly active in the dual processes of mediation and negotiation, such as the Contadora Group, and the more abstract and academic third party. The latter can only, and should only, clarify and delineate the difficult and complex passage from conflict to negotiation, to agreement, and finally to implementation. This chapter, then, is essentially an exercise in political and historical analysis, which can be no more than a modest contribution. (It does not presume to be a mediator's formula to resolve the situation.) Yet the governments and parties would entertain no loss in following a third party along the plane of 'academic objectivity' and analysis which follows.

The starting point must be primarily the very principles put forward by the Contadora Group as 'endorsed by the five governments in the region together with the various proposals and positions set forth by the governments and parties themselves'.[2] The focus of this paper is on the present conflict in Central America. The principles and processes could, however, also apply to related potential situations in the Caribbean such as occurred in Granada. We are referring to the use of third parties as fact-finders, electoral observers and peacekeepers.

The Contadora 'Document of Objectives' is well known. I quote here only the central points: (1) to 'put an end to situations of conflict in the area', which I take to mean a cessation of hostilities; (2) to 'stop the arms race'; (3) to 'end [the presence of] foreign military bases or other types of foreign military interference'; (4) 'to eliminate the traffic in arms'; (5) to give 'free access to fair and regular elections based on the full observance of citizens' rights'; (6) to 'respect and ensure the exercise of human, political, civil, economic, social, religious and cultural rights'; and lastly, and of critical importance, (7) 'the establishment of the machinery necessary to formalise and develop the objectives contained in this document, and to bring about the establishment of appropriate verification and monitoring systems'. The development of that 'machinery' and 'verification and monitoring system' then became the responsibility of the Contadora states to negotiate with the actual parties in conflict.

These objectives, seemingly endorsed by all the states of Central America, have been reflected in their individual policy statements. They are commented upon here without assessment of their sincerity. That is the business of those whose own objectives and interests are at stake.

Within weeks of the ostensible endorsement of Contadora's 21 objectives, Nicaragua presented a four-point proposal which included 'a draft treaty of respect, peace and security between Nicaragua and the United States; a draft treaty of peace, friendship and co-operation between Honduras and Nicaragua; a draft accord to contribute to the peaceful solution of the armed conflict in El Salvador; and a draft general treaty concerning the maintenance of peace and security and friendship and cooperation among the republics of Central America'.[3]

Honduras, in March 1982, before the Contadora document of objectives, put forward a peace proposal that was reiterated in December 1983 by the Permanent Representative of Honduras to the United Nations calling for, 'among other things, the withdrawal of all foreign advisors . . .; a general disarmament of the region and the establishment of mechanisms for internal political processes leading to representative pluralistic and democratic government in Central America'. He went on to say that this 'initiative, as well as the document "Permanent Basis for the Peaceful Global and Regional Solution" presented (July 1983) by Costa Rica, El Salvador, Guatemala and Honduras, have been fully incorporated into the 21 points agreed upon at the Contadora negotiations and will serve as the framework for negotiations toward a regional treaty.'[4]

In May 1983 Costa Rica, in response to allegations that anti-Sandinista military elements were operating out of Costa Rican territory, asked the OAS for a peace observer group to be sent. Eight civilian and three military observers from Mexico, Panama, Colombia and Venezuela subsequently established a Border Observation Commission.[5]

Within El Salvador, Guillermo Manuel Ungo, leader of the Democratic Revolutionary Front, stated in November 1983 that the guerrillas would take a neutral and independent position on issues such as the exclusion of foreign military bases from El Salvador and the sources and levels of military aid to a future government there.[6] In 1984 further similar apparently constructive proposals were put forward by various parties, but without major results.

The 21 objectives of the Contadora group seem to have acquired what may loosely be called 'general support' among the parties in conflict in Central America. But what do apparent statements of commitment to peaceful resolution of the conflict really mean? The government of Honduras rejected the Nicaraguan proposal of November 1983 for bilateral arrangements on border security and arms traffic, suggesting instead that such arrangements must be part of a multilateral settlement. The United States Assistant Secretary of State Langhorne A. Motley criticised the Democratic Revolutionary Front/Farabundo Martí Front for National Liberation (FDR-FMLN) which, after two meetings with the Peace Commission, 'refused even to discuss participating in the direct popular elections for president . . . set for March 25'. As to Nicaragua, Motley charged that, despite US assistance in 1979 and 1980, it continued to support the guerrillas in El Salvador, and he expressed little faith in Nicaraguan overtures concerning the withdrawal of a number of Cuban advisers and some democratic initiatives.[7] (These steps have been described in other quarters too as marginal.)

Yet what is the United States' stand on these bilateral discussions? Little can be known with certainty to the 'outside'; but the resignation of Richard B. Stone, the US special envoy to Central America, because of reported disagreements with Langhorne Motley marks a deterioration in overall negotiations in the area. The United States has itself refused to participate in the Contadora negotiations, though, according to President Reagan, it would support 'any agreement among Central American countries leading to the withdrawal of all foreign advisors and troops'. He also pleaded to help opposition groups join the political process in all countries.[8] Yet Reagan has never been satisfied with Nicaraguan initiatives. The 'dialogue' between Nicaragua and the United States is occasionally renewed, but without positive results.

For its part, the Nicaraguan government views rebellious forces on its border supported by Honduras and the United States as evidence of a determination to overthrow the Sandinista state. Then there is the counter-claim of Nicaraguan support for the FDR-FMLN in El Salvador in their determination to overthrow the government of that country. Accusations of bad faith, and of occasional rhetorical expressions of goodwill, mask deliberate contradictory behaviour. No side or interested party from within or outside the region is without fault in this complex web of the Central American conflict.

The shift from the military to the political arena

Although the Contadora Group is determined to find a political solution, there is unmistakable evidence that some parties believe in the achievement of their own goals by military means. Those who would seek to stabilise their position are caught in the vise of polarisation.

What are the general circumstances which would facilitate the shift from the military to the political arena? And what are the contrary conditions preventing the shift from occurring? Of course, both are going on at the same time, and the result is a turbulent situation.

Preventive factors are many: the irrepressible belief in the complete righteousness of one's cause; the assurance of one's own survival and victory; the determination to pursue victory at whatever cost either to the opposition or to one's own party; the certainty of omnipotence that sheer power will overwhelm and destroy the opposition; the conviction that external resources and support will be forthcoming no matter what difficulties arise; the certainty that the people's interests are being well served and that their fervour and loyalty to the cause will survive all trials and tribulations; the absolute refusal to recognise the legitimacy of the other side; the deep suspicion that any conciliatory manoeuvre of the other side is devious, a tactic to confuse or to gain time or some other advantage; and the belief that once a degree of military superiority is gained then the other side will be compelled to negotiate on one's own terms — the trouble being that if such superiority is attained, the temptation then is not to negotiate, but to plunge ahead to total victory.

We are all aware of these phenomena. But they cannot all be correct or all fulfilled. History is full of evidence to the contrary. Communists claim that the inevitability of history is on their side, but the Polish population does not subscribe to that claim. The unquestioned power of the United States could not, with the Multilateral Peace Force, ensure the peace in Beirut or restrain the civil war in Lebanon. The PLO has been defeated militarily several times, but it lives on as a strong political force. Israel and the PLO do not recognise one another; yet both survive and the Palestinian question will not go away. In Chad, for more than a decade, conflict has shifted back and forth from the battlefields to the negotiating table; but since all sides (there were eleven contending factions at one time) were at the same time convinced of the lasting support of Libya and France, they continued to fight, confident of total victory. Neither side is likely to win.

There are situations like these all over the world, a mix of civil wars, economic and human deprivation, governmental and non-governmental parties, ideological confrontations, strategic interests of major foreign power, and so on. It is much easier to see these things in 'foreign' conflicts than to acknowledge their possible relevance to one's own case. But they are there nonetheless. Conflict itself is also a fundamental manifestation of our age. And change, particularly dynamic unanticipated change, is a characteristic of each and every conflict. Outcomes are therefore unpredictable.

History is also instructive about what conditions are conducive to a negotiated settlement. There are many. Only a few essentials are mentioned here; exhaustion and belated recognition that victory in the long run is impossible and that the other side will win, as with Portugal in respect of the struggle for national independence of Angola and Mozambique; insight that more is to be gained at the bargaining table than on the battlefield, as with Anwar Sadat's visit to Jerusalem after four wars and the Camp David accords between Egypt and Israel; and, on a democratic level, the shift from historic antagonism and electoral competition to co-operation between the Communists and Socialists in France, which, for a time, brought both into a governmental coalition, without loss to the Western alliance.

The clearest contemporary case which exemplifies the conditions for the actual shift from the military to the political stage is that of Rhodesia/Zimbabwe in 1980, a case of extensive study by the writer.[9] Civil war raged there for over a decade. The white supremacist government of Ian Smith was intransigent and convinced that it could stay in power indefinitely. Indigenous black insurgent forces, with outside help from black Africa, the Soviet Union and some from China, fought for total victory. The country was devastated by the war and humanitarian concerns were set aside in the heat of battle. Smith called an election in 1979, an election boycotted by the two key insurgent forces, the Zimbabwe African National Union of Robert Mugabe and the Zimbabwe African National Union (Patriotic Front) of Joshua Nkomo. The 'democratic' results, an apparent victory for Smith, brought a black government to power, the party of Bishop Abel Muzorewa which co-operated with Smith. But the victory and new stability were an illusion. The new government did not attain national or international legitimacy, and the civil war continued.

Finally, however, all parties, even the guerrilla forces, though certain in their own minds of ultimate military success, realised that a political settlement was preferable. The conditions that brought this about were, roughly, the following: (1) there was relentless pressure from Africa, the Commonwealth and the United Nations for a political settlement; (2) all sides were growing tired of the human and physical devastation; (3) there was recognition that military victory would be too costly to either side; (4) there existed a temporary but very important equilibrium in the field of battle; (5) there was pressure on the Patriotic Front of Joshua Nkomo by its backer, the Soviet Union, and similarly on the Zimbabwe African National Union (Robert Mugabe) by China, that more was to be gained in the political arena than on the battlefield; (6) there was willingness on all sides to accept the United Kingdom as the neutral third party to conduct the negotiations and oversee the process of implementation; (7) all parties accepted a basic set of principles as the bottom line for negotiations; (8) lastly, every party recognised that a switch from the military to the political would best serve the country and all concerned.

Do these conditions prevail in Central America? They do in part. Reality, however, is how they are perceived by the protagonists.

Gateways and roadblocks

What follows, therefore, is an examination of the gateways and roadblocks, and a general guide to those who may choose to pursue the course of peaceful settlement of conflict to allow for humanitarian and economic development in a climate of stability.

Several conditions have already been met. Adoption of the Contadora objectives is the first major step. The second consists of the Contadora deliberations on political, economic, military and security matters leading to the preparation of a draft act for peace and co-operation in Central America. A concomitant factor of equal importance is the recognition in principle of third-party involvement as a critical stimulus to negotiations, as observers of elections, as a monitor or supervisor of cease-fires with particular respect to such matters as the movement of regular and irregular forces, of arms traffic, and of demilitarised border zones. Such statements have been made in several quarters, but only as initial overtures. There is still a long way to go before they can be realised, as will be discussed in later pages. But the importance of these matters should not be underestimated. The refusal to permit third-party roles in the conflict between Iran and Iraq demonstrates what a formidable barrier to resolution such refusal can be.

There is also a general understanding in the region of the vital need to foster conditions of economic rehabilitation and development, although there is severe disagreement as to how, and to what extent, the just needs of the most deprived sectors should be met. The declaration of the Kissinger Commission that 'unless rapid progress can be made on the political, economic and social fronts, peace on the military front will be illusive and would be fragile' should be taken as a fundamental prerequisite by the United States as well as the nations in the region. Still the United States proposals for large-scale infusion of aid should be welcomed, though not its reliance on military regimes to chart the course to democracy and to implement the economic programmes.

How effective this and other economic initiatives will be, when and if adopted, depends on many factors. But there can be no doubt that those parties which refuse to alter the intransigent pursuit of objectives through military means will be unable to achieve these economic and humanitarian objectives. Violence and civil war inevitably bring about economic devastation. The evidence is there for all to see in Africa and Asia, as well as in Latin America. This is one basic political truth that is not yet recognised by the parties. Until that happens the road to peaceful settlement will be blocked.

The same is true of the issue of human rights. Denial of basic human rights, and its most virulent form of indiscriminate killing, serve only to antagonise, polarise and prevent political accommodation. Whatever gateways may be opened, passage through them will be obstructed by the roadblocks of militarism, violation of human rights and state-sponsored terrorism.

And on the matter of democratic institutions — how widespread is the endorsement of the Contadora objectives? These are

to adopt measures conducive to the establishment and, where appropriate, improvement of democratic, representative and pluralistic systems that will guarantee effective popular participation in the decision-making process and ensure that the various currents of opinion have free access to fair and regular elections based on the full observance of citizens' rights.

Rhetorical support has been expressed by most parties, but neither the Nicaraguan Contra insurgent groups nor the El Salvadorean FDR-FMLN have been able, on terms agreeable to them, to gain such access. There have been critical misgivings and objections about the conditions and participation in the national elections in El Salvador and in Nicaragua. The 1984 presidential elections in El Salvador took place while a civil war was going without the participation of the FDR-FMLN, although the latter stated that the elections would not 'be the object of direct military attack'.[10] The violence and militarism in the country were hardly conducive to free and fair elections. Despite the formal process, the final political outcome is still uncertain. In Nicaragua the oscillating commitment to election of a president and a constituent legislative assembly allowed for some free access to television, radio and newspapers, but under a continued 'state of emergency' and without submission to formal international supervision. The opposition feared, however, that it was not adequately free to organise and campaign. There have been victors in each case, but substantively the pluralism of the Contadora objectives is still absent.

Protracted conflict in the area, added to the disastrous effects of the global recession, have decimated the economies of the region. The facts are well known. The suffering is enormous. Another deleterious effect is the outflow of capital and the crushing of the middle and entrepreneurial classes, which could be, in political terms, the mainstay of democratic institutions and the motor of development. Such classes survive and grow in stable conditions, but rigid military and oppressive regimes and civil war are destroying this foundation of entrepreneurial strength. The political stage under these circumstances is vacated to the extremes of left and right, a formula for chaos. Political accommodation under these circumstances becomes impossible. The struggle for power will be all that remains, in a sea of despair and disintegration. Yet one factor stands to the fore. The economies of the region are heavily interdependent. The United States is the largest trading partner with the region, but the next level of trade is intra-regional. This was succinctly put by Carlos Manuel Castillo, President of Costa Rica's Central Bank: 'If Central America is going to pull through, it will be all of us together.'[11] Evidence of this is well demonstrated by the ongoing negotiations on a new Central American Tariffs and Customs Agreement. The necessary precondition is therefore political stability brought about by political accommodation. In the Zimbabwe case, every effort was made to retain the enterpreneurial class as the vital ingredient of a stable and dynamic economy, with evident success.

Confidence building measured

What are confidence-building measures? Could they be applied in Central America, and to the Caribbean? Confidence-building measures, generally defined, are actions of an open and transparent nature designed to overcome suspicion and create sufficient levels of trust to enable communications to be sent and received with clarity, frankness and predictability. The concept has evolved from efforts to build conditions of trust and détente between the United States and the Soviet Union, between East and West, as a basis for the negotiation of arms control agreements. The United Nations, recognising their potential utility, conducted a special study in an effort to extend the applicability of the concept to other regions of the world.[12]

These measures are conceived as preliminary instruments to dampen hostility and incrementally to replenish the void of mistrust with elements of mutual reliability that could lead to actions at a higher level of co-operation. The concept is admirable, but the turmoil in Central America is very different from the situation of East-West relations in Europe. Many of the ideological and strategic elements are common to both regions, but the United States and the Soviet Union are aware of the dangers of war. They do not wish or intend to go to war with one another. But in Central America undeclared civil and cross-border warfare is a reality. War is perceived, threatened and employed as an instrument of policy. How then can confidence-building measures be applied?

A desirable and optimum course by common consent would be to set aside war as an instrument of policy. As long as hostilities continue, confidence will be elusive. But this is not likely to happen soon, if at all. Consequently, confidence-building measures of lesser magnitude might be the 'credible' affirmation of military action only in self-defence as a prelude to the conduct of negotiations. The very difficult and basic problem is how to generate confidence-building measures which could assist the parties to move hostilities from the military to the political arena.

Nonetheless, a few obvious steps that do not entail significant political cost are suggested as follows: while taking cognisance of the cautious opinion expressed by a United Nations report,

. . . it would be very difficult to point out specific measures to be implemented in a particular region for the purpose of building and strengthening confidence. As has been stressed at various points in this study, policies to be applied or measures to be taken, their nature, scope and other aspects, are to be established by the countries concerned, taking into account the particular security conditions of the region.[13]

A first step is to lower the rhetoric of accusation and vilification. Temporary moderation could help improve the political climate. A second moderate practice might be the avoidance of immediate condemnation or rejection of seemingly conciliatory words or gestures proffered by either side, because they do not meet the firm conditions of the other. United States responses to Nicaragua are a case in point. Such words or gestures could be staging-points for clarification, dialogue and potential meaningful negotiations. 'A primary requirement [as pointed out by the United Nations study] is . . . that communication and contacts between the parties to a conflict are not broken off at any time, but are improved.[14]

A real problem in Central America is the number of non-governmental and insurgency groups. Would dialogue with them mean the granting of legitimacy? Where this is a roadblock, informal channels should be opened and maintained. This has been a major problem in the Middle East. The use of third-party channels between the United States and the PLO is a case in point.

Another starting-point, where the Contadora group has made some progress in its deliberations, is on 'commitments relating to electoral processes and parliamentary cooperation'. It would be helpful, however, to draw up a model of minimum standards for elections. There does not appear to be much sense, at least from the academic point of view, in insisting on one set of standards for Nicaragua and another set for El Salvador, and at the same time ignoring the question entirely in neighbouring countries. Standards should be drawn from indigenous experience as well as foreign concepts. Furthermore, the matter of timing should not be ignored. The transition from the battlefield to the ballot-box is strewn with obstructions.

An additional confidence-building measure could well be the development of a set of basic standards for the maintenance of human rights in the region. For example, concern in the United States on the matter of human rights in El Salvador varies as between the views of President Reagan and of Congress. But it is a numbers game, more or less. The preparation of an acknowledged set of standards, as in the case of elections, could well be the focus of a set of norms to be applied to the region. Difficult as this may seem, the experience of the Conference on Security and Cooperation in Europe demonstrates that it is possible.

Security

The struggle for power is inextricably linked to the matter of security — for the antagonists as well as for the dominant power in the region, the United States. As polarisation intensifies, the antagonists seek aid, especially military aid, wherever they can acquire it. Enter the US-Soviet strategic confrontation, and arms flows increase, rhetoric escalates, and perceptions of threat become self-fulfilling prophecies. All these factors produce seemingly insurmountable roadblocks. Appeals to reason fall on deaf ears. Resort to arms becomes the only apparent means to security. In these circumstances intra-regional ambitions and struggles become subordinate to Washington's perception of US strategic interests in the area; this in spite of conflicting assessments of Soviet and Cuban influence and military penetration in the area, and of how far they will go if unchecked. But belief in the domino theory abounds, and military action is planned to counter the worst possible scenario that the future may hold. Security dominates and supersedes all other considerations.

The potential humanitarian and economic value of the Kissinger report is overshadowed by this one factor. Possible negotiations are repulsed in the face of perceived security threats.[15] An open dialogue between all concerned is therefore essential to gain time and to foster conditions of confidence that could induce direct negotiations. Independent studies should be conducted on cross-border arms flows and possible means of their curtailment through third party supervision. Such a step-by-step approach could lead to the development of innovation frameworks for the provision of regional arrangements designed to ensure the independent and sovereign security of the states in the area, whatever their political complexion, and to insulate them from non-American strategic penetration.

From here to there: The lessons of the politics of transition from Rhodesia to Zimbabwe

Our theme is that passage from open hostilities to negotiated settlement of the conflict in Cental America, 'to be successful, must move the parties from the stage of confrontation and hostilities to the medium of negotiations, from there to terms of agreement, and finally to the process of implementation.' The overall situation continues to be extremely precarious. Central America remains at a critical threshold. Either it moves toward escalation and enlargement of the area of hostilities, or towards a political settlement. Prediction is a hazardous game. The forces of war are relentless; the forces of peace are persistent too. Should the war escalate, the arguments of this paper have no current meaning. If, on the other hand, the parties choose the path of negotiations, freely or under pressure (the critical variable is the United States), then there is value in extending the foregoing analysis to an examination of what would constitute the main elements of one or several negotiated instruments, and of the process of implementation.

While there are other historical examples, the politics of transition from Rhodesia to Zimbabwe is a recent example which provides insight, valuable instruction, and warning. In 1979 Rhodesia also stood at the threshold of escalating hostilities, or of negotiations. We have earlier pointed out the eight major conditions which induced a political rather than a military solution. Most significant were a temporary equilibrium in the field of battle, general human and physical exhaustion, recognition that military victory would be too costly in the long run, and strong pressures for negotiation from outside governments and international organisations. Some of these same conditions are, in varying degrees, present in Central America. One paramount difference, however, is that while a democratic pluralist outcome is generally endorsed in Central America, as it was in Rhodesia, the United Kingdom, acting as the dominant third party in Rhodesia, adopted an impartial stand (some argue it had a preferred outcome). The dominant third party in Central America, namely the United States, appears to rule out an electoral victory or participation in government by the FDR-FMLN in El Salvador, or the continuation of the Sandinista government in Nicaragua. The United States can not be considered a 'neutral' third party and can not play the role in Central America that the United Kingdom played in Rhodesia.

The essential elements in the Rhodesian settlement were: (1) an agreement by all parties to negotiate a procedural settlement under the chairmanship of the United Kingdom at Lancaster House; (2) the establishment of a constitution before the cease-fire and elections; (3) the return of Rhodesian sovereignty to the United Kingdom for the duration of the cease-fire and elections; (4) full elaboration of the terms of the cease-fire dealing with arms traffic, deployment of opposing forces and military supervision; (5) definitive procedures to ensure free and fair elections; and (6) provision for unimpeded observation of the electoral process by the Commonwealth, other groups and the international press.[16]

The success of the Lancaster House negotiations was based, first, on the full and equitable participation of all the parties. This has not yet been possible with El Salvador or Nicaragua. Secondly, all parties agreed to the temporary transfer of sovereignty to the United Kingdom. We do not envisage, nor do we suggest, such a fundamental denial of sovereignty for any state in Central America. But that does not end the matter. Some form of third party role and international guarantees are necessary to gain the trust of the parties, to guarantee adherence to the terms of a cease-fire and procedures for free and fair elections, and to establish a political climate to allow the populace to cast ballots with the least amount of threat and intimidation. A third party, or parties, must therefore be granted a prescribed level of legitimacy, authority and assurance of operational efficacy within the domestic jurisdiction of the states concerned. How such a formula could be worked out is a matter for the parties to determine. But without it performance and credibility would be severely limited.

The key elements of the Rhodesian cease-fire agreement were: (1) All Rhodesian forces were restricted to their bases. (2) The Rhodesian air force was placed under the command of the British Governor. (3) All guerrilla forces (about 15,000) were deployed to specified assembly points under the supervision of the monitoring force. (4) A monitoring force was created 'to assess and monitor impartially all stages of the inception and maintenance of the cease-fire by forces and assist the cease-fire commission in its tasks'. The monitoring force was not an instrument of enforcement. (5) A cease-fire commission, represented by all parties, was established to consider infractions and violations of the cease-fire. (6) None of the parties was allowed jurisdiction over any zone or territory within Rhodesia. (7) The responsibility for law and order by the police force was placed under the authority and supervision of a British Governor. (8) All military operations were limited to self-defence. (9) The entire process was implemented as quickly as possible.[17]

The cease-fire arrangements were elaborate, ostensibly covering every possible need and contingency. The remarkable achievement in Rhodesia was that the cease-fire was maintained and free and fair elections were held, despite the fact that 4,000–6,000 guerrillas did not enter the designated assembly points, that a troublesome level of violence and intimidation persisted throughout the period of the cease-fire, that the Governor found it necessary to utilise part of the Rhodesian Auxiliary Forces — who were supposed to be confined to their bases — to maintain law and order, and that a serious crisis arose when it was found that all South African troops had not withdrawn as ordered by the Governor.

No two situations are the same. Those in Central America are individually unique. But however cease-fire arrangements may evolve, they should adequately cover the deployment of all regular and irregular military forces, and make provision for the maintenance of law and order and for the monitoring of cross-border arms traffic, all under careful procedures for third-party international supervision. But in each case the size, legitimacy, authority and freedom of movement of a supervisory force are absolutely critical, as in the question of the use of force. Ongoing discussions between Canada and Contadora highlight these very issues, based on Canada's extensive UN peacekeeping experience, and the frustrating non-UN experiences in Vietnam. Canadian concerns stress the critical importance of specific and firm guarantees for freedom of movement, a responsible, responsive and effective political sponsoring authority (unlike Vietnam), specified time duration, and adequate financial arrangements. Furthermore, the higher the level of trust and confidence the parties have in the process, the less likely is it that a supervisory force will be required to take military action. Should that threshold be crossed, the entire process could disintegrate.

Because it is highly unlikely that any state in Central America would or should abdicate its entire sovereignty to a third party or nation, as in Rhodesia, special provision should be made for assisting the domestic police in the maintenance of local law and order during elections. Perhaps the participation of a contingent of police from other countries might be considered as an added necessary ingredient to preclude partisan political activity by domestic police.

There were, as noted, grave problems in Rhodesia. Not all armed forces were confined to bases or assembly points, and there was frequent violence and much intimidation that threatened the legitimacy of the election. Cease-fires do not, as a rule, run smoothly; their continual violation in Beirut and generally throughout Lebanon are ample evidence of a condition not confined to that part of the world. There will always be threats and real or perceived violations. Provision for the management of unanticipated contingencies is therefore as essential as is careful advance planning.

The electoral procedures implemented under the authority of the British Governor were as rigorous as those put in place for the cease-fire. Direct responsibility for the supervision of the elections 'to the full extent necessary to ensure that they are free and fair'[18] was placed in the hands of a British Election Commissioner appointed by the British government, and with a British staff of 89. But they were dependent on the large indigenous Rhodesian staff, who had directed the election of 1979, a record that could have been a cause of trouble and certainly of apprehension, because, though trained to be impartial, their sympathies were obviously partisan.

The specific responsibilities of the Election Commissioner were: (1) to supervise the elections, directly or through members of his staff; (2) to receive any complaint concerning the conduct of the elections . . . and to investigate and take action on any such complaint; (3) to ensure the efficient functioning of the election council; (4) to cooperate and consult with the council, to have regard to its views and advice, and to receive and consider its representations and suggestions; (5) to report from time to time to the Governor on the discharge of the foregoing duties; and (6) to arrange the provision of facilities for Commonwealth and other official observers.

In addition to the Election Commission, there was an Election Council representing all the parties participating in the election. This Council had no administrative or investigatory powers of its own. But it did meet 19 times during the two months' electoral campaign and did respond to complaints. It was quite remarkable that, despite widespread intimidation throughout the election, none of the parties ever called for a special session. It was a most useful medium of communication and consultation between the parties, and helped to contain problems that might otherwise have disrupted the elections.

Other important measures were adopted to allow open campaigning by all parties, such as the conduct of rallies without hindrance (several were attended by tens of thousands), assured access to radio and the press, and so on. Moreover, exacting care was taken to prevent ballot stuffing, multiple voting, replacement or theft of ballot boxes, or any other possible means of rigging. These measures were effective. Moreover, it was essential that the populace be convinced that the elections were, in fact, 'free and fair'.

Notwithstanding all the above and more that was done to ensure 'free and fair' elections, threats, intimidation and violence occurred every day throughout the country — at times so bad that there was general concern that the election would be aborted. Parties in an election that is called when anger and the wounds of war are still fresh will use every means to gain electoral victory. But the crisis passed, the election was held and, in the words of the Commonwealth Observer Group, 'We are completely satisfied with the integrity of the conduct of the poll in all its aspects.' Further, considering the high level of intimidation conducted by all parties, 'It is the unanimous conclusion of the Commonwealth Observer Group that the election up to the end of the polling can be considered to have been free and fair to the extent that it provided an adequate and acceptable means of determining the wishes of the people in a democratic manner.'[19] In this election 2,649,529 valid ballots were cast, in comparison to 1,802,759 cast in the unsupervised election conducted in 1979 by the Smith government of Rhodesia. There were criticisms, but none of the 250 international observers questioned the legitimacy of the outcome. If all parties in El Salvador and in Nicaragua were also able to participate in 'free and fair' elections, there would doubtless be similar differences in the number of voters and in the outcomes.

It is difficult to design means to avoid all these related and unforeseen possibilities that could have disrupted the cease-fire and elections. Hence the presence of adequate, free and unfettered third-party supervision is, in our view, absolutely critical. The same is true for freedom of movement of journalists. There were so many observers and journalists in Rhodesia that any major violation of the cease-fire or act of intimidation could hardly have escaped observation. The presence of both undoubtedly contributed to the belief of the electorate that the ballot was free and fair, and to their turn-out in such large numbers in contrast to the elections held under far more restrictive circumstances in the previous year.

The entire process in Rhodesia was the subject of broad agreement, extensive pre-planning, and care in execution. All was then dependent on the firm and thorough role of the third parties, the Governor, the Monitoring Force, and the observers. The greatest credit goes to the populace which passionately desired black majority rule by means of free and fair elections.

What happens when elections are over? In Rhodesia, General Walls of the Rhodesian army is alleged to have wanted to stage a *coup* even before the victorious Zimbabwe African National Union of Robert Mugabe took office. He was restrained by the British government. No cease-fire or electoral process can guarantee an indefinite future. That is dependent on the political will of the parties.

Conclusions

We have examined those elements in Central America, of the Contadora Group, and of other states, that are conducive to political settlement of disputes. Though we have indicated counter-productive factors that foster attempts at military solutions and detract from the political process, we have not done so in depth. These factors are well known and need no recapitulation here. We have attempted to maintain a consistent focus on the political process based on historical experience and academic analysis, and have tried as much as possible to avoid judgement.

If one wants to select the essential ingredient among all the factors of the Rhodesian experience, that, in the view of this observer, was the dominant and substantially impartial third-party role. As previously asserted, it is unlikely that the same conditions could be replicated in Central America. But there are other models. The 'condominium' arrangements of a United Nations peacekeeping force for Namibia — including the special arrangements for monitoring the borders for arms and troop traffic, measures for the deployment of military units (of the South West Africa Peoples Organisation [SWAPO] , the government of Namibia and South Africa itself), and provision for the UN supervision of the elections under special co-operative arrangements with the governments of Namibia and of South Africa — are another model worthy of examination.

Which third party would be most appropriate for the conflict situation in Central America has already been made evident by the role played by the Contadora group of states. The OAS, for historical reasons, is not perceived as a fully independent organisation, and the United Nations, with the exception of a very minor role in the Dominican crisis of 1965, has not been regarded as a central political actor in the Western Hemisphere. The United States, for reasons already cited, could not play a neutral third-party role. Contadora has filled the vacuum. But it too, if it is to go beyond the conclusion of an Act for Peace and Cooperation in Central America, will have to establish a continuing competence, legitimacy and authority to execute the third-party functions enunciated in such an act.

The point is that while comparative historical analysis is very valuable, the direct parties in dispute, together with third parties, must work out agreements and processes suitable to them and to existing conditions — as long as they produce a peaceful transition from hostilities to a democratic political settlement that can satisfy the aspirations of the people and gain international legitimacy. That is an enormously complex, but historically necessary undertaking.

NOTES

1. UNDOC 5/16041, 18 Oct. 1983.
2. The writer is aware of his limited access to internal official documents setting forth the various proposals, positions and draft acts of agreement presented from time to time, and therefore acknowledges that this paper cannot take all of the necessary information into account.
3. UNDOC CA/6865, 8 Nov. 1983.
4. *New York Times*, 30 Dec. 1983.
5. *Christian Science Monitor*, 25 May 1983.
6. *Christian Science Monitor*, 8 Nov. 1983.
7. 'Is Peace Possible in Central America?', Remarks by Langhorne A. Motley before the Foreign Policy Association, New York, 19 Jan. 1984.
8. *New York Times*, 28 April 1983.
9. *From Rhodesia To Zimbabwe: The Politics of Transition*, New York, Pergamon Press, 1981.
10. *New York Times*, 19 Feb. 1984.
11. Inter-American Dialogue, *Statement*, 1 March 1983, pp. 2–3.
12. *New Directions in Disarmament*, New York, Praeger, 1981, p. 145.
13. Op. cit., UNDOC A/36/374, p. 35.
14. Ibid., UNDOC A/36/474/, p. 16.
15. Inter-American Dialogue, *Statement*, 1 March 1983, pp. 2–3.
16. *Southern Rhodesia report of the Constitutional Conference*, Lancaster House, London, Canada 7802, 1979.

17. *Rhodesia: Cease-Fire Agreement, Report of the Constitutional Conference,* ibid.
18. *Southern Rhodesia, Independence Elections 1980, Report of the Election Commissioner,* Salisbury, March 1980 (Cmnd. 7435, p. 1).
19. Statement of 2 March 1980, the day the election results were announced.

7

THE EXTENSION OF CONFIDENCE-BUILDING MEASURES: EUROPEAN EXPERIENCES, THIRD WORLD CHOICES

Falk Bomsdorf

The Confidence Building Measure (CBM) process in Europe and the Third World

It is a well-known phenomenon that political concepts and principles, set forth under quite distinct conditions and with quite definite contents, develop a life of their own and become axioms which continue to exist even when their original foundations prove false, or are no longer applicable. This phenomenon can be discerned in arms control. Everybody is in favour of arms control; everybody asks for progress in it. Yet there is no uniform understanding of what arms control really is. Everybody seems to have his own understanding, his own concept of it. It is no wonder, therefore, that in the last ten years arms control has not really made progress in the international arena.

The same phenomenon can be observed with regard to confidence-building measures (CBMs). Everybody is for peace and hence for confidence-building measures. Everybody in the East and the West, and now also in the Third World, is talking about the need for CBMs in order (to quote the UN study on the topic[1]) 'to eliminate the sources of tension by peaceful means and thereby to contribute to the strengthening of peace and security in the world'. In short, everybody is convinced that commitment to CBMs can contribute to strengthening peace and security in the world.

Yet there is no clear and common understanding of what constitutes a CBM; about what such a measure is aimed at; about its prerequisites and its area of application. In short, neither in Europe nor in the Third World is there any explicit and precise notion on the concept. There is thus a strange situation: on the one hand, there is little understanding of the essence of the CBM concept; on the other, there is an ever-growing interest in it. This is bound to lead to confusion, to a situation which may injure the CBM concept, and destroy its utility. The danger will arise that CBMs will become a

88

cheap way out for those who are not prepared to take steps on the way to disarmament, and yet want to prove their love of peace and stability; for those who want to influence their own population, as well as other states, rather than solve conflicts. Confidence-building measures may then become — and indeed have become, at least partly — a means of demonstrating at home a government's constant effort to achieve disarmament and arms control in the world, while demonstrating abroad that it is keen to make headway in maintaining peace. In the final instance, the concept of CBMs could become empty, and the politics of CBMs would then be nothing but diplomatic lacemaking.

The danger inherent in the CBM concept and its use for propaganda purposes is enhanced by another factor; the tendency to transfer a European concept of CBMs (which in itself is by no means homogeneous) to the Third World. Although the CBM concept was developed during the 1950s and 1960s in the framework of the relationship between the United States and the Soviet Union, it came to be regarded during the 1970s as a specific European contribution to international stability. This was due to the Helsinki process. In the final document of the Conference on Security and Cooperation in Europe (CSCE) a number of CBMs were agreed, and since then other CBM proposals have been negotiated in the follow-up conferences at Belgrade and Madrid. CBMs are currently being negotiated at the Conference on Disarmament in Europe (CDE) in Stockholm. A look at the literature increases the impression of CBMs as a specifically European concept. Hundreds of essays and monographs have been written on the subject, dealing almost exclusively with Europe or East-West relations generally. Writings on CBMs for the Third World are rare.[2]

In the late 1970s this Eurocentrism of the CBM concept was recognised by the arms control community in Europe, and especially in the Federal Republic of Germany. The Federal Republic, which had always had a stake in the CBM process, advanced the idea that the security of Europe and the Third World were inextricably linked, and that therefore techniques of peacekeeping like CBMs should be applied all over the world. It was the West German Chancellor Helmut Schmidt who, in his speech to the first Special Session on Disarmament (SSOD) of the UN in 1978, called for a confidence-building offensive and voiced the view that CBMs could 'serve in all parts of the world to improve the political preconditions for disarmament and arms control.'[3] Also on the initiative of the Federal Republic, a comprehensive UN report on CBMs was compiled and drafted by a group of experts from fourteen countries.[4] Finally, it was in the Federal Republic that in the spring of 1983 an international symposium on CBMs was held in which representatives of various parts of the world participated.[5]

Thus there has been a growing awareness in Europe that the concept of CBMs is not restricted to European use only, but could and should also be applied in the Third World. However, there has been a tendency on the part of the Europeans to transfer the European concept without major adaptation to the Third World; likewise there has been a tendency among Third World countries to accept this European concept without much thought about its suitability. Both attitudes are not only wrong but actually dangerous, because what has been useful in a European context (if it really has been useful) may not necessarily be applicable in another context, and may even prove counter-productive.

Both parties are to blame for the uncritical transfer of the CBM concept to the Third World. The Europeans (and the United States) have so far failed to develop a CBM concept specifically designed for the needs of these parts of the world; and although the Third World countries have criticised the European concept, they have not developed one of their own. Probably both sides have been overburdened by the task of developing universally as well as regionally applicable CBM concepts. The UN study on CBMs did not set out to design specific ones for the Third World; rather, its main function was to clarify and develop the concept of confidence-building measures in the global context to provide guidelines and advice to governments intending to introduce CBMs, and to promote public awareness of the importance of developing and fostering a process of confidence-building for the maintenance of international peace and security.[6] The motto of the study, approved by all members of the study group, was 'Even the longest journey begins with a single step.'[7] One should take the study as such a single step, and indeed a substantial one.

Equally it could not be expected of the countries of the Third World (which almost without exception had not been familiar with the CBM concept at all) to develop a specific Third World concept of CBMs at short notice. There have been more questions than answers: what precisely is the essence of the European CBM concept? Does this European concept meet the needs of the Third World? What do confidence and security mean in the specific context of Third World countries? Should the CBM be designed more in the framework of North-South relations, or more with a view to the relations between the Third World countries themselves? Such questions have to be answered before a specific concept of a Third World CBM can be developed. What is needed against this background is a forum for discussion where North and South can put forward their points of view on CBMs and where the specific requirements of the different regions of the world can be discussed with interested Third World countries.

The CBM study group of the UN was the initial step on the way to such a framework, but it was only able to generate some ideas. The second step, the discussion during the International Symposium in the spring of 1983 at Bonn, was more concrete: it was proposed that a permanent on-going process be established in the framework of which the CBM-related questions could be discussed among the Third World countries. This proposal was met with unanimous consent, but — as far as one can see — such a framework has not been established. Thus first steps still have to be taken. The various initiatives of the International Peace Academy (IPA) could well prove to be an important step in this direction.

Our main thesis here is that the CBM concept can prove its utility better in the Third World than in Europe. But in order for the CBM concept to achieve progress in the Third World, the following questions first have to be answered: What has been the European experience with CBMs? And what conclusions can be drawn from this about the utility of CBMs in the Third World? To find answers one has to go to the very basis of the CBM concept, because this field of security policy is relatively new and unfamiliar to many representatives of the Third World (as it also seems to be to many in Europe).

The experience with CBMs: Lessons to be learnt, mistakes to be avoided

To apply confidence-building measures as a peacekeeping technique may prove useless and even counter-productive if one does not stand on firm ground, i.e. if one does not have a clear notion of the CBM concept, but every international conference where CBMs have been negotiated or discussed has shown that there is by no means a clear and uniform understanding of it. This has been evident at those conferences where East and West (and neutral and non-aligned states) have been trying to solve their security problems (e.g. the Conference on Disarmament in Europe) as well as to those fora where North and South, i.e. the industrialised states and the countries of the Third World, have participated (e.g. the 1980 UN working group on CBMs, the International Symposium on CBMs at Bonn in 1983, and the IPA Workshops held in London in 1984 and Panama in 1985). Thus if we are to gain such a clear and uniform notion of the CBM concept, it is necessary to take a closer look at the experiences the Europeans have had with CBMs over the last ten years, and to take into account the attitude of Third World countries towards CBMs as they have been expressed on various occasions.

First lesson: **Before it is possible to initiate a CBM process, it
should be clear what 'confidence' means to the participating
states.**

A semantic and political problem. Neither in Europe nor in the
Third World is there a clear and uniform understanding of what the
word 'confidence' in this context really means. At first glance this
seems to be a semantic problem, but it is in fact inextricably linked
with politics. Semantics are regularly of fundamental significance in
politics — something which is widely underestimated. Particularly
in the field of CBMs, political concepts depend on semantic considerations. We must therefore look more closely at this aspect of the
problem.

When the term 'confidence' is taken literally in the context of
confidence-building measures, there is no difficulty in defining what
the latter term means. All measures that build confidence are confidence-building measures. Confidence is here seen comprehensively
and totally apart from the specific politico-military situation and the
threat to one country or another which it might imply. It is thus a
matter of confidence between countries, of the international climate, of what might finally be universal harmony. In keeping with
concepts that are so hard to pin down, there is constant reference to
the need for a process of confidence-building, a strengthening of
confidence, and an improvement in the international climate. The
aim of this process is less to reduce specific politico-military threats
than to arrive at a balance between peoples and countries. Confidence-building in this context is not a matter of restricting politico-
military options or making them more difficult, but the building of
confidence as such. The question 'confidence in whom?' or 'confidence in what?' does not usually arise.

This comprehensive and general understanding of confidence
contrasts with the traditional view of CBMs as a specific concept of
security policy and arms control. In the latter context it relates to a
specific threat to a country's security and is an attempt to eliminate
or alleviate this threat by appropriate measures. Confidence here
means confidence in the absence of certain threats posed by the
other side, so it is confidence in a specific situation. CBMs as thus
understood are intended to give the other side circumstantial evidence that the threat it fears does not exist or that a genuine threat
has been either reduced or eliminated. Confidence, or trust, between
nations is thus not the principal objective of this concept. Advocates
of this school of thought work more on the assumption — very
much in keeping with Thomas Schelling, one of the founders of
the arms control theory — that fundamental mistrust between

countries cannot be eliminated by CBMs and replaced by confidence in the wider sense of the term. This mistrust must (the argument runs) be accepted as a fact, and an attempt must be made, by reaching agreement on CBMs, to prevent mistrust from being heightened to the point where it leads to open conflict. Only in the long term, once a network of CBMs has been established and the relevant threat has been progressively reduced, can confidence in the wider sense gradually take shape. But this confidence is at best a long-term objective of CBMs. The short-term actual aim is — as has been said — to create confidence in the absence of features that are felt to constitute a threat.

Ancient CBMs: Explaining the present by going back to the past. This narrow understanding of the term 'confidence' and its consequences may be further explained by examples which stem from the distant past, when rulers — even absolute ones — may have understood better than we do how to tranquilise relations between themselves while still hating and distrusting each other.[8] They exchanged hostages, drank wine from the same glass, met in public to inhibit the murder of one by the other, and even deliberately exchanged spies to facilitate transmission of authentic information. Of these 'ancient CBMs', as they may be called, only very few have survived, and their original purpose — to demonstrate the absence of possible threats — is no longer visible today. If, for example, we lift our hats, shake hands or bow when greeting each other, we would not think that these actions constituted classical confidence-building measures originally designed to show the other party that no threat was imminent.

These actions did not create confidence in the character of the person performing them; they merely created confidence in the absence of feared threats. To elaborate one of the examples mentioned above: when two hostile tribal princes met to settle a dispute they could, for instance, drink wine from the same vessel — first the host, then the guest. This was a classical CMB in our current sense of the term: it was intended not to establish confidence between hostile tribes in the comprehensive sense, which was impossible, but to make the guest feel sure that one threat — that of poisoned drink — did not exist, so the dispute could be dealt with and settled by discussion.

To make this point clear by means of still another example, taken from our time: if two countries agree to withdraw their tanks and artillery 200 km. from each side of their common border, this does not create general confidence or trust between the political leadership or the population of the two states. What it does is to create specific confidence in the political and military leadership of each state, confidence in the absence of one threat, that of surprise attack.

Present understanding: comprehensive or narrow concept? Which version of confidence one prefers is of far-reaching significance. Those who advocate the comprehensive concept of confidence will be inclined to regard as a CBM any move that in any way tends to promote mutual understanding between countries. Thus any treaty, any negotiation, any talks, any encounter and any exchange of whatever kind between states is seen as part of the confidence-building process, and thus as part of a CBM. CBMs are not by this token limited to the politico-military sector; they may also, to the widest possible extent, apply to the economic, scientific and technological, cultural and other sectors.

In the narrower, security sense of the term, CBMs look altogether different, since they must be designed specifically to counteract a specific threat. They must be specific, because only then can the other side accept them as evidence of the absence of a certain threat. They will mainly have a military application, although measures of a strictly political character are not ruled out. On this understanding, CBMs have to fulfill a specific task, namely to influence perceptions of the security situation by creating confidence in the absence of a feared threat.

Views differ in different regions concerning the definition of confidence, and thus of CBMs to be adopted. Western and European neutral countries prefer narrow terms of reference, as do the East Bloc countries (although they have a rather diffuse understanding of the CBM concept); CBMs for them are measures which indicate or demonstrate the absence of perceived politico-military threats. Third World representatives prefer a comprehensive concept; for them a CBM connotes every step which is conducive to furthering international understanding. However, there is a growing tendency in the Third World to restrict the meaning of CBMs to measures which indicate the absence of feared threats. This notion still differs from the classical view, since it does not exclusively concentrate on politico-military threats but includes other kinds of threat, thus stressing the view that security for the Third World means much more than military security alone. This school of thought demands the inclusion of economic, scientific, technological, cultural and legal factors, and hence a definition of CBMs as measures which work toward the absence of threats to state security in the widest sense.

The attitude of the UN study. What confidence really means and what constitutes a threat in the framework of CBMs are questions that have still to be answered within the North-South relationships. The North has so far not given up its restrictive attitude, while the South still demands a wider application of CBMs. In this respect the UN study is ambivalent. On the one hand it says that international confidence cannot be established merely by gaining what it terms military confidence (paras 15, 21, 22, 158), and that the causes of mistrust have their origins in a complex of historical experiences, as well as geographical, strategic, political, economic, social and other elements (para. 18). On the other hand, the threats which CBMs are called upon to reduce or eliminate are seen primarily in the military context.[9] The study shows the same ambivalence when it comes to the question of whether measures are to be limited solely to the military sector, or should extend to the economy, science and technology, and so on. Thus, on the one hand, the concrete CBM proposals are of an exclusive military character (paras 128–134), and on the other, the study mentions proposals which aim at strengthening 'international confidence' in the economic, social and other fields (para. 135). However, these proposals are obviously not regarded as CBMs in the technical sense, but are listed as 'Policies and measures for the most part related to political, economic and social matters'. Rather vaguely, para. 159 reads: 'The group expressed the hope that, building on the results of this study, the United Nations would be able to widen further its scope and direct more attention to non-military approaches to confidence-building.'

The study thus expresses, at least by implication, a preference for the politico-military concept of CBMs. Nevertheless, the possibility of economic, social or cultural CBMs is not excluded. Obviously, this is a question about which the countries of the Third World themselves have to make up their minds.

The political possibility of CBMs in the economic, social, cultural and other fields. The Third World countries have to overcome an important methodological and political problem: they have to answer the question whether CBMs in the non-military sector are genuinely conceivable. This is a matter of whether political analogies hold good; of whether arrangements (like CBMs) made for a specific sector can be extended to others.[10] Such analogies cannot be justified simply by arguing that there are threats outside the military sector which must be reduced by means of CBMs; an analogy presupposes that CBMs in the military sector must be comparable in their objectives to those that would apply in other sectors if they are to appear feasible in those sectors.

The purpose of CBMs in an East-West context is, as the West sees it, to ensure either by negotiation or by greater transparency in the military sector, initiated by itself unilaterally, that the other side is better able to assess the military situation; or it is by regulating certain military activities or forms of deployment, to show the other side that there is no threat of the kind feared. It is assumed that neither side is interested in actually using its military power for a surprise attack or, in peacetime, to exert political pressure. It is further assumed that both sides have capabilities suitable, in theory, for military or political use. In the final analysis the aim of CBMs is to limit this threat, or intervention potential, and convert it into a defence potential. The property protected by CBMs is the inviolability and sovereignty of states whose first line of protection is the existing international legal order. Against this background, CBMs are a means of consolidating the general ban on the use of force and ensuring that states cannot, at least without difficulty, override this' ban. They are thus *protective measures.*

Turning to other potential sectors in which CBMs might be employed, and considering whether interests exist which are comparable with those existing in the military sector, it is soon clear that this is mainly true of economic sovereignty; although such options are conceivable in science, technology, the arts, law and so on, they are less potent. So the CBM concept could be applied to the economic sector, provided additional factors indicate that interests tally with those in the military sector. But this is not the case. As has already been noted, the CBM concept is based on the idea of specific moves to implement the ban on the use of force under international law. There is no general ban, controversial though it may be, on using economic power to political effect. Thus a call for CBMs in the economic sector would not help to enforce the existing order; it would be a bid to impose a legal and economic order different from the one currently existing. Such CBMs would not be designed to bolster the existing requirements for conflicts to be peacefully settled, as in the military sector; they would be *implementation measures* to arrive at arrangements which do not exist in the international economic order as it now stands.

However, formal logic is not always identical with political logic. Thus what we have said so far about the concept and field of application of CBMs may be in keeping with classical views evolved in the North, but it is far from certain that these logical deductions tally with political necessity in the framework of the North-South relationship.

Against this background, it is up to the countries of the Third World to design a CBM concept which is not solely politico-military in character. As for North-South relations, such a concept should help to solve the problem of how economic and other instabilities which stem from market power, technological superiority, monopolies over raw materials etc. can be eliminated or reduced. This is difficult, and there is a long way to go. Meanwhile there is every reason to conclude that one should concentrate on politico-military CBMs. This is all the more true if one is trying to improve peacekeeping techniques. The main arguments for such a concentration on the politico-military is that a country's external (i.e. military) security must be assured before it can develop comprehensively in other sectors. This argument seems particularly valid in the Third World. There, assets which have been gained by a country for the first time in its history and which — as industrial capacity — form the very basis of its existence may be destroyed by an act of war, with very substantial consequences. Therefore CBMs should first and foremost contribute to preventing such an occurrence.

Second lesson: **Without agreement on what constitutes a 'measure', CBMs run the risk of being misused for other than security purposes.**

As has been seen, the concept of CBMs constitutes a semantic trap: almost everybody interprets the word 'confidence' in its everyday meaning and not in the way it should be understood. Semantics also impinge on the term 'measures'; the history of negotiations on CBMs, in both the East-West and the North-South contexts, shows that this term is interpreted in different ways.

When talking of a confidence-building *measure*, the West means a concrete action which can be verified and evaluated. Only concrete actions — so the argument runs — can provide evidence for the absence of feared threats. The East on the other hand, does not restrict itself to this meaning of 'measure', but includes among 'confidence-building measures' moves which are not concrete actions but declarations. Declarations, however, cannot be verified or evaluated; you can either believe in them or not. A declaration on the renunciation of the use of force, for example, gives no indication whatever of the absence of a military threat. It is for this reason that the West has so far repudiated Eastern offers to conclude a CBM treaty on the non-use of force. Such a declaration of intent means nothing so long as the East does not change its military posture which, in case of war, would aim at a quick and decisive military offensive. Thus even if the Warsaw Pact solemnly declares that it will never attack Western forces in Europe first, the military threat to Western Europe is not diminished. Such a declaration cannot, in consequence, be regarded as a 'measure' in the CBM terminology.

There are suggestions in the UN study that countries of the Third World might likewise be inclined to classify declarations as confidence-building *measures* (e.g. paras 135, 136). Should this tendency become stronger, or — worse still — should declarations of intent become regarded as genuine CBMs, the consequences would be far-reaching. The CBM concept would no longer mean anything. It would cease to be an instrument of peacekeeping, but instead would become a propaganda tool.

Against this background the Third World countries should not repeat the mistake made in Europe, where — as the negotiations at the CDE in Stockholm are showing again and again — there is no agreed definition of the word 'measure'. They should stick to the clear and unequivocal meaning, taking their stand on the UN study, which states (paras 39 and 40) that CBMs have to be concrete measures because confidence can only be founded on concrete actions. Para. 39 of the study says plainly that neither a declaration of intent nor a repetition of generally recognised principles, nor a mere promise of good behaviour in the future, constitutes a CBM.

Third lesson: **It is very difficult to agree on CBMs if one side intends to preserve its offensive military options** *vis-à-vis* **the other side.**

The whole concept of CBMs rests on the principle that every state accepts the renunciation of the use or threat of force, as laid down in the UN Charter, and will therefore contribute to implementing that principle. One way of implementing it is to agree to specific CBMs. Every state taking part in such a CBM process proclaims (or is thought to proclaim) that it is not interested in using its military potential for an attack or, in peace-time, for exerting political pressure, and that it will use the military instrument only for defensive purposes. Only such an attitude is in accordance with the CBM concept whose aim (as has already been mentioned) is in the final analysis to limit the threat and potential for intervention of states and convert it into a purely defensive potential.

If these basic ideas of the CBM concept are not accepted by the other side, no real CBM process can be either initiated or entertained. This is the state of affairs in Europe. Here the Soviet Union has created over time, and at enormous cost, an impressive military potential which gives her the option of a surprise attack against Western Europe. The Soviet Union obviously wants to preserve this option. The West European states, which are not capable of invading the Warsaw Pact, need an assurance against the possibility of an Eastern surprise-attack. Such an assurance could be provided by CBMs which would give Western Europe warning time in order to prepare its defence. However, it is exactly such substantive measures which the Soviet Union is not prepared to take, since they would make Soviet military options more or less meaningless. From the Soviet Union's point of view this is quite understandable; it sees no reason why it should lend a helping hand to solve the military problems of Western Europe.

The consequence of this deadlock, however, is that agreed CBMs are necessarily no more than cosmetic. A close look at the CBMs agreed between East and West at Helsinki (CSCE) in 1975 shows that they are only of marginal significance. Since then no CBMs have been agreed at all. It is not difficult to predict that the Soviet Union at the CDE in Stockholm will not be prepared to accept Western or neutral proposals for substantive CBMs. The result of this conference, if any, will probably consist of more cosmetics.

What does all this mean for the Third World? Is it possible to initiate any CBM process there, given the fact that some Third World countries maintain military forces in order to use them directly or indirectly for offensive politico-military purposes? It may be, for such countries seem to be the exception. In most cases, armed forces are kept for defensive reasons, the neighbouring state being perceived as militarily aggressive. These countries face the problem of misperception, and here CBMs may prove useful. In addition, if a ruler is really willing to play the military card (without, naturally, saying so) his attitude towards CBMs may give clear proof of his real intention. CBMs in this context may serve as a diplomatic touchstone, as it were, with the help of which a state's true attitude towards the use of its military instrument may be identified.

Moreover, political attitudes of states are subject to change, to which a CBM process may well contribute in the Third World, where the capacity to learn from history sometimes seems greater than it is in Europe. Thus, while one has to doubt the prospects for genuine CBMs in Europe, the chances in the Third World seem better. This is all the more true if regional organisations (like the OAU or the OAS) or subregional groupings (like the Contadora group) offer to use their good offices and perhaps to apply pressure in bringing about a CBM process.

Fourth lesson: **A good strategy of CBMs presupposes good sociology.**

The need for identification of the type of conflict and of the threat images. The aim pursued by the CBM concept is to influence perceived or real threats by agreeing on specific measures. These will indicate either that the feared threat does not exist or that it is not as intense as perceived (information measures), or they will reduce or eliminate a genuine threat (constraints). In order to apply CBMs as a peacekeeping technique one must therefore first identify the nature of the threat. To this end two things have to be done: on the one hand, the *objective* nature of the conflict has to be identified; on the other, the *subjective* threat-image of the parties to the conflict has to be examined. Here a typology of possible conflicts would be useful. Such typologies were developed in the Latin American context,[12] which could also be applied to other parts of the world and adapted to the special circumstances and conditions prevailing there.

Threat-images are always easily identified. Particularly in ideological conflicts, it will sometimes be difficult to identify which side feels itself threatened and which actions of the other side constitute a threat. A thorough examination of the particular conflict and of the threat-images is, however, a prerequisite for the beginning of a CBM process.

The shortcomings of the European CBM process. What has not been done sufficiently in the European CBM process is the task of conflict and threat assessment. The conflict between East and West in Europe is an ideological and influence conflict, involving the superpowers. This type of conflict tends to be particularly bitter, complex and uncompromising,[13] and involvement of the United States and the Soviet Union makes it all the more so.

This insight has already given rise to scepticism as to the possibility of substantive CBMs in Europe, a scepticism increased by assessments of the respective threat-images. What is feared by West European states is that the Soviet Union may use its military power directly or indirectly. A special concern is the Soviet option of surprise-attack. On the Eastern side, it is not a military attack by the West or the political use of the military in peacetime which is really feared; the Warsaw Pact leaders know very well that NATO is not able to conduct a strategic offensive, and has no option for surprise-attack. In Eastern eyes, the real threat is not military, but rather the economic strength, wealth and civilisation of West European societies which attract and influence Eastern Europe. It is the same attraction which made hundreds of thousands of people leave East

Germany in the 1950s. Thus the West European way of life is the real danger for the East, feared particularly by the Soviet Union because it might erode its East European security glacis.

In this perspective, there are totally different threat-images on the two opposing sides, which makes the task of mitigating the two threats almost impossible. While it is feasible to reduce the Eastern military threat by way of CBMs, there is no reason why the Soviet Union should reduce its only real asset: the military instrument. On the other side, the threat which is seen in the Western way of life cannot by its very nature be reduced or eliminated.

Against this background it is clear that substantive CBMs cannot be agreed upon in Europe. What remains is, on the one hand, to concentrate on CBMs which aim at preventing the outbreak of war by accident, misunderstanding or misperception, and on the other to take refuge in cosmetic CBMs. The Europeans have so far chosen the second alternative: a number of more or less cosmetic CBMs have been agreed, but substantive CBMs which aim to prevent war by accident or misperception do not exist. Despite these short-comings, which are well known to the parties involved, the negotiating process continues. This is because the CBM process in Europe is pursued mainly for political and not for security reasons. The East's CBM strategy hopes to influence and, if possible, change political structures in the West; the West tries to counter these moves and to satisfy internal needs — namely domestic and foreign policy objectives — by its own CBM policy.

It thus seems inevitable that in Europe a real CBM process is hardly going on at present. Although the West Europeans are prepared to negotiate and agree on substantive and far-reaching CBMs, they know that this is not on the cards, because the other side is playing a different game. This is why what we see going on in Europe in this context is diplomatic posturing rather than efforts to achieve real CBMs.

The importance of conflict and threat assessment for the nature of CBMs. The European example makes clear that conflict and threat assessment is indeed necessary before a real CBM process can be initiated. When such assessments are made in the Third World the fundamental question will usually arise: where should CBMs be designed and applied — mainly in the military field or in the political field in the widest sense? The military situation in the Third World is mostly very different from that in Europe, where a whole network of war-preparedness exists[14] and where the armed forces can be mobilised to start a military action within days. Threat and conflict assessment in the Third World reveals that to try and achieve regional and sub-regional stability by means of military CBMs will usually be to put the cart before the horse. Only where there is an acute or potential danger of military conflict must the military situation be stabilised first.

This again raises the question of whether non-military CBMs are conceivable. To clarify the problem in the context of conflict and threat assessment, let us take a hypothetical example. Take two neighbouring states, where the ethnic majority of one state forms the ethnic minority of the other, and *vice versa*. At the root of such conflicts are artificial colonial borders. In this situation classical European CBMs, such as notification of manoeuvres and exchange of manoeuvre observers, will clearly have little application to the security problem. Political measures, i.e. to ensure comprehensive protection for minorities, would be better suited to create confidence. But would these measures be CBMs? What, in the Third World context, does constitute a CBM?

There is a clear need for a typology of conflicts in those regions or sub-regions. Simultaneously we need a list of possible measures which could help to solve or mitigate those conflicts. In this context the states involved should not so much stick to a theoretical concept or preconception of what might constitute a CBM, but should proceed from the clear requirement for combined and synergistic peace-making, peacebuilding, peacekeeping and confidence-building measures.[15] In any case, a measure which does nothing more than temporarily postpone a confrontation is of very limited use; it has to be accompanied by an effective search for political solutions through dialogue, and by efforts to attack the basic social and economic causes of the conflict.[16]

Fifth lesson: **Specific threats to the military security of Third World states to be assessed in the light of politico-military CBMs.**

If we concentrate on politico-military measures, CBMs should be designated with a view to the nature of the feared threat. In Europe, as was mentioned above, it is not so difficult to assess the threat and, accordingly, to design politico-military CBMs. From a Western viewpoint there are two obvious instabilities which could be mitigated by CBMs: first, the use of military imbalances, primarily through surprise or pre-emption, and secondly the use of military force for political purposes in peace-time, particularly by threatening military intervention.

In the Third World comparable situations do not usually occur; yet they exist and may even increase in number, given the extent and nature of arms supplied to Third World countries. In these cases the whole range of classical CBMs may be applied as they have been developed in the European context, and CBMs should be designed with regard to three types of perceived or feared threatening elements:

(1) *certain military activities* during periods of peace or tension;

(2) *certain forms of troop deployment* during periods of peace or tension; and

(3) *inadequate possibilities for communication* with the other side, which make impossible any decision as to whether or not any threat exists during periods of peace or tension. (In the case of a developing conflict, this third element falls into the realm of crisis management.)

In the Third World, military threats arise mainly out of disputes between two or more states, caused by conflict constellations of various kinds. The following are some of the types of conflict that may be discerned:[17]

— territorial conflicts;
— border conflicts;
— resource conflicts;
— ethnic conflicts;
— influence conflicts;
— ideological conflicts.

CBMs have to be designed according to the character of these conflicts. This goes without saying for a CBM aimed at the root of a conflict (if such a CBM is held to be possible). However, the argument is also valid for politico-military CBMs. It is to be assumed that every conflict and every resulting crisis has a certain conflict pattern, and a certain crisis structure, in which military factors play an important role. Here special attention has to be given to the so-called 'detonators'[18] – those factors which may cause the conflict to ignite and bring in military power as an instrument for the achievement of political goals in the resulting crisis. These points are particularly important for politico-military CBMs.

The difficulty in designing CBMs for the Third World lies in the fact that military power there is often used in a way which is substantially different from the European *modus operandi*. The threat of direct military intervention, though far from non-existent, tends to be exceptional; military force is employed more indirectly and sometimes more covertly. An important role is played by support for 'liberation movements' in a neighbouring country (for which — semantics play a political role here too — only 'insurgents' exist), by lending active assistance or by providing sanctuary. New types of war develop in which, as may occur in 'wars by proxy', the parties are not *de jure* at war with each other but are *de facto* waging a very real war against each other by directly or indirectly supporting insurgents within the other country. Again, there are countries which are officially at peace with each other, but of which one is financing a war which a third country is waging against the second country. These instances show that the question of how military force is employed in the Third World, and the characteristics of the various parts of the Third World in this respect, still need to be explored in depth. The same is true of CBMs aimed at preventing these military conflicts.

There is, however, one feature of Third World conflict which may profoundly change the character of a given crisis: the danger of political and military intervèntion by powers from outside the region, be they superpowers, former colonial powers or other powers. This may happen in various ways of differing intensity: from granting military aid and sending military advisers to intervening directly.

Third World countries seem unanimous in demanding the exclusion of foreign military interference, and in some cases specific objectives have been formulated.[19] However, it has been extremely difficult to embody these demands and objectives in concrete CBMs which can be applied and verified. Although eliminating, limiting or inhibiting intervention by outside powers is theoretically conceivable, putting it into effect is quite another matter, not least because extra-regional powers regard the ability to project force as an indispensable feature of their foreign policy. Here quite a number of problems have to be solved, among them how to integrate extra-regional powers into a regional CBM process.

CBMs in the Third World: A mixed bag.

Almost everywhere outside Europe CBMs can be found (without being so called). Thus they are not an exclusively European concept, but derive from an idea which is indeed age-old. What seems to be missing, however, is any awareness among Third World countries that they have been engaged in a CBM process.

In *Africa* CBMs exist to a certain extent at bilateral, continental and sub-continental (regional) levels.[20] The problem, however, has been — in the words of an African specialist on the subject[21] — 'the will to utilise the process for confidence-building'. The Charter of the Organization of African Unity (OAU) contains provisions which may well be interpreted as a mandate for agreement on CBMs. Article II, para. 2e, states that member-countries are to coordinate and harmonise their policies with special reference to cooperation and defence and security, implementation of which still seems to be lacking. Equally, in Article XIX the member-states pledge to settle all disputes among themselves by peaceful means, and agree to establish a Commission of Mediation, Conciliation and Arbitration. The Commission and various Good Offices Committees have been useful in the solution of various conflicts, but the principle — that African problems must be settled by Africans — has frequently been by-passed.[22]

As for the scope and meaning of CBMs, Africans seem to prefer a wide concept comprising the economic, the social and the cultural. The underlying idea is that joint economic projects 'will make states reflect over disputes and settle amicably'.[23] Likewise recommended is the joint development of roads and railways as well as telecommunications, 'so as to break some of the deliberate structures set by colonial powers'. These bridging facilities, as they are called, should help counter the breeding of suspicion and fear.[24]

In *Asia*, where quite a number of conflicts exist, the number of CBMs is at best marginal (the Sinai arrangements, which will be treated below, are an isolated case). This is often because one or both parties to these conflicts are not prepared to renounce the use or threat of force. However, there are conflicts or disputes which contain many opportunities for politico-military CBMs. This is particularly true of the Indo-Pakistan dispute and of the Indian subcontinent in general, where tensions have arisen between India on one side and Bangladesh and Sri Lanka on the other. Especially in the Indo-Pakistan case, some progress has already been achieved. CBMs might also prove beneficial as a step forward to an Indian Ocean peace zone. In addition to classical CBMs, it might be possible in this connection to consider conflict-regulating mechanisms between states in the region. One suggestion has been for the establishment of regional arbitration tribunals to settle existing or future disputes, especially over marine resources.[25]

For Asia, as for other parts of the world, the best way of keeping out great-power influence is to ensure the region's own independence, and create confidence through sub-regional agreements. The Association of South East Asian Nations (ASEAN), a sub-regional grouping of states which originally had a substantial conflict potential, is an excellent example. An entire range of CBMs had been agreed between ASEAN countries without actually being designated in that way.

Asia, with the case of ASEAN, not only provides a good example of the CBM concept functioning in the framework of sub-regional political and economic cooperation, but has also shown that the concept is working in bringing about peace between long-standing enemies, as in the CBM regulations contained in the 1979 Peace Treaty between Egypt and Israel.[26] They give a good example of the essential nature and goals of CBMs. First, the agreement of CBMs between the two states, although mutual distrust continues, shows that CBMs do not aim at establishing confidence between states in a comprehensive sense. Rather — as we have mentioned — they aim at creating confidence in the absence of specific threats to the security of the respective countries. Secondly, the CBMs agreed upon result from a correct threat assessment. What was feared most by Egypt and Israel alike was a surprise-attack by land across Sinai; 'consequently, the Treaty's most important measure was the partial demilitarisation of Sinai, which not only took into account the threat perceptions of each side, but also increased the stability of the deterrence balance between them. On the one hand the threat of a surprise attack has been considerably reduced, and on the other hand, if such an attack should happen anyway, the absence of adequate infrastructure in the desert will make it difficult to maintain the logistics to extend a battle much beyond Sinai. A battle confined to Sinai itself makes no sense to either party.

Further, the Treaty and the subsequent political developments show that it is not enough to mitigate the military dimension of a political conflict. The time provided by the peace regime and its CBMs must be used to tackle the political problems. Here CBMs of a political character are called for; at least, anything which might imperil the peace regime has to be avoided. A CBM process thus creates political obligations for the participating countries.

In *Latin America* the so-called Inter-American System, with its consultation and arbitration mechanisms, contains the beginnings of conflict settlement by CBMs. This system has been successful in a number of cases.[27] Moreover, CBMs similar to those practised in Europe have long operated in Latin America: joint manoeuvres, invitations to send manoeuvre observers, exchanges of military missions, training foreign officers at military academies, and joint annual conferences of the Chiefs of Staffs of all services in different Latin American capitals.[28] These and other measures may be unnecessary, given the fact that with two exceptions (Bolivia/Paraguay in the 1930s and Peru/Ecuador in the 1940s) international peace has been the rule at least in South America.[29] But CBMs by no means presuppose a danger of war.

There are two other instances that should be mentioned. One is the Treaty of Tlatelolco, of which Articles 12–16 contain provisions which may be regarded as CBMs in that they require nuclear energy to be used only for peaceful purposes. The other is the Declaration of Ayacucho (1974), in which eight Latin American states pledged themselves not to purchase 'offensive weapons of a sophisticated nature'. However, this could not be regarded as a CBM, because it was not a 'measure' but a declaration of intent; as such, it needed to be translated into an internationally binding instrument, with precise provisions for implementation, including verification measures. If these conditions had been met, one could have talked of a complex CBM. Although a number of conferences were subsequently held at which the principles of Ayacucho were stressed again and again, the Declaration has apparently not yet yielded concrete results.[30]

At this moment, the whole complex of CBMs plays a significant role in attempts to mitigate the conflict in Central America and prevent the outbreak of open war. The proposals made by the Contadora Group (although in very general language, and without designating specific measures) contain quite a number of CBM-goals;
— prevention of the installation of foreign military bases, and of any other type of foreign military interference;
— reduction (with a view to elimination) of the presence of foreign military advisers and other foreign elements involved in military and security activities;
— establishment of an internal control machinery to prevent arms traffic between countries in the region;
— elimination of arms traffic, whether within the region or from outside it, intended for persons, organisations or groups seeking to destabilise the governments of Central American countries, and refusal to provide them with, or allow them to receive, military or logistic support;
— refraining from incitement of, or support for, acts of terrorism, subversion or sabotage in the countries of the region; and
— establishment and coordination of direct communication systems with a view to preventing or, where appropriate, settling incidents between states of the region.

In addition, a number of economic measures are mentioned which can be called CBMs if one advocates such an extension of the concept, as is widely done in Latin America.[31]

The proposals of the Contadora Group (which are only designated as objectives to be achieved) constitute the most comprehensive and ambitious set of CBMs ever put forward for consideration in an acute crisis. This is by no means a fault, since the objectives are those which have to be achieved if the conflict is to be solved peacefully. However, everything depends on whether the parties involved — and these are not only the Central American states themselves, but also extra-regional states and 'liberation movements' — are prepared to accept such regulations. Moreover it will not be easy, to say the least, to translate the objectives of the Contadora Group into concrete and verifiable CBMs. To this end, a first step was taken by the joint meeting of the Central American and Contadora Group foreign ministers in January 1984. The ministers recognised the necessity to take steps to implement the commitments in the Document of Objectives, and adopted several principles for immediate application.

The need for analytical and conceptual work: Some recommendations

The world faces many conflicts, and it is easy to predict that their number will grow. The need for CBMs to prevent these crises from occurring or from being solved by military means will grow commensurately. However, if CBMs are to help solve the many conflicts of the future, Third World countries will have to make a contribution of their own. *They* are the ones who define what they understand by 'security'; *they* decide which measures are best suited for tackling their security problems; *they* have to agree on specific CBMs and implement them. Moreover, most future crises will probably (and regrettably) occur in the Third World.

What is needed against this background is a specific Third World contribution. It is not enough merely to accept the European CBM concept and make minor adaptations to it; on the other hand it is not enough to criticise and finally reject this European concept (well founded though this criticism may often be). Concepts which meet the specific requirements of the various regions of the Third World need to be developed. We offer below some thoughts and recommendations.

1. The principal question to be answered by Third World countries is whether CBMs should merely be politico-military or whether economic, social, cultural and other areas should be included.

Here Third World states will surely point out that military CBMs do not tackle the real problems; what is needed is to tackle the roots of tension and threats and deal with the causes of economic, social, ethnic and cultural instability. To give one concrete example, numerous Third World states do not feel much threatened by the military power of their immediate neighbours; instead the real danger to their sovereignty is seen in debts owed to creditors outside the region.

It is hard to disagree with these and similar threat-perceptions of Third World countries. But if one tries to design CBMs to alleviate them, one must be aware that the attitude just described causes a change in the political function as well as the conceptual character of CBMs as they have been known for the last 30 years. First, they cease to be a means of consolidating the general ban on the use of force; but become a political instrument which may be used in the political struggle between North and South. Secondly, CBMs would no longer presuppose (as in the military sector) the existence of threat-options open to both or all partners in such measures. Instead, it would merely be a matter of reducing threats felt by only *one* side to be genuine and serious.

Against this background, the task of analysing the specific threat-perceptions of Third World countries and designing CBMs which correspond to the perceived threats is very difficult. This does not mean that there is no place for economic and other CBMs (which, by the way, must certainly not be seen solely in a North-South context, but would also be important in a South-South context). It only means that the burden of proof, so to speak, for the feasibility of such measures rests with those who reject the narrow CBM concept concentrated on politico-military measures. In other words, if Third World countries decide to favour the wide CBM concept, it is up to them to work it out in detail. In particular, they must decide which economic (and social, cultural, ethnic etc.) principles are acknowledged by the parties concerned and thus could be protected and implemented by CBMs.

2. Until such a wide CBM concept has been worked out in detail and until CBMs in other fields have proved their feasibility, the countries participating in the CBM process would be well advised to restrict themselves to politico-miliary measures since these meet the most urgent needs. In doing so one should not repeat the mistake made by the European countries in concentrating on purely military measures and neglecting the political side. In many cases, especially in the Third World, it is not the military confrontation which causes tensions as much as lack of communication, which can ignite a latent or acute conflict.

Thus the purely political aspect of the CBM concept should be stressed. Talks at all levels, between representatives of the states participating in the CBM process, as well as direct or indirect communication between the respective peoples through meetings or through the media should be promoted as a priority. Indeed it is a principal instrument of prudent CBM diplomacy. Because the mass media can influence a latent or acute conflict, the development of so-called enemy images should be analysed; ways should be explored of playing down these images and so forestalling their fatal consequences. Finally, more attention should be given to crisis management; CBMs should be designed to create and enhance crisis stability.

3. In analysing the threat, countries will sometimes recognise that their security is endangered not by an external threat but an internal one. At the roots of most threats of this type are ethnic problems: minorities are fighting for rights and for a just share in the economic and social life of their country. Here it is useless to design CBMs aimed at the neighbouring countries; it is the internal security problem that needs to be solved. Internal CBMs should at the same time satisfy the security needs of the ethnic minorities themselves (as well as those of their ethnic kin in neighbouring states who may also be minorities there but who may also be in a majority) and provide no incentive whatever for extra-regional states to intervene. In designing CBMs for internal needs the scope of the CBM concept would be extended; moreover, these CBMs would lend themselves more to unilateral than to mutually agreed application which in no way diminishes their potential usefulness.

Notwithstanding the importance of these internal, unilateral measures, the main problem with CBMs for the Third World will in future be how to eliminate, limit or inhibit intervention by extra-regional powers. The difficulties here lie not so much in the conceptual as in the political realm: do extra-regional powers really have the political will to abstain from various kinds of intervention? And do Third World countries in every case wish to keep these powers out?

4. To examine and elaborate · the practical questions affecting CBMs in the Third World, an ongoing process needs to be established.[32] Working groups might be set up (possibly in the framework of the Non-Aligned movement and/or regional organisations like the OAU or OAS) in which the countries of the various regions or sub-regions first seek to identify the major threats to security and stability in their region and then try to design suitable CBMs: a directory or inventory of appropriate CBMs related to the security needs of each region could be developed.

Moreover, it would be very important for the whole process if the CBM, concept could prove its effectiveness in practice. To this end workshops and conferences should be held in crisis regions where all parties concerned would have the opportunity to express their threat-perceptions and propose corresponding CBMs. It would be hoped that these workshops would result in specific CBMs which could then contribute to solving the conflict in question peacefully.

5. In a prudent CBM strategy, declaratory politics should always be avoided. Rhetoric, as well as the repetition of generally accepted principles, are not conducive to solving inter-state conflicts. What matters is implementing these principles through agreement on concrete measures. A German saying neatly sums up the whole CBM process: *'Es gibt nichts gutes, ausser man tut es'* — 'Nothing good happens unless someone is doing it.'

NOTES

1. UN Document A/36/474, para. 4
2. To these rare exceptions belong the following essays: Hugo Palma, 'El fomento de la confianza: un punto de vista del Sur' in *Desarrollo*, 1982, 2; Fuad Hassan, 'The Potential Role of Confidence-Building in the Crisis Areas for the Prevention or Settlement of Regional or International Disputes and Armed Conflicts'; Alexandre S.C. Barros, 'Confidence-Building Measures in South America: Some Notes on Opportunities and Needs'; Oscar O.B. Ede, 'The Potential Role of Confidence-Building in Crisis Areas for the Prevention or Settlement of Regional or International Disputes and Armed Conflicts: The African Dimension'; Donald Mills, 'Report on the Discussions'; all in Karl Kaiser (ed.), *Confidence-Building Measures*, Bonn, 1982; Falk Bomsdorf, 'The Confidence-Building Offensive in the United Nations', in *Aussenpolitik* (English edn), Bonn, 1982, 4; Jack Child, 'The Use of Confidence-Building Measures as a contribution to Peace in Central America', paper presented to the Conference on Maintenance of Peace and Security in the Caribbean and Central America sponsored by the International Peace Academy, Bridgetown, Barbados, 28–30 May 1983; Hugo Palma, 'Confidence Building: Present Situation and Future Prospects', in *Disarmament*, Autumn 1984.
3. Cf. Bulletin of the Federal Government, no. 55, 30 May 1978, p. 534.
4. Austria, Canada, Czechoslovakia, Ecuador, Finland, Federal Republic of Germany, Ghana, Peru, Romania, Soviet Union, Thailand, United States, Zaire.
5. The proceedings of the Symposium were edited by Karl Kaiser, see note 2, above.
6. Cf. para. 171 of the Study.
7. Obviously a variation of Lao Tse's saying that even a journey of 1,000 miles begins where you stand; cf. Lau Dse (Lao Tse), Dau Do Djing (Tao Te King), saying 64.
8. Thomas Schelling, 'Reciprocal measures for arms stabilization' in Donald Brennan (ed.), *Arms control, disarmament and national security*, New York, 1961, p. 169.
9. Cf. Bomsdorf (see note 2). pp. 375ff.
10. Ibid., pp. 379ff.
11. Cf. Erwin Muller, 'Non-Military Confidence Building Measures', in Wolf Graf Baudissin (ed.), *From Distrust to Confidence: Concepts, experiences and dimensions of confidence-building measures*, vol. II, Baden-Baden, 1983, pp. 113–20.
12. Cf. Jack Child, 'The applicability of peacekeeping techniques to Central American conflicts', in Jack Child (ed.), *Maintenance of peace and security in the Caribbean and Central America*, Report of International Peace Academy Workshop, Cancun, Mexico, 7–9 Oct. 1983, p. 45ff.
13. ibid, p. 46.
14. Cf. Alexandre Barros (see note 2), p. 193.
15. Jack Child (note 12), p. 57.

16. Ibid.
17. Cf. ibid., p. 46.
18. Cf. Jack Child, Summary of the Workshop and the discussions (see note 12), p. 9.
19. Cf. the Document of Objectives of the Contadora Group, published as an annex to Jack Child (ed.), *Maintenance of Peace and Security* (note 12). pp. 89–93.
20. Cf. Oscar Ede (note 2), pp 211ff.; Falk Bomsdorf (note 2), pp. 387ff.
21. Oscar Ede, p. 210.
22. Ibid., p. 212.
23. Ibid., p. 219.
24. Ibid., p. 219.
25. Cf. Philip Towle, 'The United Nations Ad Hoc Committee on the Indian Ocean: Blind Alley or Zone of Peace?' In Larry Bowman/Jan Clark (eds), *The Indian Ocean in Global Poltics*, Boulder, Colo., 1981, p. 218 *et seq*. A comprehensive confidence-building measures strategy in this sub-region is advocated by Dieter Braun in *The Indian Ocean: Region of Conflict or 'Zone of Peace'?*, London/New York, 1983, pp. 180ff.
26. Cf. Yair Evron, 'The CBM impact of the Israeli-Egyptian Peace Treaty' in Wolf Graf Baudissin, *From Distrust to Confidence* (note 11), pp. 87–99.
27. Cf. Jack Child (note 12), pp. 46ff.
28. Cf. Jozef Goldblat/Victor Millan, 'Militarization and Arms Control in Latin America', in *SIPRI Yearbook 1982*, Stockholm/London, 1982, p. 393 (422).
29. Cf. Alexandre Barros (note 2), p. 185
30. Cf. Jozef Goldblat/Victor Millan (note 28), pp. 420ff.
31. Cf. Hugo Palma, 'El Fomento de la confianza: un punto de vista del Sur', in *Desarrollo*, 1982, 2.
32. As was proposed by Working Group IV (CBMs in the Third World) during the CBM Symposium at Bonn in 1983; see Donald Mills (note 2), p. 232.

8

A CONFIDENCE-BUILDING APPROACH TO RESOLVING CENTRAL AMERICAN CONFLICTS

Jack Child

Introduction

The early 1980s have seen a dramatic increase in interstate tensions and violence in Central America. Equally dramatic has been the intense search for a peaceful resolution of the major disputes which have given rise to this tension and violence. The search for peace has involved many nations and non-state actors; it has included a wide variety of techniques and approaches involving mediation, conciliation, negotiation, negative and positive peace, peacekeeping, peacemaking, peacebuilding, and so on.

Despite this intense and wide-ranging search for approaches towards peace and stability in Central America, there is one technique which has received relatively little attention: that of confidence-building measures (CBMs) designed to lower tensions by increasing the trust between adversaries.[1] The reasons for this lack of attention are somewhat obscure, but perhaps they stem from the fact that they are usually linked to analyses of high-intensity warfare (nuclear and non-nuclear) in the NATO-Warsaw Pact European Theatre and would thus seem to have little applicability to the low-intensity warfare characteristic of Central American conflicts.

The central thesis of this paper is that CBMs *can* be applied to Central American tensions, and, if used in conjunction with other diplomatic and political approaches, can make an important contribution to peace and conflict resolution in the area. Further, the paper argues that some basic CBMs have in fact been proposed (although not explicitly identified as such), and that some of the mechanisms for implementing them are already in existence in the Western Hemisphere.

The Theory of Confidence Building Measures[2]

The basic concept and its origin. The fundamental concept of confidence-building measures stems from a competitive international

environment in which potential adversaries mistrust each other's intentions and have inadequate information about their capabilities. This mistrust and lack of adequate information are strong incentives to improve one's own capabilities for war and surround one's own intentions with secrecy, thus contributing to a rising cycle of tension, suspicion and costly arms races, and increasing the possibility that one or more international actors will start a war through misunderstanding, uncertainty or accident. The purposes of CBMs are thus:
— to reduce the risk of war stemming from misunderstanding or misinterpretation;
— to lower international tensions by slowing down or reversing the spiraling interaction of tensions, suspicion and armaments;
— to contribute to arms control and disarmament.

Alford[3] proposes an analogy of two swordsmen with weapons raised to strike; neither one wants the conflict, but neither one is willing to let his guard down. The process of avoiding the conflict involves a slow and formal ritual in which the swordsmen slowly back away until outside striking range, then a slow and mutual lowering of the swords, the sheathing of the weapons, which are still at hand if the adversary moves aggressively, and then finally the unbuckling of the scabbards. Each step in the process involves caution and verification that the other side is making an equally significant move away from the conflict. Alford notes that this simple analogy is imperfect since in international relations the asymmetries of doctrine, power and force postures make the creation of this ritual framework an extremely difficult process. The process involves a great deal of imagination as the adversaries search for small but meaningful ways to build up verifiable steps down the road towards peaceful resolution of their differences. The role of CBMs is to provide some of these steps.

Historical precedents. As the analogy of the swordsmen suggests, CBMs have probably existed for as long as conflict itself. The term 'confidence- building measures' in its present context emerged from the Final Act of the Conference on Security and Cooperation in Europe (CSCE) in Helsinki in 1975,[4] although most observers would probably agree that the concept and techniques were a by-product of the Cold War and US-Soviet rivalry. In the 1950s the precursors of today's CBMs focused on reducing the possibilities of surprise attack by exchanging observers and suggesting aerial inspection of strategic force sites. After the Cuban missile crisis of 1962, the emphasis changed and concentrated on preventing war through misunderstanding or accident; this emphasis produced the 'hot line' direct link between the United States and the Soviet Union, and 1971 brought about the 'Agreement on Measures to Reduce the Risk of Outbreak of Nuclear War between the United States and the Union of Soviet Socialist Republics'. More recently, the Strategic Arms Limitations Talks (SALT) and the Strategic Arms Reduction Talks (START) have included a number of CBMs.

Types of confidence-building measures. The general categories of CBMs considered in the European and US-Soviet contexts have included:
— announcement of exercise and manoeuvres;
— notification of other military activities;
— verification through exchange of observers;
— non-interference with national verification means;
— communications between potential adversaries;
— information exchange;
— explanation of strategic and tactical doctrine;
— notification of major weapons programs.

Capabilities, intentions, perceptions and the arms spiral. The theory (and practice) of CBMs frequently runs counter to conventional views held by military planners and national leaders because of the different weight given to intentions and capabilities in strategic analysis. Strategic planners, intelligence analysts and national leaders have traditionally dealt with the adversaries' capabilities and not their intentions, because the former are generally based on physical entities (population, size, economy, men under arms, weapons systems etc.) which can be measured, while intentions involve psychological and abstract values which are rarely expressed openly. This emphasis on measurable capabilities over intangible intentions almost inevitably leads military planners (and the national leaders they advise) to worst-case analysis and pessimism which is most readily countered by a build-up of one's own capabilities. Most arms control proposals also deal with physically measurable capabilities (i.e. numbers of missiles, quantities of warheads, launching platforms etc.) rather than with intentions.

The emphasis on the capabilities of one's potential adversary strongly influences one's perceptions of his possible intentions. There is a tendency to assume the worst possible intention and distort and filter incoming information to support this pessimistic view. This in turn leads to fear and mistrust of the adversary and the emphasis on building up military responses to the worst case. This build-up has a tendency to be perceived by the adversary as a threatening increase in capabilities which should be countered by a further arms build-up — hence, the spiral of mistrust, fear and armaments.

In sharp contrast, the confidence-building approach focuses on intentions and on verifiable non-aggressive postures which, if matched by the potential adversary, can lead to further non-aggressive steps and a reversal of the arms spiral. The key to the CBM approach is the verifiable and credible nature of the CBM, as well as the balance and symmetry of the measures taken by each side. Like the two swordsmen of the analogy, each adversary must be able to monitor the non-aggressive steps taken by the other before a further action is taken. At any moment in the process there is enough time and space available to permit rapid recovery of an adequate defensive posture if the adversary launches a surprise attack.

The process of confidence-building is thus a slow, cautious and cumulative one in which the nations involved gain confidence in their own defences and the process itself as they perceive that violations or threats can be detected soon enough to permit an adequate response.

The components of confidence-building measures. Successful CBMs must include the following:

(*a*) *Transparency and openness.* The measure or step must be obvious and unambiguous. There must be no way to hide or distort the capability or intention in question. A convincing argument against secrecy here is that the measure will probably become public knowledge anyway, so why not announce it and take credit for the announcement as a CBM?

(*b*) *Predictability.* The actors involved must be convinced that aggressive actions (their own or their adversary's) cannot be carried out secretly, but instead carry their predictable indicators which will give the adversary adequate time to respond.

(*c*) *Mutuality, balance and symmetry.* Any steps taken towards a CBM must be perceived as a fair *quid pro quo*, with balanced and symmetrical concessions on either side.

(*d*) *Communication and verification.* There must be adequate channels for notifying the potential adversary of any moves which might be misperceived; these communications channels must be adequate in both the technical and perceptual sense (i.e. the transmission means must be adequate and the message must be credible and logical to the recipient — it must fit into one of the 'pigeonhole' categories he is expecting).

(*e*) The ultimate goal of CBMs should be an actual reduction of capabilities for making war; this is possible only if the reduction is mutual and verifiable, and if the means exist for detecting and countering violations.

Limitations. CBMs have a number of limitations; among them

(*a*) The adversaries involved must genuinely want to avoid the conflict. If one of the adversaries believes in the cost-effectiveness of aggression, or if he is motivated by strong ideological convictions which permit him no compromise, or if he sees conflict as a zero-sum game in which he has a reasonable chance to win something at the adversary's expense, then any CBMs will quickly break down.

(*b*) CBMs will be strongly opposed by individuals whose training and experience have given them a strong sense of secrecy and a profound distrust of the perceived enemy. Although these attitudes are particularly strong in military and intelligence institutions (and especially so in closed totalitarian regimes), these perceptions also extend to many civilian political leaders and to general public opinion as well.

(*c*) CBMs in and of themselves cannot resolve the basic causes of conflict. They are, in this sense, instruments of 'negative peace' which can help prevent a conflict from breaking out, but do nothing about its roots. This suggests that they should be combined with 'positive peace' instruments which deal with the underlying causes of conflict: injustice, ideological crusades, imperialism and underdevelopment.

(*d*) Although CBMs can contribute to the lowering of tensions, their effective employment is basically a function of the general status of international politics at any given moment. Thus too much must not be expected of them.

Pace. Dramatic and bold CBMs are unlikely to produce results. The process of confidence-building is inherently a slow and cautious one in which individual phases must be tested and verified by both sides before proceeding onwards to the next phase. This suggests that it is advisable to begin CBMs at a low and modest level where mistakes or losses would not be fatal. These low levels may in fact involve no more than social and non-substantial contacts which begin to show adversaries that their opposite numbers are like them and have compatible goals. This low-level educational process can then be gradually expanded to the point where liaison and exchanges of personnel and observers slowly build up the network of communication and understanding that is necessary in order to sustain more meaningful CBMs.

The European experience with CBMs

The Final Act of the 1975 Helsinki Conference on Security and Cooperation in Europe included a number of provisions for military CBMs:[5]
— notification of manoeuvres of more than 25,000 men (with 21 days advance notice);
— they should apply to all of Europe, and 250 km. into the Soviet Union;
— nations were encouraged (but not obliged) to invite and send observers to these manoeuvres;
— optional notification requirement for smaller manoeuvres (understood to be within the range of one division, from 10,000 men up to the 25,000 point where notification was required and not optional);
— notification of other military activities, referred to as 'out of garrison activities';
— exchanges of military visits.

Assessment of their effectiveness. Most assessments of the effectiveness of the 1975 Helsinki CBMs agree that they have been no panacea and that the results have been mixed. While there has been fair compliance with the provisions for notification of major manoeuvres, the other measures have had uneven results and even some deliberate evasions. Western observers conclude generally that the compliance has been much greater by NATO than by the Warsaw Pact. There have also been complaints of petty irritations, such as when Soviet binoculars provided to NATO observers were supposedly unserviceable.[6] Concern has been expressed that the 1975 Helsinki accords placed too much emphasis on ground manoeuvre notification and did not include naval forces or the broader questions of communciations links or further steps to reduce tensions.[7]

Future prospects for European CBMs. The prospects for additional CBMs or the more effective implementation of existing ones obviously depend on the general tone of East-West relations. A number of possible additional CBMs have been proposed in the following categories:[8]
(*a*) notification of smaller manoeuvres and exercises;
(*b*) notification of other military activities, such as whenever a unit left its normal garrison;
(*c*) notification of mobilisation exercises (routine alerts and deployments);

(*d*) extended notification period (from the present 21 days to possibly 30, 45, or 60 days);

(*e*) notification of certain naval and air activities;

(*f*) inviting more foreign observers to military manoeuvres, treating them better and giving them greater freedom of movement;

(*g*) improving communications between nations involved, including the setting up of 'hot lines' between opposing military headquarters or tactical units in physical proximity;

(*h*) ground or air inspection for verification;

(*i*) information exchange on military forces, budgets, locations etc.;

(*j*) extension of the geographic areas of the Helsinki CBMs to all of Europe and possibly to other areas;

(*k*) non-interference with national technical verification means (i.e. no destruction or jamming).

The United Nations interest in CBMs

The possibility of extending CBMs beyond the NATO-Warsaw Pact context has received considerable attention at the United Nations, and a summary of this interest is a useful transition from the European environment to our consideration of the applicability of CBMs to the Central American situation.

The UN General Assembly decided (Res. 34/87B of 11 December 1979)[9] to undertake a comprehensive study using a group of qualified experts, with due regard for geographical balance. The 'Group of Governmental Experts on Confidence Building Measures' met four times in 1980 and 1981, and produced a study (UN Document A/36/474). This UN Study defined the objectives of CBMs as:[10]

. . . . to contribute towards reducing or eliminating the causes for mistrust, fear, tensions and hostilities as significant factors behind the international arms build-up. Generally speaking, confidence-building measures aim at fostering a climate of trust and international co-operation among States in order to facilitate progress in the disarmament field.

The recent United Nations study represents a first attempt to clarify and develop the concept of confidence-building measures in a global context. It is intended to provide guidelines and advice to Governments for the introduction and implementation of confidence-building measures and the promotion of public awareness of the concept with a view to contributing to the maintenance of international peace and security.

The Group went on to observe:[11]

Among the principal causes of mistrust is the lack of reliable information on the military activities of other states and on other matters pertaining to mutual security. The destabilization caused by insufficient knowledge about opposing military forces is often aggravated by subjective misconceptions and a resulting lack of trust concerning the intentions of states. Consequently, one of the main objectives of confidence-building measures must be to reduce the elements of fear and speculation in order to achieve a more accurate and more reliable reciprocal assessment of military activities and other matters pertaining to mutual security, which may cause mutual apprehensions and increase the danger of conflict. Although all experts agreed in principle on the need for an exchange of information on the military activities of states and matters related to mutual security, there were differences of view concerning the degree of openness necessary for building confidence.

The Group agreed that the seriousness, credibility and reliability of the state's commitment to confidence-building can only be demonstrated by the continuous, regular and full implementation of confidence-building measures and policies, and accordingly, constitute another important characteristic of the confidence-building process.

According to the Group, regular personal contacts at all levels of political and military decision-making should be encouraged and promoted with a view to achieving a better understanding of reciprocal concerns and to foster co-operation in the field of security-related communication. All measures enhancing communication and information assume a particularly important function in times of crisis.

Confidence-building measures cannot, however, replace measures which would directly limit and reduce military potentials. If one were to misunderstand confidence-building measures as a substitute for disarmament measures one would not only over-estimate their inherent positive potential, but might also run the risk of their being used as a pretext for avoiding real progress in arms control and disarmament or even to legitimize a continuing arms build-up.

Among some of the specific ideas considered by the Group and the Committee on disarmament are several which would, on initial examination, appear to be applicable to Central America:[12]
— publication and exchange of information on security-related measures incuding matters of arms control and disarmament;
— regular bilateral and/or regional consultations of governmental representatives on such security-related matters;
— provisions of scholarships in military schools for the military personnel of other states;
— exchanges of military delegations and military attachés;
— indication of normal military conduct and information on scope and extent of specific military activities like manoeuvres, specified movements, etc. according to pre-established procedures;
— limitations of certain military activities and movements;

— establishment of procedures for the containment of conflicts, including the establishment of hot lines;
— agreement of steps conducive to the relaxation of tensions and the settlement of conflicts;
— achievement of greater transparency of military postures, i.e. the establishment of a standardised and verifiable reporting system for military expenditures enabling their comparison as a step to their balanced reduction on a multilateral level;
— establishment of registers within the framework of the United Nations for the recording of data necessary for transparency and comparability of military postures.

The Contadora process as a CBM approach

We propose in this section that the Contadora efforts should be envisioned essentially as a confidence-building process in the broadest sense, and be employed as such in the search for a reduction in tensions and a peaceful resolution of Central American conflicts.

The general steps and elements of the process would include the following:

(*a*) The Contadora Group (Mexico, Panama, Colombia, Venezuela) is accepted by all concerned as the catalyst that brings the parties to agreement and oversees compliance and verification. Implicit in this understanding is that Contadora must be prepared to exercise pressure and make public any violations.

(*b*) The United States accepts the legitimacy of the FSLN regime in Nicaragua and ceases overt and covert attempts to intimidate it and bring it down.

(*c*) Nicaragua accepts the legitimacy of the elected regimes in the Isthmus and ceases overt and covert support for insurgencies in these countries.

(*d*) Implicit in the latter two points is the agreement to cease the illegal trafficking in arms and other support to destabilising groups.

(*e*) Agreement is reached on limits on arms, troop levels and foreign military advisers; an open registry is maintained by Contadora, which verifies compliance.

(*f*) Contadora puts into place a conflict resolution mechanism by interposing third-party neutrals in areas of high tension where adversaries are in contact (peacekeeping). In zones of lower tension smaller peace-observing groups aided by technological means can verify compliance with the Contadora provisions.

(*g*) Contadora group representatives (aided by international organisations and other neutral observers) observe (and, if necessary guarantee) the free electoral process in those countries where regimes have come to power by means other than elections.

(*h*) Contadora is the vehicle for continuing negotiations to settle the various issues between the parties in conflict.

(*i*) A confidence-building regime is established in Central America to lower tensions and reduce the possibility of conflict through misunderstanding, accident or misreading of actions. Contadora assists in the establishment of this regime (specific measures which might be considered are contained in the following section, as well as in the Contadora documents found in the Appendixes to this book). As a minimum this CBM regime would include communication links ('hot lines'); verification of limits on troops, arms and advisers; advance notification of manoeuvres and exercises; and exchanges of information and personnel. Other measures might involve the establishment of demilitarised zones, bilateral (joint) border patrols, and increased military-to-military contacts through periodic conferences, sporting events and attendance at regional military training institutions.

(*j*) A major development and economic integration effort is launched to attack the socio-economic problems underlying much of the conflict in the area. Although most of the funding for this effort will inevitably have to be from the United States, the bulk of the financing should be channelled through multilateral agencies.

To protect the interests of the Central American nations as well as the United States, the process must be cautious, balanced, incremental and verifiable. As an interim measure, existing levels of external military assistance and advisers should be frozen while negotiations are worked out for agreed-on levels and their eventual reduction. Contadora's verification measures should be credible, pressures on violators should be meaningful, and there should be an understanding that consistent violation by one side leaves the other side free to increase its own efforts.

As can be seen from the outline of the Contadora process sketched out above, peacekeeping and peace-observing play an important role in the implementation and verification process. Peacekeeping is a controversial topic in the inter-American system because of the way it has been used in the past to mask intervention, and because of a commonly-held perception that this type of initiative has tended to serve US interests. Thus many Latin Americans recall the intervention in the Dominican Republic in 1965 as a case of unilateral US action which was subsequently made more palatable by the 'figleaf' of multilateral OAS support (obtained by the thinnest of margins). As a result, when the United States proposed in July 1979 that an OAS peacekeeping element be sent to Nicaragua in the final days of the Somoza regime, there was much suspicion that this masked a US attempt to preserve *Somocismo*. These sensitivities, and current realities in Central America, suggest that the United States would not be able to play much of a role in any of these Contadora peacekeeping and peace-observing initiatives, other than perhaps a logistical and technical support function outside the area. Thus the search for acceptable third-party neutrals willing to perform this function and capable of doing so may be difficult. The Contadora countries are a logical starting-point; others, such as Canada and some of the European countries, are possible candidates, along with some of the Hemisphere states. However, the technical, logistical and administrative problems of peacekeeping should not be minimised; there exists the dismaying possibility of reaching a political agreement via Contadora and then having it break down at the practical and operational level.

In May 1984 three Central American nations (El Salvador, Honduras and Costa Rica) proposed that the Inter-American Defense Board serve as a verifier of the Contadora process in a peace-observing function, and the proposal was rejected by Nicaragua.[13] The proposal and the rejection serve to illustrate some of the characteristics of the Board and the inter-American military system of which it forms a part. Essentially, the military system's history is that it was created under US aegis during the Second World War as an instrument for Hemisphere defence against the Axis. This orientation shifted to anti-Communism aimed at Marxist-Leninist insurgencies during the Cold War. In the context of current Central American tensions, the Board cannot realistically play a peace-observing or peacekeeping role as long as it retains this anti-Communist orientation and the historically high US profile.

In the constant focus on the crisis of the moment, it appears that the US government may not have fully appreciated that the Contadora process has acquired a broader significance which transcends immediate Central American problems. Contadora has become to many Latin Americans a symbol of greater maturity and independence. It is also seen as an indication that solutions proposed and implemented by regional Latin American powers may be more effective than the traditional solutions advocated by the United States, either unilaterally, bilaterally through selected allies, or multilaterally through the Organization of American States. Each of the four Contadora countries (Mexico, Panama, Colombia and Venezuela) has a special significance in the regional context, and the four acting collectively represent an important segment of Latin America. Contadora has also acquired a kind of mystique and

aura as an important Latin American initiative supported enthusiastically by a broad range of most of the Hemisphere and West
European nations.[14] At the pragmatic level the Contadora process
involves a significant number of individuals from the four countries
including their Presidents (who have committed personal and
national prestige), their foreign ministers, and a large number of
lower-level officials. In and of itself, Contadora thus represents a
major integrative endeavour for the region, and the contacts made
in the process of working out the agreements are an important
reality. Furthermore, Contadora is consistently described as a
'process' which will not end when agreement is reached on its major
points; presumably the verification and confirmation process will
continue to keep the players active, and the integrative effect will
thus continue.

The significance of this integrative effort is all the more important
in the light of the decline of the traditional instruments of the Inter-
American System. Damaged by the Malvinas/Falklands crisis of
1982, and again by the intervention in Grenada in 1983, the System,
and the Organization of American States as its principal institution,
seem more and more irrelevant to the Central American crisis and to
the Hemisphere's needs. The Contadora process is thus, to some
extent, a replacement for the old and now increasingly anachronistic
vehicles for inter-American cooperation and security. As a result,
Contadora presents the United States with both a challenge and an
opportunity to accept a new type of Latin American initiative, a new
measure of Hemisphere diversity, and a new cooperative approach
to problems.

The Contadora process and the proposed CBM regime thus go
beyond Central America's current crises and the need for an
immediate and relevant policy. There are distinct benefits and costs
for the US in this situation. Acceptance of the basic Contadora
proposals implies that the United States will eventually give up significant instruments of its traditional influence and power in
Central America, especially those associated with the Security
Assistance Program. Carried to their fullest, the Contadora proposals meant that the US military presense will end in the area. Further,
the symbolism and mystique of Contadora may exert considerable
pressure on the United States and may force it to accept agreements
that in the long run may be disadvantageous; the 'cut and run' fears
of US conservatives may not be unfounded. There is, moreover, a
certain analogy to the Panama Canal negotiating process: the
United States can dig in and attempt to hold on to a situation which
is becoming less and less tenable, or it can adopt a more enlightened
position giving the Latin Americans a greater share of benefits and

responsibility. The costs and benefits of the Contadora proposals and the ensuing CBM regime must thus be carefully weighed.

There is one final element of the Contadora process that also must be considered: the psychological and propagandistic one. Because of the importance Contadora has acquired as a symbol of a cooperative Latin American effort to solve its own problems, there will be a high price to pay if the effort fails and the United States is portrayed as the chief reason for that failure. There is a substantial body of public and official opinion in Latin America that the United States is only paying lip-service to the Contadora process, and is in fact finding ways quietly to scuttle it. If Contadora fails and this opinion prevails, there may be strong Latin American resentment and the United States may find itself even more isolated than it did during the Malvinas/Falklands and other crises in recent years.

Applicability of CBMs to Central-America

This section will list a number of possible CBMs with relevance to Central America, will suggest some complementary measures aimed at reducing tensions in the area, will mention institutions with a role to play in this process, and will identify some areas in which caution is advised.

CONFIDENCE-BUILDING MEASURES WITH RELEVANCE TO CENTRAL AMERICA

CBMs dealing with troop movements and exercises:
(*a*) notification of manoeuvres (with different procedures and length of advance notice for different types and sizes of manoeuvres);
(*b*) notification of alert exercises and mobilisation drills;
(*c*) notification of naval activities outside of normal areas;
(*d*) notification of aircraft operations and flights near sensitive and border areas;
(*e*) notification of other military activities ('out of garrison') which might be misinterpreted.

CBMs dealing with exchanges of information
Information should be exchanged on a *quid pro quo* basis in the following areas:
(*a*) military budgets;
(*b*) new equipment and arms;
(*c*) unit locations;

(*d*) significant changes in a unit's size, equipment or mission;
(*e*) the major elements in the military's strategic and tactical doctrine.

CBMs dealing with exchanges of personnel

These personnel exchanges should be balanced in terms of numbers and duration, and could include:

(*a*) inviting observers at manoeuvres, exercises, and 'out of garrison' activities (the observers could be from neighbouring states, a third-party neutral country, or an international organisation);

(*b*) stationing permanent liaison observers at major headquarters (the observers could be from neighbouring states, from a third party neutral nation, or from an international organisation);

(*c*) exchanging personnel as students or instructors at military academies, military schools, and war colleges;

(*d*) exchanging military attachés from all three services (land, sea, air) to all the area countries. These attaché positions should be filled by highly qualified personnel, and not be used as 'gilded exiles' to get rid of officers who are politically undesirable.

CBMs dealing with the assembly, collation and dissemination of data

(*a*) A central registry should be set up (perhaps as an OAS entity) to assemble, collect, analyse and publish information on armaments, organisation and disposition of military units.

(*b*) Independent national technical means should be available to verify this information; there should be agreement on the nature of these means and an understanding that there will be no interference with them.

CBMs dealing with border tensions

(*a*) Joint patrols should be established along sensitive borders (with or without the participation of third party neutrals or international organisation observers).

(*b*) Neutral third party or international organisation observers should be available to man permanent posts in historically disputed and troubled areas.

(*c*) Unmanned ground sensors could be used to supplement observers.

(*d*) Buffer or demilitarised zones (DMZ) could be established along sensitive borders for certain types of equipment with strong offensive capabilities (armour, artillery, naval combatants, attack etc.), or for all military activites.

CBMs dealing with actions which might be interpreted as provocative
(*a*) Agreement should be reached on acceptable and unacceptable military activities in terms of a 'code of conduct' of rules of engagement.
(*b*) Clear limits should be placed on those military activities (such as mobilisation, calling up of reserves etc.) which could lead to misunderstandings.

CBMs dealing with communications
(*a*) Establish communication 'hot lines' between:
— heads of state;
— chiefs of military forces (defence ministers);
— units in contact across a border;
(*b*) limit the use of coded (on-line and off-line cryptography) military message traffic;
(*c*) increase the miltiary-to-military contacts through the various organs of the Inter-American Military System (Inter-American Defense Board, Inter-American Defense College, Service Chiefs Conferences, exercises, etc.).

CBMs dealing with arms
(*a*) Reach an agreement on levels and types of arms, with emphasis on the exclusion of high-performance and expensive weapons systems;
(*b*) encourage the procurement and deployment of defensive weapons systems in lieu of offensive weapons systems;
(*c*) reach agreement on military budgets for arms.

CBMs dealing with extra-military contacts
(*a*) Exchange visits by military athletic teams;
(*b*) encourage social and professional contacts through the attaché network and the various elements of the Inter-American Military System.

CBMs dealing with training and education
(*a*) Teach CBM approaches in national military academies, staff schools, and war colleges, as well as in multinational military schools (such as the US Army School of the Americas and the Inter-American Air force Academy) and colleges (such as the Inter-American Defense College);
(*b*) examine primary and secondary school curricula for aggressive, hostile or false information on potential adversaries;
(*c*) apply CBM techniques in command post and field exercises;

(*d*) encourage the development of military trans-nationalism (i.e. a sense of military professionalism and mutual respect that transcends national boundaries).

CBMs dealing with the role of superpowers
(*a*) De-link local and Central American issues from East-West superpower concerns;
(*b*) reduce military ties between the Central American nations and the superpowers;
(*c*) explore the possibility of extending CBMs geographically beyond the Central American area (i.e. the Caribbean and South America).

CBMs dealing with ways of expanding CBMs
(*a*) Establish a regional or subregional mechanism, similar to the Conference on Security and Cooperation in Europe (CSCE) to study confidence-building measures and ways to improve and increase them;
(*b*) discuss CBMs at the periodic Service Chiefs' Conferences;

COMPLEMENTARY MEASURES

There are a number of measures which, while not strictly within the definition of 'confidence-building', could contribute to peace in Central America and reduce the possibility of escalation and a military confrontation. These would
(1) control the political-military actions of exiles;
(2) renew the historic inter-American commitment to non-intervention and respect for sovereignty;
(3) involve military establishments of possible adversaries in exercises where there is a mutually profitable result. Such exercises could involve search and rescue (SAR) of aircraft and shipping, disaster relief, hurricane tracking, humanitarian actions, control of arms and drug trafficking, etc.;
(4) internationalise the United States military schools formerly located in Panama (the Army's School of the Americas — USARSA; the Air Force's Inter-American Air Force Academy — IAAFA; and the Navy's small craft training team — SCIATT) and bring these schools under a multi-national board of directors, using the Inter-American Defense College as a model;
(5) consider moving the Inter-American Defense Board or Inter-American Defense College to a Latin American nation and rotate the key positions among the Hemisphere nations (at present all the key positions are held by US military officers).
(6) Countries in Central America with pending border or territorial

disputes should be encouraged to resolve them using all methods available (third party mediation, arbitration, conciliation etc.). At present these disputes include: Guatemala-Belize, Nicaragua-Colombia, Honduras-El Salvador.

(7) All the countries in the Hemisphere should be encouraged and permitted to join the OAS, article 8 of the OAS Charter being amended to permit the entry of Belize and Guyana; Cuba should be invited to return to the OAS. All OAS members should be encouraged to sign the Rio Treaty and use it as the principal vehicle for peaceful settlement of disputes.

INSTITUTIONS FOR FACILITATING THE IMPLEMENTATION OF CBMs

The Hemisphere has available an Inter-American Military System which can, with certain modifications, play a valuable role in implementing CBMs in the Central American context. The following are among some of the necessary modifications:

1. Reduce the high profile of the United States in the System. This high profile (in which the United States provides the key officers and the military doctrine and much of the equipment) is a relic of the Second World War and the Cold War years when the United States set up and gave direction to most of the organs of the System. To function effectively in today's politico-military environment the Latin Americans must play the dominant role and assume greater responsibilities for their own security and peacekeeping.

2. Re-orient the thrust of the Inter-American Military System away from its narrow anti-communist concern to a much broader and more realistic role as a forum and channel of communications for dealing with contemporary security problems and issues such as peacekeeping and confidence-building.

3. The Inter-American Military System should permit a much larger role for third-party neutral mediators, especially in terms of their role in conflict resolution.

4. All the Hemisphere nations should participate in the Inter-American Military System. This premise seems ridiculous if the System is seen as an anti-communist alliance (which it indeed was in the early 1960s). However, in the current politico-military context the System is no longer credible in these terms; however, it can and should play a role in conflict avoidance, conflict resolution and confidence-building.

5. In the Central American subregion there should be a subregional security coordinating institution. The old Central American Defense Council (CONDECA) once performed this function, but did so within the narrow confines of an anti-subversive, anti-communist and counter-insurgency alliance. Its replacement (or

revival) must be based on a broader vision of mutual security and mutual confidence among the various states and ideologies of Central America.

A CAVEAT: THE LIMITATIONS

The preceding list of possible CBMs and complementary measures and institutions to carry them out is extensive and even utopian. It represents an attempt to identify as many areas as possible in which the concept of CBMs may play a role in Central America's tortuous path towards peace, stability and security. The European experience shows us that cooperative steps are indeed possible even between bitter adversaries. The European experience also shows how slow the pace is, and how one must initially be content with very modest and low-level steps towards mutual self-confidence.

The Latin American experience would add the limitation that any movement towards peace in Central America through CBMs or other techniques must not be dominated by the United States (although it can and must play an important role). No regional state should be excluded; some approaches (such as the use of large peace-keeping contingents with a heavy US representation) are not possible because of long historical memories of abuses of this technique. The immediate goals must be limited and modest; but the confidence-building measure approach is one that merits attention and serious consideration.

NOTES

1. Few scholars have explicitly applied CBMs to Latin America. One is Victor Millan of the Stockholm International Peace Research Institute (SIPRI). His preliminary ideas were contained in a paper prepared for the 1982 Latin American Studies Association (LASA) meeting in Washington, DC. Millan also has a chapter 'Regional Confidence-building in the Military Field: the case of Latin America' in the book *Controlling Latin American Conflicts* by Michael A Morris and Victor Millan (Boulder, Westview Press, 1983).
2. This section draws from: Jonathan Alford, 'Confidence-building Measures', *Adelphi papers*, no. 149 (London, International Institute for Strategic Studies, 1979). Abbot Brayton, 'Confidence-building Measures in European Security'; *World Today*, October 1978, pp. 382–91; Johan Jorgen Holst, 'Confidence-building Measures: a Conceptual Framework', *Survival*, Jan./Feb. 1983; IPRA Disarmament Study Group, 'Building Confidence in Europe', *Bulletin of Peace Proposals*, no. 2, 1980.
3. Alford, op. cit., p. 2.
4. IPRA, op. cit., p. 226.
5. Same sources as in note 2, above, plus: US Congress, Comission on Security and Cooperation in Europe, Implementation of the Final Act of the Conference on

Security and Cooperation in Europe: Findings and Recommendations Five Years After Helsinki, August 1980.

6. Alford, op. cit., p. 4.
7. Holst, op. cit., p. 226.
8. Brayton, op. cit., pp. 387–91.
9. United Nations, *Disarmament Yearbook*, Vol, 5, 1980, p. 409.
10. United Nations, *Disarmament Fact Sheet* no. 20, 'Study on Confidence-building Measures: A Summary', Jan. 1982, pp 2–3.
11. Ibid., pp. 4–5.
12. UN, General Assembly, Report of the Committee on Disarmament, Official Records, 36th Session, Supp. no. 27 (A/36/77), pp. 100–1.
13. *Washington Post*, 2 May 1984, p. A1. US Department of State, Current Policy, no. 572, 'US Central American Policy at a Crossroads', 2 May 1984, pp. 7–8.
14. For expressions of this support, see *Washington Post*, 1 May 1984, p. A1; ibid., 13 May 1984, p. A32; International Peace Academy, *Summary Report of Regional Cooperation in Peace and Security in Central America and the Caribbean*, 1984; *La Nación* (Costa Rica), 28 Dec, 1983, p. 2 29 Feb. 1984, p. 4 7 March 1984, pp. 1; *El País* (Madrid), 21 May 1984, p. 7 4 June 1984, pp. 3, 11; *La Nación* (Buenos Aires), 26 March 1984, p. 5 24 July 1983, p. 1; *Excelsior* (Mexico), 22 Sept. 1983, p. 1.

9

NEGOTIATION AND COOPERATION AS A STRATEGY FOR DEVELOPMENT IN THE CARIBBEAN BASIN

Helen McEachrane Dickson

The current economic crisis and more recent upheavals in the Caribbean Basin, heightened by the drop in oil prices, has increased the already serious debt problems in Mexico, Venezuela and Brazil, to name the major middle-sized nations of concern to US economic interests and ultimately its political interest. This situation has in turn increased tensions and highlighted differences in the interpretation as to how US policy for the area is formulated and applied. In addition, the Falklands/Malvinas crisis resulted in considerable realignment in the hemisphere in favour of Latin American solidarity and anti-US feeling.

In addition to border confrontations, territorial disputes which continue to plague the area with the dangerous reminder of the Falklands/Malvinas spectre, military intervention in Central America escalated at an unprecedented level from the beginning of the 1980s. Regional organisations, such as the OAS, have been unable to respond to the complexity of this situation, and localised conflicts are being polarised into East-West-type conflicts with what is seen as a return to Cold War rhetoric.

This changing situation, which began in 1979 with the Nicaraguan and Grenadian revolutions, is the crux of the deterioration of relations between the United States and the countries of the region. If indeed the United States (notably the Carter and Reagan administrations) has been correct in seeing a serious challenge to its hemispheric interests in the actions of the Soviet Union and its surrogates Cuba, Nicaragua, Grenada and anti-government forces fighting in El Salvador, Guatemala and Honduras, should we not assume that there is a need for change in the area and that a better way to respond might be to negotiate multilaterally?

What is absolutely certain is that the repercussions of the aforementioned aspects of the economic crisis are being felt inside the US borders (in Miami, Houston and other border towns real estate and related businesses have virtually collapsed) and the export, foreign investment and banking systems are seriously jeopardised and threatened. The unprecedentedly high interest rates in the United States, coupled with the sharp drop in oil revenues in the case of Mexico and Venezuela, have brought the IMF to reconsider its usually tough conditions for loans and caused it to negotiate the rescheduling of external debts for countries like Costa Rica and Mexico. This close financial interlinked system could well be much more of a threat than the political loss of hegemony in the Basin perceived by the Reagan Administration. The possibility of Mexico — experiencing its most severe economic crisis this century with its population of 70 million, its extensive border with the United States and its migration problems — eventually having to call a moratorium is dangerous. Further, Mexico would almost certainly be followed by Venezuela, Brazil and Argentina, thereby causing a major disruption of the world financial system and adding to unemployment and migration factors in US domestic policy.

What does all this point to? Our thesis is that the cost of failure to resolve this situation is as great for the Caribbean Basin countries as it is for the United States with which its future is inextricably linked, and we therefore propose cooperation at both political and economic levels as a strategy for development. Further, we suggest that attempts to integrate the region through economic cooperation have largely failed in the past because of the lack of political will and the more recent emphasis given to bilateral aid and relations developed by the Reagan Administration. It is our firm belief that the role of multilateral development banks such as the Caribbean Development Bank and the IBRD should be expanded as a reflection of the region's needs as a whole, without countries regarded as friends of the United States being singled out as beneficiaries of selective bilateral aid. This kind of policy lends itself to divisiveness and can only further heighten tensions and polarise local conflicts into regional confrontation with dire consequences for the United States. The Basin's economic problems require a long-term strategy and not merely a response to emergency situations with emergency measures. If these problems are not addressed bearing in mind the dangers of superimposing austerity programmes on an infrastructure where there is already seriously inequitable income distribution, the consequences for democracy as espoused by the West will be open to hemispheric confrontation, leading to violent opposition and, as a consequence, increased repression.

The fight for democracy as understood in the West should not be aligned with totalitarian regimes which oppose the less advantaged groups in their society, but rather with the cause of those very groups and their changing needs, both social and institutional. Tolerance of political differences is part and parcel of the democratic process, necessary for countries wishing to conserve democracy. The key words in the fight for the conservation of democracy, then, must be negotiation and cooperation. It is in this context that we wish to focus on the nature of the politics of the basin. 'Political community is a condition in which specific groups and individuals show more loyalty to their central political institutions than to any other political authority in a specific period of time and in a definable geographic space'; this is the strategy and precondition for political cooperation leading to economic development.[1]

One should not assume that the existence of dissenting countries whose ideologies vary from the larger unit of the Basin precludes the possibility of cooperation. Indeed conflict, consensus and diversity are the hallmarks of existing Western European political communities with which the Basin is partly integrated through the existing French, British and Dutch territories and the various internal groupings such as the ACP and the Commonwealth, to name but two. Unfortunately, this has not been the view of the US government — notably the Reagan Administration,[2] although it sees itself as committed to the region through the Caribbean Basin Initiative (CBI) package: the 'resource availability at one billion dollars a year of economic and military assistance for the Caribbean Basin[3] has not been forthcoming so far except in the form of military aid for El Salvador, which requires financial year supplementals beyond 1984. The 1983 request fell substantially short of the $300 million of the required $1,000 million level in 1982 dollars.'

Quite contrary to repeated statements by President Reagan and members of his Administration on development and cooperation in the Basin, the press (and even a number of CIA officials) have indicated that there is growing concern that the covert operations which have been denied officially may have gone beyond the limitations stated in Presidential documents and intelligence briefings to Congressional Committees. (By law, the President is required to notify the House and Senate Intelligence Committees of covert actions.[5]) In other words, the notion of a political community and cooperation as a strategy for development in the Basin is viewed by the Administration conceptually as a 'security community'. That is to say that violence is a necessary means of maintaining the *status quo*, as opposed to 'political community' which understands the need for social change in the developing countries.[6]

If ideological pluralism is a vital characteristic of Western Europe, why are the Caribbean countries denied it? Why are the Basin countries not extended the same privileges of conducting their national affairs free of intervention and of punishment, both political and economic, if they dare to imagine that cooperation and peaceful

coexistence independent of ideology are possible and indeed
salutary in this conflict-plagued zone?

Either cooperation or integration, if it is to work successfully,
must have a political base, which in turn engenders political consequences. In addressing the concept of cooperation as a strategy for
development, it should therefore be stressed that the probable outcome will be measured by the opposing factions in terms of military
successes rather than the political or economic revival and development of the region. This is a truly disastrous trend.

Difficulties arising from US foreign policy for the Caribbean Basin

No democratic system of government can exist without dialogue
between its constituent parts, that is to say without the participation
of dissenting voices which are allowed to express themselves and
their point of view freely in an atmosphere where there is some
possibility of a reasonable response from those elected to govern.
This principle, which is valid as a principle, becomes essential when
in moments of crisis the joint broad political responsibility fails to
converge in national, regional and international objectives, converting these into hemispheric as opposed to national and regional
programmes. There are no technical solutions, however elaborate
they may be, which could be effective if they were not adopted
without broad consent. Hence dialogue is a necessity to overcome
the crisis, as several attempts to start one between countries, governments and pressure groups in the region have indicated.[7] The
fundamentally political character of the crisis and the absence of
any need for the US Administration to justify to the region its actions
once these have been endorsed domestically obviates the glaring call
for dialogue and cooperation. The absence of dialogue has generated
increased anxiety regionally and internationally because of the failed
attempts to arrive at a negotiated political consensus. Some of these
attempts won the blessing and cautious interest of the Administration; nearly all have been partial in some way. What is clear is that
the differences in national policy within the region, as reflected in
regional and international policy, prevent the real issue of the social
and economic viability of these states from being discussed. In this
context, cooperation as a strategy for overcoming the developmental
crisis becomes a clear alternative to the current strategy of the
Administration whereby only a few countries benefit to the detriment of the whole. What then might be considered such a strategy
for cooperation, considering the options available to the region, and

what are the tactical advantages of those so far implemented? There are four main points to consider as a framework before any realistic options can be adopted:

(1) The recent belligerent Cold War rhetoric which has been used by the Administration as well by the Nicaraguan, Grenadian and Cuban governments must be toned down. President Reagan's speech defending his military programme and appealing for increased military spending, during which he showed declassified photographs which he claimed to be proof of a Soviet build-up in the Caribbean, did not offer an opportunity, for example, to discuss increased US economic and military aid to 'friendly governments' in the region. This was probably designed to win a 'first victory in Congress'[8] rather than to threaten a full-scale US military intervention, which is the way the rhetoric could be and was read.[9]

(2) Current US policy for the region which treats the Caribbean Basin as an area of special interest is merely an extension of what President Carter set up in the last months of his Administration, with the important difference that the emphasis has been shifted away from regional cooperation and development[10] to the CBI, which focuses mainly on stimulating private investment for friendly countries. This shift away from cooperation and aid for the region channelled through multilateral organisations to incentives for US investors in friendly countries has not met with the resounding success either in the United States itself or in the Caribbean anticipated by the Reagan Administration.[11] Caribbean governments have been forced to give public approval to the notion of the CBI on pain of losing aid. However, the large majority have not received the so-called benefits to date despite having given almost unconditional political commitment. The reasons for their doing so are not the subject of this paper, although it should be pointed out that private investors appear afraid of the long-term instability of the region, coupled with a lack of infrastructure.

(3) Both the US public and the better-informed interest groups and opinion-makers across the region have become increasingly aware of converging interests as well as the threat of localised conflicts being regionalised. The current economic crises in Venezuela, Mexico and Brazil (the so-called middle powers), important actors in policy for the region, have only served to heighten local tensions still further and increase speculation over the long-term stability of the region. It would appear that once again the cart is being put before the horse. It is likely that the economic crises of these countries present a much more serious and deep threat for the United States than the military-strategic situation of the less

friendly countries. It should be remembered that before the Falklands/Malvinas crisis Mexico, Venezuela and Brazil (particularly the latter two) were considered relatively strong allies of the United States. The Latin American solidarity no longer permits a more or less monolithic public applause for US policy at regional and international levels. Despite the change in rhetoric, the Administration's main thrust continues to be based on military and strategic considerations, paying little heed to the causes of the region's crises or to cooperation and development.[12]

(4) The situation in El Salvador has been admitted by many US policymakers to be that of 'a holding operation' and has to date been a political and military stalemate. In addition, the embarrassment caused to the Administration by the human rights situation in El Salvador and Guatemala has increased the difficulties for the Administration in getting monies approved domestically or its Central American policy for the area approved at any level.

Finally, it is hard to see in this broad political framework, how the policy contradictions created by incorrect political analysis and assessment can be resolved if the region is not encouraged by the United States at least to formulate a list of what it views as its own priorities rather than making a conditioned response to the Administration's exigencies which are based on a perceived loss of hegemonial interest and the relentless advance and gains of Soviet surrogates.

The challenge of filling the geopolitical space using cooperation as a strategy for development in the Basin.

There is an urgent need for the region to evaluate and declare its priorities on a broad regional basis, recognising the need for political cooperation to include all nations based on development as a strategy for scaling down local conflicts, and emphasising and focusing on the very real problems of unequal distribution of wealth and growth. What must be the priorities of such a broad-based policy? There have been many meetings of experts, wise men and groups of nations who have passed resolutions and made declarations denouncing negative factors and attempting to lay down guidelines for future action. However, those attempts have excluded either Grenada, Cuba and Nicaragua or, worse still, the most important actor, the US Administration and its advisers.

It is hard to imagine any negotiated settlement or even partial solution being reached if the constituent actors do not all take part whatever the format. The Administration has refused dialogue on many occasions except on its own terms,[13] and it really should now be clear that this strategy is not conducive to the peace it claims to seek, and that far from banishing the problem, it has spurred on anti-government forces backed by the socialist governments of the region and the rest of the world.

Priorities for the region are and must be the same as those of the Administration, since common interests converge on such themes as the national crises (both economic and political), human rights, democracy and social stability. Where they differ is on interpretation, emphasis and modalities of implementation. For example, while the United States talks of preventing outside interference and halting the relentless growth of communism, the more progressive governments and groups in the region reject this interpretation and advance the opinion that, whether it is the New Jewel Movement in Grenada or the Sandinista government in Nicaragua, countries not only have the right to determine how they wish to be governed but question the change of attitude of successive governments on the issues of their not so tacit disapproval of the *anciens régimes* of Somoza in Nicaragua and Eric Gairy in Grenada. Indeed the attitude which Mexico has adopted all along, and in which it has been joined most recently by Venezuela, Colombia and Panama (the Contadora group), may well be the only salvageable option — that of non-intervention. US policy in the past has been that Mexico be ·kept isolated from the Central American issues;[14] however, the US Secretaries of State, Treasury and Commerce visited Mexico City to discuss the possibility of a negotiated settlement of the crisis, which itself indicated a change of attitude by the Reagan Administration. Secretary Schultz appeared to have the notion that Mexico should not be 'isolated' if it were able to come up with explorative ideas for a peaceful settlement. Yet with a deep economic crisis on its hands, Mexico's bargaining position has been considerably reduced, and its own priorities will perhaps have to be reflected in milder rhetoric and a less visible role in this region.

Regional efforts to use cooperation as a strategy for negotiation (largely headed by Mexico) have not been well received by the US Administration, and President Reagan's hard-hitting speech to an unconvinced Congress to salvage his Central American Program on 28 April 1983 (the House Foreign Affairs Committee voted 19–16 denying the Administration's request for an additional $1 million in military aid for El Salvador that fiscal year) did not offer much hope. In addition, the Administration was seeking permission to transfer $60 million from aid scheduled to other countries. The House Appropriations subcommittee held up approval of this so-called 'reprogramming', but it was approved by the Senate Appropriations subcommittee, while the Senate Foreign Relations Committee recommended not $60 million but $30 million. This would mean that El Salvador would get reprogrammed funds totalling $86.5 million for the year.[15] In other words, the difference in approach is that of a political approach versus the military one favoured by the Administration.

Then the issue arises of whether a region so balkanised and plagued by the economic and social problems of development can realistically be expected to formulate regional policies based on a wide consensus where the practice of 'democracy' and institutional change is the exception rather than the rule. Here it would seem that the United States as well as governments in the region must bring to bear new concepts and approaches other than those of the Western-style ballot box and the 'Westminster model', which have clearly failed to bring about the necessary reforms in an area plagued by a different tradition, that of political violence and pretorianism. The complexity of the region's economic and consequent political problems are then oversimplified in reductionist classical arguments of free economy against totalitarian models.

What we here propose, and indeed what seems to be the main thrust of the report 'The Americas at a Crossroads'[16] to which citizens from many different countries in the hemisphere and with various political perspectives and professional backgrounds contributed, is that the profound doubts held in the US Congress, Mexico and the rest of the region as to the economic and political future of the hemisphere will not be dispelled by promises of a modified Caribbean Basin Initiative which only provides aid for friendly countries and more money for El Salvador. What is needed is more emphasis on cooperation and less talk about Cuban subversion, more money for economic development and less for covert activity and counter-insurgency.

Finally, all governments in the Basin, including that of the United States, would do well to consider two further reports: Willy Brandt's second report, 'Common Crisis', and that of the Committee for Development Planning of the United Nations (a group of international economists headed by William G. Demas, President of the Caribbean Development Bank) entitled 'Overcoming International Economic Disorder'. The latter argues that if developed countries do not cooperate with the developing countries, the poor will sink the rich and in this context the recovery started in the United States and the industrial North will most certainly be threatened by persisting depression and threat of universal financial ruin. The Caribbean Basin is the first testing ground for these theses.

The grave geopolitical panorama should not overshadow the economic base of the conflict. No single political action can hope to achieve true peace in the region if it is not accompanied by economic and social initatives. So it is that brief mention of the more recent initiative for Central America proposed by the Inter-American Development Bank and supported by six of the Central American countries, as well as Mexico, Venezuela and Brazil, should be seriously considered. This idea and initiative emerged as a consequence of the the Contadora negotiations. It reflects the regional approach to development in the form of a massive economic plan to rebuild the area which will be launched at the EEC in Brussels. The Plan stresses the importance of an economic and not a military approach to the current crisis in the region. The current state of the CBI does not address itself to the issues and problems in the same way.

NOTES

1. Ernst B. Haas, *The Uniting of Europe: Political, Social, Economic Forces, 1950–57* (Stevens, 1958), p.5.
2. See National Security Council document 'U.S. Policy in Central America and Cuba Through FY 84 [Summary Paper]' on a meeting of the National Security Planning Group, April 1982.
3. President's approval of policy of preventing Cuban-model states, *New York Times*, April 7, 1983, pp. A1 and A16.
4. *Ibid*.
5. *New York Times*, April 7, 1983, p. A16.
6. See Karl Deutsch, *Political Community at the International Level* (New York: Doubleday, 1954).
7. *Congressional Record*, 18 March 1983, H1389. The need for dialogue, to include as third parties Mexico, Venezuela, Canada and Spain, aimed at producing a series of security guarantees or conventions between Nicaragua and Costa Rica, Nicaragua and Honduras, Honduras and El Salvador, and Nicaragua and El Salvador. These agreements would prohibit the use of military force against each other, limit weapons and arms and halt cross-border activities from each other's territories. Other parties might undertake the task of 'obtaining Cuban acquiescence in the agreements, absent direct negotiations between the US and Cuba'. See also Appropriations Subcommittee on Foreign Operations, 20 March 1983, to consider the President's request to reprogramme economic and military assistance to El Salvador (S 2985–6, 16 March 1983). Mr Inouye's request for a tripartite commission in Panama City to include the United States, Mexico and Venezuela with a 3-point proposal: (1) reduction of foreign military sales reprogramming $60 million to $30 million; (2) limitation of US military trainers and advisers in El Salvador to no more than 55; and (3) enlistment of Venezuela and Mexico for peace talks with the United States.
   In addition to these attempts there were many efforts by the region in the early 1980s, the last being the Contadora Group. Further, Honduras called on the countries of Central America to meet as soon as possible to work out a settlement to bring peace to the region. The proposal was made to a special meeting in Washington of the Thirty-Nation Council of the OAS. *New York Times*, 6 April 1983.

8. The Senate Appropriation subcommittee approved $60 million to be diverted from military assistance elsewhere. *New York Times*, 28 January 1983: 'Salvador Aid Backed in Senate'.
9. See Jeane Kirkpatrick's speech to the UN on the Nicaraguan government's accusation of destabilisation being a US obsession. *New York Times*, 24 March 1983.
10. Caribbean Basin Economic Recovery Act S1436–S1440, and Amendments H9940, 13–29 December 1982. House Resolution 629 for consideration of HR 7397 to promote economic revitalization in the Caribbean Basin H10123. *97th Congressional Record*.
11. *97th Congressional Record*, pp. H10131, H10136, H10138.
12. See transcript of a response to President Reagan's address, 27 April 1983, on behalf of Congressional Democrats by Senator Christopher J. Dodd as recorded by the *New York Times*, 28 April 1983: 'The President's request for El Salvador alone will bring the total aid to that country during his term to more than $1 billion. . . . after 30,000 deaths, after hundreds of millions of dollars, with the ante going up, with no end in sight, with no hope for change, real change, the time has come for a different approach. . . we must restore America's role as a source of hope and a hope for progress in Central America. We must help governments only if they will help their own people. . . we must make violent revolution preventable by making peaceful revolution possible.'
13. President Reagan's Address on Central America, 27 April 1983, Joint Session of Congress as recorded by *New York Times*, 28 April 1983: 'To support these diplomatic goals, I offer these assurances: (1) The US will support any agreement among Central American countries for the withdrawal — under fully verifiable and reciprocal conditions — of all foreign military and security advisers and troops. (2) We want to help opposition groups join the political process in all countries and compete by ballots instead of bullets. (3) We will support any verifiable, reciprocal agreement among Central American countries on the renunciation of support for insurgencies on neighbors' territory. And finally, we desire to help Central America end its costly arms race and will support any verifiable, reciprocal agreements on the nonimportation of offensive weapons.' Nowhere in the President's speech is there any mention of cooperation, development, or the deep economic distress the region is in, or alternatives in that direction.
14. See 'Fight or Negotiate?' by James Reston, *New York Times*, 20 April 1983.
15. *New York Times*, 20 April 1983.
16. A report of the Inter-American dialogue held at the Woodrow Wilson Center for Scholars in April 1983.

10

ANALYSIS AND CONCLUSIONS

Jack Child

The Central American Conflict Environment

As the preceding chapters have suggested, the present conflict environment in Central America is a complex and many-faceted one which defies the best efforts of a broad range of peacemakers. Not only are the conflicts complex, but they are also layered and inter-linked, so that tensions in one part of the region tend to reverberate in other areas, and an outbreak of hostilities at one point can escalate so as to involve numerous regional and extra-regional actors.

Many of these conflicts begin in the social, cultural, economic and political milieu of a single country, and are frequently the result of the breaking up of an anachronistic oligarchic order which had managed to endure for centuries. Revolutionary and counter-revolutionary ideologies and guerrilla warfare supported (to a greater or less degree) from outside tend to exacerbate and internationalise these essentially internal conflicts.

This type of conflict must be set against a second kind which frequently blends with it: the historic quarrels between neighbours in the Central American area. Over the years these have involved disputes over territory, strains at borders where sovereignties collide, and tensions caused by currents of human migration, smuggling, gun-running, and the activities of political exiles operating from supposed safe havens across borders.

To these two categories of conflict in Central America a third, sadly, must now be added: superpower tensions. These appear either directly — through ideologies, military presence or covert destabilising acts — or indirectly through economic and diplomatic pressures and the activities of allies or surrogates. In either case they add a new and dangerous geopolitical dimension to what has historically been a purely local set of conflict relationships. What could once be described as a region of frequent but local and low-level conflicts is now one where the East-West conflict influences regional problems. The nature of this influence has to be assessed.

Any consideration of conflict in the Central American region must now also contend with a bewildering array of combatants. The Central American military has always played a special political role, and now the concept of 'military' must extend beyond the notion of regular organised forces to include the irregulars, be they known as guerrillas, liberation fronts or 'Contras'. No solution to conflict in the area can afford to ignore the presence of large numbers of well-armed and highly experienced groups of combatants who might or might not respond to the conventional niceties of diplomacy, and who might or might not be acceptable to the regular military in any Zimbabwe-like schemes to integrate them into national forces.

The search for peace and security in Central America, then, must be concerned not only with the resolution of internal strains. It must also find ways of keeping these internal strains from crossing borders, as well as ways to keep local and regional tensions from involving the superpowers. Central America now finds itself at the juncture of an increasing number of East-West strains as well as the more traditional North-South ones.

The superpowers, and other extra-regional actors, tend to see the current crisis in a relatively narrow security perspective distorted by the lenses of East-West relationships and tensions. In contrast, the Central American countries and their immediate neighbours tend to take a considerably broader view of peace and security which includes economic, social and political facets as well as the more traditionally military and security ones. This viewpoint stems from a more sweeping interpretation of what constitutes threats to security, which for Third World countries includes considerations of basic human needs, food supplies, medical services, refugee problems, and other humanitarian concerns.

Seen in this perspective, peace and security in Central America must also involve consideration of such problems as the instabilities caused by demographic changes and important rural-urban population shifts; the militarisation of the Central American social, economic and political environment; the perils and opportunities offered by proximity to a superpower and the related issue of dependence versus interdependence; the effect of inefficiency and corruption on the capacity of the Central American countries to absorb development aid: and the special problems of financing energy needs and of servicing overwhelming foreign debts.

Attempts to deal with these underlying problems lead one to the notion of 'peacebuilding': the idea that stable and enduring peace requires strong economic, social and psychological foundations. The challenge, as suggested in McEachrane's chapter, is to find ways of filling the vacuum created by the erosion of an old order, using regional cooperation and development. Such a regional approach, if able to tap the profound roots of Central American integration movements, may be a strong contributor to peace.

144 *Jack Child*

Requirements for Central American peace and security

The fundamental requirement for regional peace and security is for the principals involved to conclude that a military victory is no longer possible, and that a negotiated solution is the best way to protect their interests. However, as suggested above, the present situation also requires that outside powers permit a Latin American solution to the area's conflicts, and avoid converting purely local issues into East-West ones. This does not imply abandoning Central America to its own resources, since long-term solutions to problems of development and integration will require substantial amounts of outside assistance.

As previous chapters have indicated, political will on the part of the parties involved in the Central American conflict may not be enough. The present conflict has facets and depths that outstrip the capacity of traditional regional conflict-resolution mechanisms to deal with it. Inevitably, one must turn to third-party neutrals and a complex mechanism in order for the Central Americans to be helped to move down the path toward peace and security. Since 1983 the Contadora process has emerged as the most promising such mechanism.

The Contadora process

The Contadora process has been variously described as 'the last best chance for peace', and 'the most complex and far-reaching negotiation the Latin Americans have ever undertaken'. Since its beginning in January 1983 it has had its periods of dramatic progress and disappointing stagnation; and it has produced several remarkable documents which are appended to this book: the 21-point 'document of objectives' (September 1983); the 'implementing principles' (January 1984); and the draft Contadora Act on Peace and Cooperation in Central America (October 1984).

These three documents reveal that Contadora is far more than a peace treaty to resolve a specific conflict. It contains both short and long-term objectives which can be characterised as an immediate truce followed by a disarmament effort and a major economic, political and social development effort aimed at solving the root causes of conflict in the region. In a sense it is both a 'containment dam' and a defusing effort directed at the immediate causes of conflict as well as a mechanism for producing long-term and fundamental changes. Put another way, it is both 'pacifier' (in the sense of establishing the immediate conditions to limit hostilities) and 'democratiser' (as a stimulant for the building of the social, economic and political foundations for democracy).

Contadora also reiterates a number of basic principles of American international law which grew out of the Latin American nations' need to protect themselves by juridical means against intervention. Thus respect for the sovereign equality of states and non-intervention are woven through many of the articles of the Contadora documents. This aspect of Contadora inevitably raises the question of its relationship to the Organization of American States. Unfortunately, as will be assessed below, Contadora also reflects the inability of the Hemisphere organisation to resolve the crisis, and in that sense is a possible harbinger of new forms of international law and organisation in the inter-American system.

Because Contadora has been a major sustained effort over a prolonged period of time, it has come to be seen (especially in Latin America) as a significant force in its own right. It is frequently described as a 'process', with momentum and impact beyond the immediate issues it deals with. Over the period since January 1983 it has absorbed the energy and attention of a substantial number of senior Latin American officials, who have increased their contacts and knowledge of each other in the process. In this sense Contadora is an integrative force, one that has raised the region's own consciousness and identity and forced it to face many of its problems and failures realistically. Because of the demands of the Contadora verification process, the effort will not end when signatures are affixed to the Treaty; this process of integration and strengthening the regional identity will continue and will reinforce the feeling that Contadora is a symbol of Latin American maturity and ability to solve its own major problems.

This optimistic perception of the Contadora process has been sustained by many Latin Americans despite a number of setbacks. Their optimism has been fed by the perception that Contadora has indeed survived its setbacks, and remains the best hope for a peaceful resolution of regional tensions. This current of opinion tends to give Contadora credit for a sort of Central American détente that has been established during its existence. Thus there was no introduction in this period of advanced weapons systems (i.e. high-performance aircraft) by the Nicaraguans, nor was there an introduction of a permanent US troop presence in the region. Contadora has been given credit for sorting out a series of tensions, and for defining more clearly many of the issues separating the Central American countries.

Pessimists, on the other hand, can point to the fact that even after the painful negotiations that have gone on since early 1985, no signed treaty and no permanent solutions have come into being. Even if a Contadora Treaty were to be signed and ratified, there are many doubts as to the verification and confirmation process, suggesting that many of the parties involved may only give lip-service to Contadora, and attempt to use the treaty as an instrument for strengthening their own positions.

The lack of a signed treaty after so much effort and so much rhetorical support for Contadora leads to an inevitable question regarding obstacles in its way. At various points in the development of the Contadora process, accusing fingers have been pointed at several participants. In 1984 the United States and its regional allies consistently accused Nicaragua of stalling, but when Nicaragua abruptly indicated her willingness to sign a draft treaty in late 1984, the psychological tables were turned and the United States found itself diplomatically on the defensive. In early 1985 the Urbina Lara asylum case blocked the forward movement of Contadora, and both sides used the incident to accuse the other of stalling once again. For the Nicaraguans the incident was being exaggerated in order to block the treaty; for the Costa Ricans, the Salvadoreans and others, the asylum case demonstrated that Nicaragua was not willing to live up to a treaty and could not be trusted.

The question of how sincerely the United States was really supporting Contadora has been raised from the beginning of the process, and serves to emphasise the delicacy of many of the areas which Contadora covers. The Reagan Administration has consistently given rhetorical support to Contadora, and explained its lack of more direct involvement in the process by saying that it is a regional initiative in which a greater US role would not be appropriate. Despite official US protestations, it is hard to see much real enthusiasm for Contadora on the part of the Reagan Administration. Carried to its logical conclusion, the full implementation of Contadora would represent a dramatic decline in an historic US military, strategic and diplomatic presence in the area.

Seen in this light, Contadora also represents a Latin American challenge to the United States in that is is a purely Latin American initiative whose implementation leads to a lessening of dependence on the United States and a greater sense of maturity and regional autonomy. Contadora has thus acquired an important value as a symbol of Latin American independence, and to reject or dismiss it is also to reject the idea that the nations of the area have the capacity to work out their own problems. The nations involved are not only the five Central American countries and the Contadora Four (Mexico, Colombia, Venezuela and Panama); they also include almost all the Latin American countries that have given their enthusiastic support to Contadora, as well as a large number of European and Third World countries. Because of this commitment, the failure of Contadora carries with it a high price, especially if the failure is perceived as being the fault of the United States.

The holistic versus incremental approaches to Contadora

An emerging major issue surrounding Contadora is whether it should be seen (and implemented) as a single sweeping whole, or approached rather as a series of goals which should be arranged in some kind of order of priority and attacked in sequence and incrementally.

This 'simultaneity versus piecemeal' issue is important because each side has proponents who argue convincingly that the process will fail if it is not properly approached. The advocates of simultaneity firmly believe that Contadora's strength derives from the visionary and all-encompassing scope of its proposals, and that to attempt to implement the proposals by the 'salami tactics' of incrementalism would be to lose that vision and severely weaken the chief strength of the Contadora process. The other side argues that Contadora is a mix of some eminently practical and feasible elements which could be implemented immediately, and others which are long-range ideals which might or might not be feasible, and in any case would need a great deal of time. For those who hold this view Contadora's chief strength lies in its functional and pragmatic incremental nature by which a few practicable steps toward peace can be the foundations for constructing the following more difficult steps, and so on until the final goals are eventually reached.

The issue can also be framed in terms of the twin Contadora goals of pacification and democratisation. The incremental pragmatists argue that the first priority lies in the pacification goals in order to stop the violence and reduce tensions in the region. Once this immediate goal is achieved, and a suitable framework of confidence-building measures is constructed, then the actors can proceed on to the more complex and inherently more difficult goal of rebuilding Central America's shattered economic, social and political infrastructure in the search for democracy. In any case, they argue, the very term 'democratisation' is a highly subjective one which can give rise to endless arguments on meaning and implementation.

As one observer has put it, *'En el proceso de Contadora, lo perfecto es enemigo de lo bueno'* ('In the Contadora process, the perfect is enemy of the good'). The danger is that in the search for the perfect vision of a peaceful and democratic Central America, one might lose the opportunity to put into place a series of more modest but achievable goals which could lower tensions and make at least some progress toward enhancing peace and security.

An example of this approach would be the issue of withdrawal of all foreign military advisers in the region. Contadora calls for a complete withdrawal. However, even if all concerned agreed to this goal, there would be many opportunities to cheat or misrepresent one's advisers by using retired military personnel, paramilitary advisers, or personnel operating independently. The pragmatic approach would begin by inventorying the various categories of personnel, then calling for phased and partial reductions on each side; as each phased reduction was verified, then both parties could proceed to the next step in the incremental process.

The incrementalist and pragmatic approach can also be expressed in terms of the idea of decoupling or de-linking certain issues. Thus it would make sense to decouple efforts to enhance military stabilisation (i.e. preventing the outbreak of hostilities) from the longer-range efforts at rebuilding the economic and political infrastructure and the democratisation process. Likewise, peace and security in the region would be enhanced by decoupling foreign issues from domestic ones, and the outside actors from the parties directly involved in Central American conflicts.

The incremental approach has the added virtue of recognising that a partial achievement of Contadora goals may be possible as an interim measure. Indeed, as in many situations of conflict in the world, it may never be possible to solve all the strains and achieve a full measure of peace and security. But prior experience with peace-keeping and peacemaking suggests that even partial goals are worth striving for and can be important factors in preventing a bad situation from becoming worse.

The role of the superpowers

As was noted above, one of the major exacerbating factors in the Central American conflict scenario is the undercurrent of super-power competition which fuels several of the conflicts. Not surprisingly, the superpowers have acted like superpowers in Central America in the last few years, with one (the United States) forcefully defending its ground while the other (the Soviet Union) exploits an area of instability close to its adversary's heartland. If the countries of Central America and the Caribbean Basin are forced to play out roles as pawns in a superpower geopolitical chess game, the chances of peaceful settlement in Contadora terms are minimal. Other and grimmer possibilities also emerge: if reduced to a superpower conflict, Central America and the Basin have the potential to become a site for a direct or indirect clash between the United States and the Soviet Union, with potentially disastrous consequences for all concerned. The concept of superpower symmetry could also become real, with the Soviet Union regarding its possibilities in Central America (close to the US heartland) as being parallel to those of the United States in places such as Afghanistan and Eastern Europe.

In many ways it is the United States that is being asked to make the major sacrifice of historic interests if Contadora is to be fully implemented. This has been, after all, a region in which the United States has had an overwhelmingly dominant position of power, and where that power has been defended and supported by instruments such as military assistance, military advisers and covert intelligence operations. To accept Contadora means giving up many of those instruments of power, and in that sense represents a low-cost victory for the other superpower. Yet to many observers the US attempt to hang on to its traditional role in the area using military and covert pressures is a dangerous dead-end policy which runs counter to Contadora and poses the real possibility of escalation and ultimately a direct US military intervention. A relevant precedent here is the Panama Canal Treaty negotiating process in the period 1964–77. The United States could have clung to its Canal Zone enclave through military means and ignored Panamanian requests for a return of the Canal. Instead, a more enlightened US policy prevailed and the end-result was a cooperative approach whereby the United States and Panama share control over an extended transition period which will end with complete Panamanian control. The result to date has been to defuse the Panama Canal issue as a potential major irritant in US-Latin American relations.

Similarly, it is in the best interests of the United States in the long run to accept Contadora's diminution of the historic US hegemony in Central America as the price for peace and stability in the area, and as recognition of the emerging maturity of the Latin American countries concerned. Such an acceptance by the United States requires guarantees and verification that the Soviet Union and its regional allies do not take advantage of the lowering of the US profile to make geopolitical gains at the expense of the United States. Hence the crucial role of verification in the Contadora process.

In superpower terms the Contadora process is an enlightened

attempt to let Central America be Central America, and to reduce superpower interests in the region so that tensions, and the techniques to resolve them, can be kept at traditional Central American levels.

The role of the Organization of American States

Along with the United States, another historic actor in Central America must also view the current situation as a challenge to its traditional role: the Organization of American States (OAS). Indeed, a notable feature of the crisis in the region since 1979 is the extremely low profile of the OAS (some would say its irrelevance). This is ironic because Central America is the part of Latin America where the OAS has had its more impressive successes as a peacemaker and peacekeeper.

This traditional OAS role in Central America was made possible by the fact that up to the late 1970s the typical Central American conflict involved territorial or border issues, was not ideological and was generally bilateral; if it ever reached the shooting stage, only very modest military establishments were usually involved and both sides were equipped and advised by the United States. Furthermore, outside powers (notably the Soviet Union and its surrogates) were kept out and it was easy for the United States to bring its overwhelming influence to bear in conjunction with OAS peacekeeping and peacemaking efforts.

The current conflict environment in Central America has little resemblance to what has just been described. Border or territorial issues, while present, are not as significant as ideological ones linked to outside powers, including the superpowers. Bilateral issues, also still present, are overwhelmed by a series of layered and inter-linked regional tensions. The military forces at work now include guerrilla elements which can sustain levels of conflict for a long time, with or without outside help. Lastly, the regular military establishments now include one linked to the Soviet Union through arms supplies; even the military establishments linked to the United States have shown a considerable degree of independence and can no longer automatically be assumed to be under US control.

This author has argued elsewhere (1) that the OAS and the inter-American security system have suffered a serious decline in their ability to function effectively due to the impact of three crises: the Malvinas/Falklands conflict of 1982, the Grenadian invasion/rescue effort of 1983, and the enduring Central American crisis. Furthermore, the traditional success of the OAS was largely due to the influence the United States could bring to bear, and to the logistical, administrative and diplomatic support which it gave to OAS efforts at conflict resolution. For any number of reasons the United States cannot credibly play this role in the present Central American conflict environment, and the effectiveness of the OAS suffers as a result.

Contributing to the ineffectiveness of the OAS are two membership problems. On the one hand the sudden influx of Caribbean mini-states in the 1970s and 1980s lowered the value of the Organization to the traditional Latin American membership. At the same time the absence of four Hemisphere states from the OAS (Cuba, Guyana, Belize and Canada) diminishes its credibility and possible role.

Yet, despite its limitations in the present Central American crisis, the OAS holds considerable promise in the implementation phase of Contadora. Its long experience in Central American peacekeeping suggests that it may be of value in assisting the verification elements of Contadora in their difficult task. If Contadora continues its efforts over a long period, the four key nations (Mexico, Panama, Colombia, Venezuela) may find the burden onerous and may seek to institutionalise the process in an international organisation. The OAS is the obvious choice for this purpose.

The role of other outside parties

An important new development in the history of Central American conflict and international relations is the increasingly significant role played by outside actors which previously showed little interest in the region. A number of West European nations (as well as Canada and several Commonwealth states) have increased their diplomatic and economic contacts in the region; the East European nations are also present in terms of support for and presence in Nicaragua. At the NGO level there are many unofficial relationships between bodies such as the Christian Democrat and Social Democrat political organisations in Europe, South America and Central America. The Catholic Church and labour groups provide another category of actors in the crisis. The participation of these entities does, in a way, complicate matters; but fundamentally it is a positive sign suggesting that there are contacts and resources other than the traditional ones.

These parties have been playing roles as channels of communication in Central America in the present crisis. Many of them also provide important quantities of development or security assistance.

152 *Jack Child*

Ultimately, they may be the logical sources of the third party neutral contingents required to provide effective monitoring and verification of the more delicate portions of the Contadora agreement.

The verification problem

As suggested at several points in the preceding analysis, the verification problem looms as a key element in the success or failure of the Contadora process. The need for credible verification mechanisms has been defined as absolutely essential, especially for the United States and its regional allies. Without them there is the possibility of wholesale treaty violation without the aggrieved party knowing until it is too late. Proponents of this viewpoint argue that a Contadora Treaty without adequate verification measures would be worse than no treaty at all since it would give rise to false hopes and serve as a screen for further aggresion. There is a real danger that the psychological pressures and desire for peace might lead to a premature commitment to the Treaty which, if not protected by adequate verification mechanisms, would only lead to further conflict in the future. Holders of this view argue that the worst possible outcome to Contadora would be to have a signed Treaty which fails because of poorly thought-out verification measures.

Another perspective has held that this is merely a device for blocking the Contadora process. The Nicaraguans, for example, have suggested that since it is politically difficult to attack Contadora directly, the vehicle used for this purpose is the verification issue. Thus, by requiring impossibly difficult verification conditions, the United States can ensure that Contadora never comes to pass.

Regardless of which of these two views is valid, it is clear that the complexity of the Central American conflict environment and the broad scope of Contadora will require an unprecedented verification effort. The draft Treaty contains the mechanism (the Verification and Control Commission for Security Matters), but in the latter part of 1985 there were still many unanswered questions concerning the Commission. How, for example, would it get its administrative, logistical and transportation support? How would it be financed? To what political authority would it report? And what would be the timing and scope of its activities?

Peacekeeping, Peace-observing, Peacemaking

The basic concept: peacekeeping. Peacekeeping draws its conceptual basis from conflict resolution theory. This argues that conflicts cannot be mediated, conciliated, arbitrated or otherwise resolved unless the parties actively involved in the conflict lower their level of violence or hostility to the point where meaningful communication about their differences can take place. They frequently need assistance in doing this, and the peacekeeper's role is to act as a third-party neutral to separate the parties, defuse the violent aspects of the conflict, and allow the other conflict resolution mechanisms to go to work to solve the basic causes of the conflict. Although the peacekeeper may be armed, his basic weapons are moral and psychological ones and not his guns, grenades or cannons. The effectiveness of the peacekeeper depends more on his perceived impartiality and his presence than on his military potential. Peacekeeping must also be distinguished from any attempt to impose or enforce peace by an outside power acting in a police role. Seen in this light, peacekeeping is not the imposition of peace and order by a supra-national force with a mandate to oblige the parties in conflict to cease their violence. The international peacekeeping element should be equipped and ready to deal with minor military threats, but cannot keep a third-party neutral stance in the face of a significant attack by one of the parties involved in the conflict.

Relevant definitions[2]
(1) Peacekeeping is that set of measures and techniques aimed at preventing, containing, moderating and terminating hostilities through peaceful third-party intervention. The peacekeeping mission does not seek to enforce peace or impose solutions to the conflict; rather, the thrust is to create the conditions which would lead to dialogue and eventual resolution to the conflict.
(2) Peace-observing has the same basic purposes as peacekeeping, but differs from it in that it is usually a much smaller effort, with somewhat different functions on the ground. While peacekeeping contingents may be fairly large (ranging from hundreds to thousands of men), peace-observer missions are usually much smaller, and may even consist of only one or two individuals whose function is to act as the 'eyes and ears' of the international body that sent them to the scene of a conflict. As such, their efforts are mainly aimed at investigating, observing and reporting.
(3) Peacemaking, which in the Western Hemisphere system is sometimes called 'peaceful settlement of disputes', is that collection of techniques and institutions available to resolve conflicts through

negotiation, mediation, amelioration, arbitration and conciliation.
(4) Peacebuilding is the development effort, principally in social
and economic dimensions, by which it is hoped to ameliorate conflict by improving basic conditions and meeting fundamental
human needs. While traditionally focused on economic and social
conditions, peacebuilding also has a political, military and diplomatic dimension in terms of the assumption and hope that cooperative development efforts will increase mutual trust and build confidence and thus make conflicts less likely.
(5) Confidence-building measures (CBMs) are certain techniques
(such as direct 'hot lines', arms registries and advance notification
of manoeuvers) designed to lower tensions and make it less likely
that a conflict would break out by misunderstanding, mistake, or
misreading of the actions of an adversary.

Peacekeeping, Peace-observing, Peacemaking and Contadora. The
Hemisphere's past experience with peacekeeping has unfortunately
been conditioned by the Inter-American Peace Force which operated in the Dominican Republic in 1965. On that occasion a
unilateral US intervention was subsequently made more palatable
by adding a token Latin American element, obtaining a favourable
OAS vote, and creating a multilateral peacekeeping force under
effective US control. The end-result was that any future attempts at
creating a peacekeeping element were suspect, especially if there was
a strong US presence. Thus, when the US Secretary of State suggested a peacekeeping element in Nicaragua during the final days of
the Somoza regime, his suggestion was quickly rejected by the Latin
American countries because it seemed like a transparent attempt to
repeat the Dominican experience and guarantee the survival of
Somocismo.
    In the present-day context of the Contadora process, the
memories of US-dominated peacekeeping elements continue to be
fresh and relevant. Any such initiatives will be suspect if the United
States promotes them or if there is a heavy US representation in the
contingent. Given the present close US involvement in several of
Central America's conflicts, there is little chance that any US
presence at all would be acceptable.
    The search for relevant Central American peacekeeping or peace-
observing precedents yields little of value for today's much more
complex situations. The El Salvador-Honduras conflict of 1969
resulted in a long-lasting OAS peace-observer mission which
patrolled the disputed border areas by helicopter for almost a decade. But this was a bilateral problem of the traditional Central
American type, and involved considerably fewer parties, arms and

tensions than the present conflicts. The logistics, communications and transportation equipment used in that peace-observer effort were principally of US origin, although the helicopters carried OAS markings, and the cost of the effort was borne by the two countries involved.

Peacekeeping and peace-observing missions are extraordinarily difficult in situations of guerrilla warfare where there are no fixed fronts or definable borders: the peacekeeper has great difficulty identifying the forces in conflict, and may not be able to interpose himself effectively between the various factions. The relevant example here, as Henry Wiseman suggests above, may be Zimbabwe.

Given limited resources, the peace-keeping elements in a Contadora verification mission might have to concentrate on what could be called the 'detonators': those high-tension situations and sites where confict is most likely to break out. In Central America these would involve sensitive issues such as the flow of weapons across borders, attempts to destabilise other governments in the area, and the presence of outside military advisers. Geographically the most sensitive areas are the Gulf of Fonseca (where El Salvador, Honduras and Nicaragua meet) and extensive parts of the Honduras-Nicaragua and Nicaragua-Costa Rica borders.

The United Nations experience with peacekeeping suggests that one of the most difficult problems is finding suitable, willing and acceptable third-party neutrals for such missions. For reasons explained above, the United States would not be acceptable. The Contadora countries would be an appropriate starting-point, as would other Latin American countries not directly committed in the area. However, with the exception of Brazil, Panama, Peru and Colombia, none of these nations has had any peacekeeping experience of this type, and it will probably be necessary to call on outsiders. Among the obvious candidates for this role are Canada and a number of European states.

The potentially negative effects of international peacekeeping must also be considered. Among them is the possibility that third-party neutral peacekeeping may in fact only serve to prolong the conflict if the underlying causes of the conflict are not addressed through dialogue and political, social and economic channels. It is not enough simply to establish a superficial peace based on stability, if underlying social and economic injustices and political oppression remain.

This survey of the Central American conflict environment and recent developments relevant to peacekeeping provides ample evidence of the extraordinary sensitivity of the concept of 'peace-keeping', especially if it in any way involves the United States or serves US policy objectives. The past history of US interventions, and the use made in the past of 'peacekeeping' as a convenient cover for unilateral national objectives continues to cast a pall on the mere possibility of using an approach which in principle could be very useful. And yet, despite the aversion to using the concept, the record shows that the idea continues to crop up in both bilateral and multilateral proposals for peace in the area. Thus, some way must be found to permit Central America to have access to the peacekeeping it so badly needs without calling it by that name.

The semantic considerations stated at the beginning of this section may offer a way out. Because of the sensitivities to the term 'peacekeeping' (to say nothing of the idea of a 'peace force' or, worse still, an 'Inter-American Peace Force'), it is clear that these terms cannot be used. Instead, the element should be called a 'peace-observing mission', or a 'technical group', or an 'international verification group', or by some term that stresses the limited observation and verification function. An expansion of the term 'confidence-building measures' to cover some of the areas traditionally associated with peacekeeping might also offer a solution. It would also be advisable to keep the military side of the contingent as small as possible, and make the civilian and diplomatic side as large as possible, to stress further that the group has an observation and verification function, and not one involving force. The 'three-flag solution' is also an attractive one: the contingent could fly the flag of the international organisation and the flags of the two countries involved (e.g. Costa Rica and Nicaragua or Nicaragua and Honduras). In this arrangement the bulk of the contingent could be from the two countries involved, with the international organisation providing a symbolic civilian and military third presence.

The role of technology

Recent work done by the International Peace Academy suggests that developments in sensor technology can be applied to peacekeeping in ways that have special political significance in Central America.[3] Arrays of ground, tethered-balloon and airborne sensors, when linked to dependable communications networks, permit a relatively small group of peace-observers to cover much more territory than was previously feasible. Thus it may be possible to reduce the size of the required contingent and make it politically more acceptable by the Central American nations and more feasible from a financial and diplomatic perspective.

The most relevant recent experience in this connection has come from the Sinai Field Mission which acted as third-party peace-observing force between Israel and Egypt. The Field Mission made extensive use of sensor technology to carry out its functions, and was aided by a favourable political climate and a physical environment almost ideal for sensors (i.e. open desert terrain with little vegetation and few inhabitants). The tropical rain forests of much of the Central American conflict region, the high population densities of many areas and the difficult political environment would all greatly complicate the task of employing technology in the peacekeeper's task. But the potential for sensor-aided surveillance in support of Contadora verification is a real one which should be more adequately explored.

Toward a CBM regime in Central America

Two previous chapters in this book (by Bomsdorf and Child) have explored the concept of confidence-building measures (CBMs), and have considered how an idea which grew out of US-Soviet and Nato-Warsaw Pact strains might be applicable to Third World conflicts in general and those in Central America in particular. The report of the 1984 United Nations Disarmament Commission suggested that CBMs might be very relevant to conflicts far removed from Europe.

A basic problem in this connection is that of definition. CBMs in the European context have a rather narrow and technical definition stemming from specific military applications, such as hot lines, notification of manoeuvres, limits on troop strength and types of weapons, and so on. Attempts to apply the CBM concept to Third World conflicts have resulted in a tendency to broaden the concept to the point where almost anything that increases contact between potential adversaries is quickly labelled a confidence-building measure. Thus the concept has been used to cover all kinds of diplomatic, social, cultural and even athletic contacts.

The suggestion has been made that the Contadora process be viewed as an imaginative and innovative attempt to replace a conflict regime in Central America with a 'CBM regime'. Such a regime would apply the full range of CBMs contained in Contadora to establish a 'zone of peace' in which attempts to violate the specific provisions of Contadora would be detected and publicly exposed by a sophisticated network of sensors and observers manned by third-party neutrals. The Contadora process, as laid out in its three key documents (see Appendixes), establishes the conceptual framework for such a zone of peace protected by CBMs. Linked with appropriate technology and the experience of third-party neutrals from outside the region, there exists the possibility of establishing a foundation for permanent peace, security and development in the region.

Moreover, like the Treaty of Tlatelolco, such a zone of peace based on Contadora CBMs could serve as a relevant example of a Third World solution to conflict and might be applicable to other areas of the world.

In this sense, rather than merely copying an idea imported from Europe, Latin America would be expanding on it and adapting it to a vastly different set of conditions. This process would be facilitated by the fact that the inter-American system has in fact been using confidence-building measures for many years, although they have not been called by that name.

NOTES

1. Jack Child, 'Present Trends in the Inter-American Security System and the Role of the Rio Treaty' in *Anuario Juridico Interamericano, 1983* (Washington: Organization of American States, 1984), pp. 43–82.
2. These definitions are adapted from those used by the International Peace Academy in its *Peacekeeper's Handbook*, and in the author's article, 'Peacekeeping in the Inter-American System' in *Military Review*, October 1980.
3. International Peace Academy Report no. 8, *Weapons of Peace: How New Technology can Revitalize Peacekeeping* (1980), and Report no. 17, *Peacekeeping and Technology: Concepts for the Future* (1983).

APPENDIX A
THE CONTADORA 'OBJECTIVES DOCUMENT'
September 1983

UNITED
NATIONS

 Security Council

Distr.
GENERAL
S/16041*
18 October 1983
ENGLISH
ORIGINAL: SPANISH

THE SITUATION IN CENTRAL AMERICA
Note by the Secretary-General

1. Since the Security Council adopted resolution 530 (1983), on 19 May 1983, I have endeavoured to keep in contact with the Governments of Costa Rica, El Salvador, Guatemala, Honduras and Nicaragua, as well as with the Governments of Colombia, Mexico, Panama and Venezuela, which comprise the Contadora Group, in order to keep informed of the efforts made to find a negotiated political solution to the problems in the Central American region and of the developments in the area. On two occasions, on 28 June and 13 July 1983, I reported orally on the situation to the members of the Council.

2. Within the framework of the Declaration adopted at Isla de Contadora on 9 January 1983,[1] there was an initial phase of official contacts and visits by the Ministers for Foreign Affairs of the Contadora Group to the countries directly concerned, on 12 and 13 April.[2] As a result of the consultations held, it was agreed to initiate a new phase of joint meetings of the Ministers for Foreign Affairs of the Group with the Ministers for Foreign Affairs of the five Central American countries. The first three meetings were held in Panama City on 20 and 21 April,[2] from 28 to 30 May[3] and from 28 to 30 July 1983,[4] respectively.

3. On 17 July 1983, the Presidents of Colombia, Mexico, Panama and Venezuela met in Cancun, Mexico. The Declaration issued on that occasion proposed guidelines for the negotiating process as well as specific commitments the implementation of which would ensure peace in the region.[5]

4. On the basis of the Cancun Declaration, the Ministers for Foreign Affairs of the Contadora Group and of the five Central American countries met again in Panama City, from 7 to 9 September 1983, and adopted a Document of Objectives.[6] On 6 October, I received a visit from the Minister for Foreign Affairs of Mexico and the Permanent Representatives of Colombia, Panama and Venezuela to the United Nations, who handed me the Document, which, I was informed, had been approved by the Heads of State of Costa Rica, El Salvador, Guatemala, Honduras and Nicaragua.[7] At the request of the Contadora Group, the Document is transmitted to the Security Council as an annex to this note.

5. On that occasion, the Minister for Foreign Affairs of Mexico pointed out that the Document of Objectives is a single consensus text, which sets out the positions and the concerns of the Governments directly concerned and the proposals of the Contadora Group, and which contains the principles on which the eventual solution of the Central American problems will have to be based. The Document also contains a definition of the specific areas of negotiation and the terms of reference for the formulation of the legal instruments and the machinery which would be essential in order to ensure harmonious coexistence in the region. I expressed to the Minister for Foreign Affairs of Mexico my fervent hope that the Group's activities would soon achieve substantive and concrete results. I also emphasized on that occasion that any attempt at a solution should take into account the profound economic and social imbalances with which the Central American peoples have always struggled.

*Second reissue for technical reasons.

6. In transmitting the Document of Objectives to the Security Council, I consider it my duty to express my profound concern at the grave and prolonged tension which persists in the area. In view of the nature and possible ramifications of the convulsive situation currently prevailing in the Central American region, the unavoidable conclusion is that it threatens international peace and security.

7. In communications addressed to the President of the Council and to the Secretary-General, there have been frequent accusations and counteraccusations of foreign interference in the region and complaints of numerous border incidents as well as incursions by sea and by air, causing deplorable loss of life and material damage.[8] In the view of some Governments, the military and naval maneouvres now in progress add to tensions in the region. It has also been pointed out that the presence of military advisers and training centers, the traffic in arms and the activities of armed groups, and the unprecedented build-up of arms and of military and paramilitary forces constitute further factors of tension. On 13 September, the Security Council met at the urgent request of a Government of the region, which complained of what it described as a further escalation of acts of aggression against its country.[9] Although the Secretary-General has no way of reliably verifying each and every one of the components of this situation and is therefore unable to make definite judgments, there is no doubt that an alarming picture is emerging in the area.

8. The five Governments of Central America have assured me on a number of occasions of their firm commitment to contribute in good faith to the search for peaceful solutions. In that connection, they have also reiterated their determination to cooperate with the Governments of the Contadora Group in their efforts for peace. The Governments of Colombia, Mexico, Panama and Venezuela are motivated by an earnest desire to find solutions adapted to the realities of the region, without any intrusion derived from the East-West conflict. That is why they have the manifest support of the international community as a whole.

9. In accordance with the terms of resolution 530 (1983), I shall continue to keep the Council informed as and when necessary.

NOTES

[1] A/38/68.
[2] S/15727.
[3] S/15809.
[4] S/15900.
[5] S/15877.
[6] S/15982.
[7] The texts of the communications from the Governments of Nicaragua and Honduras on this subject were circulated to the Security Council as documents S/16006 and S/16021 respectively.
[8] Documents S/15780, S/15787, S/15806, S/15808, S/15813, S/15816, S/15817, S/15835, S/15836, S/15837, S/15838, S/15839, S/15840, S/15855, S/15857, S/15858, S/15879, S/15893, S/15899, S/15930, S/15952, S/15973, S/15979, S/15980, S/15986, S/15993, S/15995, S/16007, S/16011, S/16012, S/16013, S/16016, S/16018, S/16020, S/16022, S/16024, S/16025, S/16026, S/16030, S/16031, S/16032.
[9] Document S/PV. 2477.

ANNEX

Document of Objectives

Considering:

The situation prevailing in Central America, which is characterized by an atmosphere of tension that threatens security and peaceful coexistence in the region, and which requires, for its solution, observance of the principles of international law governing the actions of States, especially:

The self-determination of peoples;

Non-intervention;

The sovereign equality of States;

The peaceful settlement of disputes;

Refraining from the threat or use of force;

Respect for the territorial integrity of States;

Pluralism in its various manifestations;

Full support for democratic institutions;

The promotion of social justice;

International cooperation for development;

Respect for and promotion of human rights;

The prohibition of terrorism and subversion;

The desire to reconstruct the Central American homeland through progressive integration of its economic, legal and social institutions;

The need for economic cooperation among the States of Central America so as to make a fundamental contribution to the development of their peoples and the strengthening of their independence;

The undertaking to establish, promote or revitalize representative, democratic systems in all the countries of the region;

The unjust economic, social and political structures which exacerbate the conflicts in Central America;

The urgent need to put an end to the tensions and lay the foundations for understanding and solidarity among the countries of the area;

The arms race and the growing arms traffic in Central America, which aggravate political relations in the region and divert economic resources that could be used for development;

The presence of foreign advisers and other forms of foreign military interference in the zone;

The risks that the territory of Central American States may be used for the purpose of conducting military operations and pursuing policies of destabilization against others;

The need for concerted political efforts in order to encourage dialogue and understanding in Central America, avert the danger of a general spreading of the conflicts, and set in motion the machinery needed to ensure the peaceful coexistence and security of their peoples;

Declare their intention of achieving the following objectives:

To promote détente and put an end to situations of conflict in the area, refraining from taking any action that might jeopardize political confidence or prevent the achievement of peace, security and stability in the region;

To ensure strict compliance with the aforementioned principles of international law, whose violators will be held accountable;

Appendix A

To respect and ensure the exercise of human, political, civil, economic, social, religious and cultural rights;

To adopt measures conducive to the establishment and, where appropriate, improvement of democratic, representative and pluralistic systems that will guarantee effective popular participation in the decision-making process and ensure that the various currents of opinion have free access to fair and regular elections based on the full observance of citizens' rights;

To promote national reconciliation efforts wherever deep divisions have taken place within society, with a view to fostering participation in democratic political processes in accordance with the law;

To create political conditions intended to ensure the international security, integrity and sovereignty of the States of the region;

To stop the arms race in all its forms and begin negotiations for the control and reduction of current stocks of weapons and on the number of armed troops;

To prevent the installation on their territory of foreign military bases or any other type of foreign military interference;

To conclude agreements to reduce the presence of foreign military advisers and other foreign elements involved in military and security activities, with a view to their elimination;

To establish internal control machinery to prevent the traffic in arms from the territory of any country in the region to the territory of another;

To eliminate the traffic in arms, whether within the region or from outside it, intended for persons, organizations or groups seeking to destabilize the Governments of Central American countries;

To prevent the use of their own territory by persons, organizations or groups seeking to destabilize the Governments of Central American countries and to refuse to provide them with or permit them to receive military or logistical support;

To refrain from inciting or supporting acts of terrorism, subversion or sabotage in the countries in the area;

To establish and coordinate direct communication systems with a view to preventing or, where appropriate, settling incidents between States of the region;

To continue humanitarian aid aimed at helping Central American refugees who have been displaced from their countries of origin, and to create suitable conditions for the voluntary repatriation of such refugees, in consultation with or with the cooperation of the United Nations High Commissioner for Refugees (UNHCR) and other international agencies deemed appropriate;

To undertake economic and social development programs with the aim of promoting well being and an equitable distribution of wealth;

To revitalize and restore economic integration machinery in order to attain sustained development on the basis of solidarity and mutual advantage;

To negotiate the provision of external monetary resources which will provide additional means of financing the resumption of intra-regional trade, meet the serious balance-of-payments problems, attract funds for working capital, support programs to extend and restructure production systems and promote medium- and long-term investment projects;

To negotiate better and broader access to international markets in order to increase the volume of trade between the countries of Central America and the rest of the world, particularly the industrialized countries; by means of a revision of trade practices, the elimination of tariff and other barriers, and the achievement of price stability at a profitable and fair level for the products exported by the countries of the region;

To establish technical cooperation machinery for the planning, programming and implementation of multi-sectoral investment and trade promotion projects.

The Ministers for Foreign Affairs of the Central American countries, with the participation of the countries in the Contadora Group, have begun negotiations with the aim of preparing for the conclusion of the agreements and the establishment of the machinery necessary to formalize and develop the objectives contained in this document, and to bring about the establishment of appropriate verification and monitoring systems. To that end, account will be taken of the initiatives put forward at the meetings convened by the Contadora Group.

Panama City, 9 September 1983

THE CONTADORA 'IMPLEMENTATION PRINCIPLES'
January 1984

[Principles for the Implementation of the Commitments Undertaken in the Document of Objectives," adopted as the final resolution of the joint meeting of the Central American and Contadora Group foreign ministers' in Panama City on 8 January 1984]

[Text] The Governments of Costa Rica, El Salvador, Guatemala, Honduras, and Nicaragua, considering:

1. That in September 1983 the five governments approved the Document of Objectives, which is the frame of reference for the regional peace agreement;

2. And that it is necessary to take measures to implement the commitments contained in that document, resolve to:

I. Adopt the following principles for immediate application:

1. *Security Affairs*

a. To prepare a registry or detailed inventory of military installations, weapons, and troops by each of the Central America states, in order to establish the foundations for a policy to control and reduce these things, providing ceilings and resulting in a reasonable balance of forces in the region.

b. To prepare a census in each country and to adopt a calendar of reduction with an eye to the elimination of foreign military advisers and other foreign individuals who are participating in military or security activities.

c. To identify and eradicate all forms of support, encouragement, and financing for or tolerance of irregular groups of forces involved in the destabilization of Central American governments.

d. To identify and eradicate irregular groups of forces that, acting either from or through the territory of any Central American state, participate in destabilizing actions against another government in the region.

e. To localize the areas, routes, and means used for illegal intraregional and extra-regional arms traffic, in order to eliminate it.

f. To establish direct communication mechanisms for the purpose of preventing and resolving incidents among states.

2. *Political Affairs*

a. To promote national reconciliation on the basis of justice, freedom, and democracy, and, to that effect, to create mechanisms that permit dialogue within the countries in the region.

b. To guarantee full respect for human rights and, to this end, to comply with the obligations contained in international legal documents and constitutional provisions on the subject.

c. To enact or review electoral legislation for the convocation of elections, so as to guarantee effective popular participation.

d. To create independent electoral bodies that will establish reliable electoral registries and ensure the impartiality and democracy of the processes.

e. To dictate, or when applicable update, regulations that guarantee the existence and participation of political parties that are representative of the various sectors of opinion.

f. To establish an electoral calendar and to adopt measures that will ensure that political parties can participate under conditions of equality.

g. To strive to carry out actions that will permit the attainment of true political confidence among the governments of the area, in order to contribute to detente.

3. *Socioeconomic Affairs*

a. To intensify the program of aid for Central American refugees and to facilitate voluntary repatriation through the cooperation of the governments involved, in communication or coordination with national humanitarian organizations and the appropriate international organizations.

b. To grant full cooperation to the Central American Integration Bank, ECLA, the Action Committee for Suport to the Socioeconomic Development of Central America, and SIECA (Secretariat of Central American Integration).

c. To jointly negotiate for foreign resources that permit the revitalization of Central American integration processes.

d. To encourage intra-zonal trade and to promote greater and better access to international markets for Central American products.

e. To promote joint investment projects.

f. To establish just socioeconomic structures that consolidate genuine democratic systems and permit full access of their peoples to their right to work, education, health, and culture.

II. Authorize the technical group, which is the advisory body for the joint meeting of the foreign ministers of Central America and the Contadora Group, to follow up on the actions provided for in this document on security, political, and socioeconomic affairs. The technical group will inform the meeting of ministers on the progress made in the implementation of these measures.

III. Create, within the framework of the Contadora Group, three working commissions charged with the preparation of studies, legal briefs, and recommendations that develop the areas of security, political, and socioeconomic affairs, and proposals for the verification and supervision of compliance with the agreed upon measures.

The working commissions will be governed by the following rules:

a. They will consist of the representatives of the Central American governments. Each country may appoint no more than two advisers per commission.

b. The Contadora Group will convoke and participate in the session of those commissions, so that it may continue to extend its active cooperation in the discussion of the assigned topics and in the preparation of agreements.

c. Foreign advisory services, whether provided by individual personalities or representatives of international organizations, must be previously approved by consensus.

d. The working commissions will be installed in office no later than 31 January 1984. To this end, the participating governments will appoint their representatives and advisers and opportunely inform the Foreign Ministry of the Republic of Panama.

e. Each commission will draft and present its respective calendar and working program before 29 February 1984.

f. The working commissions will carry out their duties within the framework established by the Document of Objectives, will have their tasks coordinated by the technical group, and will present their studies, legal briefs, and recommendations to the joint meeting of foreign ministers no later than 30 April 1984.

APPENDIX C
THE CONTADORA ACT
October 1984

**UNITED
NATIONS**

 General Assembly   Security Council

Distr.
GENERAL

A/39/562
S/16775
9 October 1984
ENGLISH
ORIGINAL: SPANISH

GENERAL ASSEMBLY
Thirty-ninth session
Agenda item 25
THE SITUATION IN CENTRAL AMERICA:
  THREATS TO INTERNATIONAL PEACE
  AND SECURITY AND PEACE INITIATIVES

SECURITY COUNCIL
Thirty-ninth year

Report of the Secretary-General

1.   This report is submitted in accordance with General Assembly resolution 38/10
of 11 November 1983 and Security Council resolution 530 (1983) of 19 May 1983.

2.   Since the adoption of the latter resolution I have sought to keep the Security
Council informed - by means of the notes in documents S/16041, S/16208 and
S/16633 - of developments in Central America and of the efforts of the Governments
constituting the Contadora Group to find a political solution to the problems
affecting the region. I wish to make it clear that these notes are based mainly on
the information submitted to me in interviews with the Heads of State, Ministers
for Foreign Affairs and Permanent Representatives of the four countries which make
up the Contadora Group and of the five Central American countries. This report
also reflects actions of and communications from organs of the United Nations.

3.   Under cover of the notes referred to above the following documents were
transmitted to the Security Council: (a) the Document of Objectives adopted in
September 1983 at Panama City by the Ministers for Foreign Affairs of the Contadora
Group and of the five Central American countries; (b) a communication submitted by
the Ministers for Foreign Affairs of the Contadora Group to the General Assembly of
the Organization of American States, together with the text of the resolution
adopted at the seventh plenary meeting of the thirteenth regular session of that
Organization, held on 18 November 1983, entitled "Peace Efforts in Central
America"; and (c) the communication of 9 June 1984 under cover of which the
Ministers for Foreign Affairs of the Contadora Group transmitted personally to the
Heads of State of the five Central American countries the draft comprehensive
agreement entitled "Contadora Act on Peace and Co-operation in Central America".

A/39/562
S/16775
English
Page 2

4.   On 25 September 1984 I received a visit from the Ministers for Foreign Affairs of Colombia, Mexico, Panama and Venezuela, who delivered to me the draft Contadora Act on Peace and Co-operation in Central American (revised version), the text of which is annexed to this report at the request of the Ministers for Foreign Affairs.   The Ministers informed me that at the Seventh Joint Meeting of Ministers for Foreign Affairs of the Contadora Group and of the Central American countries, held on 7 September at Panama City, they had delivered the document in question to their Central American counterparts together with a communication addressed to the five Heads of State of Central America.   At that Joint Meeting, 15 October 1984 was fixed as the deadline for the Central American Governments to make known their views on the matter.

5.   The Ministers for Foreign Affairs of the Contadora Group indicated that, in accordance with the joint communiqué issued at the conclusion of the Seventh Joint Meeting (A/39/495-S/16742, annex II), the revised version of the Act is the result of a process of intensive consultations and a broad exchange of views with all the Central American Governments and reflects an effort to integrate the various contributions and reconcile those aspects on which divergencies remained.   Part III of the Act states that the commitments made in that document are legally binding on the Parties.   The Act, which is not subject to reservation, would enter into force when the five Central American signatory States have deposited their instruments of ratification, but the Parties, as from the date of signature, would be required to refrain from any acts which ran counter to the objectives and aims of the Act.   The Act contains an Additional Protocol, open for signature by all States desiring to contribute to peace and co-operation in Central America, under which those States would undertake to refrain from any acts that would serve to frustrate the object and purpose of the Act.

6.   Up to the date of this report, the Governments of Costa Rica, Honduras and Nicaragua have transmitted their comments on the revised Act to the Security Council and/or to the General Assembly (see documents A/39/555-S/16770, A/39/512 and S/16756).

7.   I wish to express my profound satisfaction with regard to the intelligent and vigorous contribution made by the Governments of the Contadora Group with a view to giving momentum to the process of negotiation among the Central American countries and finding formulas which would enable the causes of tension in the region to be eliminated.

8.   The efforts of the Contadora Group are especially important in view of the persistent gravity of the situation in Central America.   In fact, since the adoption of General Assembly resolution 38/10, the accusations and counter-accusations concerning acts of armed aggression, frontier incidents and acts of subversion and sabotage with the consequent losses in human life and material damage have continued and, in certain cases increased.   In addition, the presence of military forces from outside the region continues.

9.   The Security Council met on three occasions this year in order to consider complaints by Nicaragua relating mainly to the northern area of that country. Owing to the mining of a number of Nicaraguan ports, in April the Council

A/39/562
S/16775
English
Page 3

considered a draft resolution sponsored by Nicaragua (S/16463), which, because of
the negative vote of a permanent member, was not adopted. With regard to the
southern area of Nicaragua bordering Costa Rica, it should be noted that a
Commission for Supervision and Prevention has been set up under the auspices of the
Contadora Group which appears to have facilitated a reduction in the frontier
incidents involving the two countries.

10. On 10 May 1984, at the request of the Government of Nicaragua, the
International Court of Justice indicated certain provisional measures by virtue of
Article 41 of the Statute of the Court in the case concerning Military and
Paramilitary Activities in and against Nicaragua (Nicaragua v. United States of
America). The Order of the Court was trasmitted to the Security Council in
accordance with Article 41, paragraph 2, of the Statute of the Court. 1/

11. As a result of the visit to Managua by the United States Secretary of State, a
two-way dialogue has been initiated since the end of May between the United States
and Nicaragua. To date, six meetings have been held, under the auspices of Mexico,
between the United States Special Envoy for Central America and the Deputy Minister
of Foreign Affairs of Nicaragua. Both sides have welcomed the fact that these
talks have entered their substantive phase.

12. I have followed attentively the electoral process which took place recently in
El Salvador and the steps taken by President Duarte with a view to the country's
political stabilization. The fact that a political segment abstained from
participating in the elections, as well as the continuation of armed conflict, make
it difficult to bring about a broad, effective and lasting political
reconciliation. To date, the efforts to bring about a dialogue between the
Government and the Frente Democrático Revolucionario-Frente Farabundo Martí para la
Liberación Nacional (FDR-FMLN), including those sponsored by foreign Governments,
have not met with the success that was hoped for. While this report was being
finalized, on 8 October, President Duarte made a proposal in this respect during
his statement in the General Assembly (see A/39/PV.24).

13. It is encouraging that electoral processes are in the course of being
conducted in Guatemala and Nicaragua. Where Nicaragua is concerned, negotiations
have been proceeding in order to achieve the broadest possible participation in the
election. I hope that the holding of these elections will promote a genuine
process of democratization in the area.

14. The continuation of the upheaval in Central America, with its grievous impact
on the civilian population, is still causing a flood of refugees. According to
figures provided by the host countries, the number of refugees in the Central
American area is estimated at some 350,000, of whom 104,900, as of the end of
September this year, were receiving assistance from the Office of the United
Nations High Commissioner for Refugees (UNHCR).

15. On 28 and 29 September a Conference of Foreign Ministers was held in San José,
Costa Rica, between the member countries of the European Economic Community, Spain
and Portugal and their counterparts from the five States of Central America and the
Contadora States. I value highly the support of the 12 Western European countries

A/39/562
S/16775
English
Page 4

for the work of the Contadora Group and for the objectives of peace, democracy, security and economic and social development in Central America, as well as their rejection of any solution based on the use of force. The undertakings agreed upon in respect of economic co-operation, with provision for the participation of the five Central American States (see A/39/539, annex), are also a source of satisfaction.

16. I wish to take the opportunity afforded me by the submission of this report to appeal to the countries of the region, as provided for in Security Council resolution 530 (1983), to pursue their efforts to negotiate a comprehensive solution to their problems under the auspices of the Contadora Group.

Notes

1/ The full text of the Order of the Court has been reproduced in document S/16564.

A/39/562
S/16775
English
Page 5

ANNEX

CONTADORA ACT ON PEACE AND CO-OPERATION
IN CENTRAL AMERICA

(REVISED VERSION)

172   *Appendix C*

A/39/562
S/16775
English
Page 6

CONTENTS

A/39/562
S/16775
English
Page 7

CONTENTS (continued)

A/39/562
S/16775
English
Page 8

PREAMBLE

The Governments of the Republics of Costa Rica, El Salvador, Guatemala, Honduras and Nicaragua:

1. AWARE of the urgent need to strengthen peace and co-operation among the peoples of the region, through the observance of principles and measures that would facilitate a better understanding among the Central American Governments;

2. CONCERNED about the situation in Central America, which is characterized by a serious decline in political confidence and by frontier incidents, an arms build-up, arms traffic, the presence of foreign advisers and other forms of foreign military presence, and the use by irregular forces of the territories of certain States to carry out destabilizing operations against other States in the region;

CONVINCED

3. That the tension and the present conflicts may worsen and lead to widespread hostilities;

4. That the restoration of peace and confidence in the region may be achieved only through unconditional respect for the principles of international law, particularly the principle which concerns the right of peoples to choose freely and without external interference the form of political, economic and social organization that best serves their interests, and to do so through institutions which represent their freely-expressed will;

5. Of the importance of creating, promoting and strengthening democratic systems in all the countries of the region;

6. Of the need to create political conditions designed to guarantee the security, integrity and sovereignty of the States of the region;

7. That the achievement of genuine regional stability hinges on the conclusion of agreements on security and disarmament;

8. That, in the adoption of measures aimed at halting the arms race in all its forms, account should be taken of the national security interests of the States of the region;

9. That military superiority as a political objective of the States of the region, the presence of foreign advisers and other foreign elements and the arms traffic endanger regional security and constitute destabilizing factors in the region;

10. That the agreements on regional security must be subject to an effective system of verification and control;

11. That the destabilization of the Governments in the region, generally taking the form of encouragement or support of the activities of irregular groups

A/39/562
S/16775
English
Page 9

or forces, acts of terrorism, subversion or sabotage and the use of the territory of a State for operations affecting the security of another State, is contrary to the fundamental norms of international law and peaceful coexistence among States;

12. That it is highly desirable to set maximum limits for military development, in accordance with the requirements of stability and security in the region;

13. That the elaboration of instruments to permit the application of a policy of détente should be based on the existence of political trust among States which would effectively reduce political and military tension among them;

14. RECALLING the provisions adopted by the United Nations concerning the definition of aggression, in particular General Assembly resolution 3314 (XXIX), and the relevant resolutions of the Organization of American States;

15. TAKING INTO ACCOUNT the Declaration on the Strengthening of International Security, adopted by the United Nations General Assembly in resolution 2734 (XXV), and the corresponding legal instruments of the inter-American system;

16. REAFFIRMING the need to promote national reconciliation in those cases where deep divisions have occurred within society, so as to permit the people to participate, in accordance with the law, in political processes of a democratic nature;

CONSIDERING:

17. That, on the basis of the United Nations Charter of 1945 and the Universal Declaration of Human Rights of 1948, various international organizations and conferences have elaborated and adopted declarations, covenants, protocols, conventions and statutes designed to provide effective protection of human rights in general, or of certain human rights in particular;

18. That not all Central American States have accepted the entirety of the existing international instruments on human rights, and that it would be desirable that they should do so in order to bring the human rights régime closer to the goal of universality in the interests of promoting the observance and guarantee of human, political, civil, economic, social, religious and cultural rights;

19. That in many cases the deficiencies of outdated or inadequate domestic legislation interfere with the effective enjoyment of human rights as defined in declarations and other international instruments;

20. That it should be the concern of each State to modernize and adapt its legislation with a view to guaranteeing the effective enjoyment of human rights;

21. That one of the most effective ways of securing the enjoyment of human rights embodied in international instruments, political constitutions and the laws of individual States lies in ensuring that the judiciary enjoys sufficient authority and autonomy to put an end to violations of those rights;

A/39/562
S/16775
English
Page 10

22. That, to that end, the absolute independence of the judiciary must be guaranteed;

23. That that guarantee may be achieved only if judicial officials enjoy security of office and if the judiciary is ensured budgetary stability so that it may be absolutely and unquestionably independent of the other authorities;

CONVINCED:

24. Of the need to establish equitable economic and social structures in order to promote a genuinely democratic system and permit full enjoyment by the people of the right to work, education, health and culture;

25. Of the high level of interdependence of the Central American countries and the prospects which economic integration offers small countries;

26. That the magnitude of the economic and social crisis affecting the region has highlighted the need for changes in the economic and social structures that would reduce the dependence of the Central American countries and promote regional self-sufficiency, enabling them to reaffirm their own identity;

27. That Central American economic integration should constitute an effective tool for economic and social development based on justice, solidarity and mutual benefit;

28. Of the need to reactivate, improve and restructure the process of Central American economic integration with the active and institutional participation of all the States of the region;

29. That, in the reform of the existing economic and social structures and the strengthening of regional integration, the Central American institutions and authorities are called upon to assume primary responsibility;

30. Of the necessity and appropriateness of undertaking joint programmes of economic and social development which would help to promote economic integration in Central America in the context of the development plans and priorities adopted by each sovereign State;

31. Of the urgent need for substantial investment for the development and economic recovery of the Central American countries and of the efforts undertaken jointly by these countries to obtain financing for specific priority projects, and in view of the need to expand and strengthen international, regional and subregional financial institutions;

32. That the regional crisis has provoked massive flows of refugees and that the situation demands urgent attention;

33. CONCERNED about the constant worsening of social conditions, including the situation with regard to employment, education, health and housing in the Central American countries;

A/39/562
S/16775
English
Page 11

34. REAFFIRMING, without prejudice to the right of recourse to other
competent international forums, their desire to settle their disputes within the
framework of the negotiation process sponsored by the Contadora Group;

35. RECALLING the support given by the Contadora Group to United Nations
Security Council resolution 530 (1983) and General Assembly resolution 38/10, as
well as to resolution AG/RES 675 (XIII-0/83) adopted by the General Assembly of the
Organization of American States; and

36. BEING READY to implement fully the Document of Objectives and the norms
for the implementation of the undertakings made therein, adopted by their Ministers
for Foreign Affairs in Panama on 9 September 1983 and 8 January 1984 respectively,
under the auspices of the Governments of Colombia, Mexico, Panama and Venezuela,
which comprise the Contadora Group;

Have agreed as follows:

CONTADORA ACT ON PEACE AND CO-OPERATION IN CENTRAL AMERICA

PART I

COMMITMENTS

CHAPTER I

GENERAL COMMITMENTS

Sole section. PRINCIPLES

THE PARTIES undertake, in accordance with their obligations under international law:

1. To abide by the following principles:

(a) The principle of refraining from the threat or use of force against the
territorial integrity or political independence of States;

(b) The peaceful settlement of disputes;

(c) Non-interference in the internal affairs of other States;

(d) Co-operation between States in solving international problems;

(e) The equal rights and self-determination of peoples and the promotion of
respect for human rights;

(f) Sovereign equality and respect for the rights inherent in sovereignty;

(g) The principle of refraining from discriminatory practices in economic
relations between States by respecting their systems of political,
economic and social organization;

A/39/562
S/16775
English
Page 12

(h) The fulfilment in good faith of obligations assumed under international law.

2. In pursuance of the foregoing principles:

(a) They shall refrain from any action inconsistent with the purposes and principles of the Charter of the United Nations and the Charter of the Organization of American States aimed against the territorial integrity, political independence or unity of any State, and, in particular, from any such action involving the threat or use of force.

(b) They shall settle their disputes by peaceful means in accordance with the fundamental principles of international law embodied in the Charter of the United Nations and the Charter of the Organization of American States.

(c) They shall respect the existing international boundaries between States.

(d) They shall refrain from militarily occupying territory of any other State in the region.

(e) They shall refrain from any act of military, political, economic or other form of coercion aimed at subordinating to their interests the exercise by other States of rights inherent in their sovereignty.

(f) They shall take such action as is necessary to secure their frontiers against irregular groups or forces operating from their territory with the aim of destabilizing the Governments of neighbouring States.

(g) They shall not permit their territory to be used for acts which violate the sovereign rights of other States, and shall see to it that the conditions obtaining in their territory do not pose a threat to international peace and security.

(h) They shall respect the principle that no State or group of States has the right to intervene either directly or indirectly through the use of arms or any other form of interference in the internal or external affairs of another State.

(i) They shall respect the right of all peoples to self-determination free from outside intervention or coercion by refraining from the threat or the direct or covert use of force to disrupt the national unity and territorial integrity of any other State.

A/39/562
S/16775
English
Page 13

CHAPTER II

COMMITMENTS WITH REGARD TO POLITICAL MATTERS

Section 1. COMMITMENTS WITH REGARD TO REGIONAL DETENTE AND CONFIDENCE-BUILDING

THE PARTIES undertake:

3. To promote mutual trust by every means at their disposal and to refrain from any action which might disturb peace and security in the Central American region;

4. To refrain from issuing or promoting propaganda in support of violence or war, and hostile propaganda against any Central American Government, and to abide by and foster the principles of peaceful coexistence and friendly co-operation;

5. Towards that end, their respective governmental authorities shall:

    (a) Avoid any oral or written statement which might aggravate the situation of conflict in the area;

    (b) Urge the mass media to help to promote understanding and co-operation between peoples of the region;

    (c) Promote increased contacts between their peoples and a better knowledge of each other's peoples through co-operation in all spheres relating to education, science, technology and culture;

    (d) Consider together future action and mechanisms for bringing about and solidifying a climate of stable and lasting peace;

6. Join together in seeking a regional settlement which will eliminate the causes of tension in Central America by safeguarding the inalienable rights of its peoples from foreign pressure and interests.

Section 2. COMMITMENTS WITH REGARD TO NATIONAL RECONCILIATION

Each PARTY recognizes vis-à-vis the other Central American States the commitment assumed vis-à-vis its own people to ensure the preservation of domestic peace as a contribution to peace in the region, and they accordingly resolve:

7. To adopt measures for the establishment or, as the case may be, the further development of representative and pluralistic democratic systems guaranteeing effective participation by the people, through political organizations, in the decision-making process, and ensuring the different currents of opinion free access to honest and periodic elections based on the full observance of the rights of citizens;

A/39/562
S/16775
English
Page 14

8.   Where deep divisions have come about within society, urgently to promote
     actions of national reconciliation which will make it possible for the people
     to participate, with full guarantees, in genuine democratic political
     processes on the basis of justice, liberty and democracy, and, towards that
     end, to create mechanisms making possible, in accordance with the law,
     dialogue with opposition groups;

9.   To adopt and, as the case may be, endorse, broaden and improve legal measures
     for a genuine amnesty which will enable their citizens to resume full
     participation in political, economic and social affairs, and similarly, to
     guarantee the inviolability of life, the liberty and the security of person of
     those to whom such amnesty is granted.

Section 3.   COMMITMENTS WITH REGARD TO HUMAN RIGHTS

THE PARTIES undertake, in accordance with their respective national laws and their
obligations under international law:

10. To guarantee full respect for human rights and, towards that end, to comply
     with the obligations laid down in international legal instruments and
     constitutional provisions relating to human rights;

11. To set in motion the constitutional procedures necessary for them to become
     parties to the following international instruments:

     (a) The 1966 International Covenant on Economic, Social and Cultural Rights;

     (b) The 1966 International Covenant on Civil and Political Rights;

     (c) The 1966 Optional Protocol to the International Covenant on Civil and
          Political Rights;

     (d) The 1965 International Convention on the Elimination of All Forms of
          Racial Discrimination;

     (e) The 1951 Convention Relating to the Status of Refugees;

     (f) The 1967 Optional Protocol relating to the Status of Refugees;

     (g) The 1952 Convention on the Political Rights of Women;

     (h) The 1979 Convention on the Elimination of All Forms of Discrimination
          Against Women;

     (i) The 1953 Protocol Amending the 1925 Slavery Convention;

     (j) The 1956 Supplementary Convention on the Abolition of Slavery, the Slave
          Trade and Institutions and Practices Similar to Slavery;

     (k) The 1953 Convention on the Civil and Political Rights of Women;

A/39/562
S/16775
English
Page 15

(1) The 1969 American Convention on Human Rights, taking note of articles 45 and 62;

12. To prepare the necessary draft legislation and submit it to their competent internal organs with a view to accelerating the process of modernizing and updating their legislation, so as to make it more capable of promoting and guaranteeing due respect for human rights;

13. To prepare and submit to their competent internal organs draft legislation aimed at:

(a) Guaranteeing the stability of the member of the judiciary, so that they can act without being subjected to political pressures, and themselves guarantee the stability of officials of lower rank;

(b) Guaranteeing the budgetary stability of the judiciary itself, so that it may be absolutely and unquestionably independent of the other authorities.

Section 4. COMMITMENTS WITH REGARD TO ELECTORAL PROCESSES AND PARLIAMENTARY CO-OPERATION

Each PARTY shall recognize vis-à-vis the other Central American States the commitment assumed vis-à-vis its own people to guarantee the preservation of internal peace as a contribution to peace in the region and to that end shall resolve:

14. To adopt the appropriate measures that guarantee the participation of political parties in electoral processes on an equal footing, ensuring that they have access to the mass communication media and enjoy freedom of assembly and freedom of expression.

15. They likewise commit themselves to:

(a) Take the following measures:

(1) Promulgate or revise the electoral legislation with a view to the holding of elections that guarantee effective participation by the people;

(2) Establish independent electoral organs that will prepare a reliable voting register and ensure the impartiality and democratic nature of the process;

(3) Formulate or, where appropriate, update the rules guaranteeing the existence and participation of political parties representing various currents of opinion;

(4) Establish an electoral timetable and adopt measures to ensure that the political parties participate on an equal footing;

A/39/562
S/16775
English
Page 16

(b)   Propose to their respective legislative organs that they should:

    (1)   Hold regular meetings at alternating sites that would enable them to exchange experience, contribute to détente and foster better communication with a view to <u>rapproachement</u> among the countries of the area;

    (2)   Take measures aimed at maintaining relations with the Latin American Parliament and its respective Working Commissions;

    (3)   Exchange information and experience on the matters within their competence and collect with a view to comparative study, the electoral legislation in force in each country, together with related provisions;

    (4)   Follow, as observers, the various stages in the electoral processes taking place in the region. To that end, the express invitation of the Central American State in which the electoral process is taking place shall be essential;

    (5)   Hold periodic technical meetings in the place and with the agenda determined by consensus at each preceeding meeting. The arrangements for the first meeting shall be made through consultations among the Central American Ministers for Foreign Affairs.

CHAPTER III

COMMITMENTS WITH REGARD TO SECURITY MATTERS

In conformity with the obligations they have contracted in accordance with international law, the PARTIES assume the following commitments:

Section 1.   COMMITMENTS WITH REGARD TO MILITARY MANOEUVRES

16.   To comply with the following provisions as regards the holding of military manoeuvres:

    (a)   When national or joint military manoeuvres are held in areas less than 30 (thirty) kilometres from the frontier, the appropriate prior notification to the neighbouring countries and the Verification and Control Commission, mentioned in Part II of this Act, shall be made at least 30 (thirty) days beforehand.

    (b)   The notification shall contain the following information:

        (1)   Name;

        (2)   Purpose;

A/39/562
S/16775
English
Page 17

(3) Participating forces;

(4) Geographical location;

(5) Timetable;

(6) Equipment and weapons to be used.

Invitations shall be issued to observers from neighbouring countries.

17. To prohibit the holding of international military manoeuvres in their respective territories. Any manoeuvre of this kind which is currently under way shall be suspended within a period of not more than thirty days after the signing of this Act.

Section 2. COMMITMENTS WITH REGARD TO ARMAMENTS

18. To halt the arms race in all its forms, and begin immediately negotiations on the control and reduction of the current inventory of weapons and the number of troops under arms;

19. Not to introduce new weapons systems that alter the quality or quantity of current inventories of war materiel;

20. Not to introduce, possess or use chemical, biological, radiological or other weapons which may be deemed to be excessively injurious or to have indiscriminate effects;

21. To send to the Verification and Control Commission their respective current inventories of weapons, installations and troops under arms within a period of not more than 30 (thirty) days from the date of the signing of this Act. The inventories shall be prepared in accordance with the definitions and basic criteria agreed on in the Annex and in paragraph 21 of this section. On receiving the inventories, the Commission shall carry out within a period of not more than 30 days the technical studies that will be used for the purpose of setting maximum limits for the military development of the States of the region, taking into account their national security interests, and of halting the arms race.

On the basis of the foregoing, the PARTIES agree on the following implementation stages:

First stage: Once they have submitted their respective inventories, the PARTIES shall acquire no more military materiel. The moratorium shall continue until limits are agreed on in the following stage.

Second stage: The PARTIES shall establish within a maximum period of thirty days limits for the following types of armaments: fighter aircraft and helicopters, tanks and armoured vehicles, artillery, short-, medium- and long-range rockets and guided missiles and launching equipment, ships or vessels that are of a military nature or can be used for military purposes.

A/39/562
S/16775
English
Page 18

Third stage: Once the preceding stage has been completed and within a period of not more than thirty days, the PARTIES shall establish limits for military forces and for installations that can be used in military actions.

Fourth stage: The PARTIES may begin negotiations concerning those matters with which it is considered essential to deal. Notwithstanding the foregoing, the PARTIES may, by mutual agreement, change the periods set for the negotiation and establishment of limits.

22. The following basic criteria shall determine the levels of military development of the Central American States, in accordance with the requirements of stability and security in the region:

   (a) No armed institution shall have as a political objective the pursuit of hegemony over the other forces considered individually;

   (b) The definition of national security shall take into account the level of economic and social development attained at a given time, and the level which it is desired to attain;

   (c) For the purpose of formulating that definition, studies shall be carried out covering the following aspects in a comprehensive manner:

      (1) Perception of the internal and external security needs of the State;

      (2) Area of the territory;

      (3) Population;

      (4) Nation-wide distribution of economic resources, infrastructure and population;

      (5) Range and characteristics of land and sea boundaries;

      (6) Military expenditure in relation to gross domestic product (GDP);

      (7) Military budget in relation to public expenditure and other social indicators;

      (8) Geographical features and position, and geopolitical situation;

      (9) Level of advanced military technology suited to the region.

23. To initiate constitutional procedures so as to be in a position to sign, ratify or accede to treaties and other international agreements on disarmament, if they have not already done so.

Section 3. COMMITMENTS WITH REGARD TO FOREIGN MILITARY BASES

24. Not to authorize the installation in their respective territories of foreign bases or foreign military schools.

A/39/562
S/16775
English
Page 19

25. To close down any foreign bases or foreign military schools in their respective territories within six months of the signing of this Act.

Section 4. COMMITMENTS WITH REGARD TO FOREIGN MILITARY ADVISERS

26. To provide the Verification and Control Commission with a list of any foreign military advisers or other foreign elements participating in military and security activities in their territory, within 30 days of the signing of this Act. In the preparation of the list, the definitions contained in the annex shall be taken into account.

27. With a view to the removal of foreign military advisers and other foreign elements, to set a timetable for phased withdrawals, including the immediate withdrawal of any advisers performing operational and training functions. To that end, the studies and recommendations of the Verification and Control Commission shall be taken into account.

28. As for advisers performing technical functions related to the installation and maintenance of military equipment, a control register shall be maintained in accordance with the terms laid down in the respective contracts or agreements. On the basis of that register, the Verification and Control Commission shall seek to set reasonable limits on the number of such advisers.

Section 5. COMMITMENTS WITH REGARD TO THE TRAFFIC IN ARMS

29. To stop the flow of arms, within and outside the region, towards persons, organizations, irregular forces or armed bands trying to destabilize the Governments of the States Parties.

30. To establish for that purpose internal control mechanisms at airports, landing strips, harbours, terminals and border crossings, on roads, air routes, sea lanes and waterways, and at any other point or in any other area likely to be used for the traffic in arms.

31. On the basis of presumption or established facts, to report any violations to the Verification and Control Commission, with sufficient evidence to enable it to carry out the necessary investigation and submit such conclusions and recommendations as it may consider useful. Whenever appropriate, the following elements, among others, shall be taken into account for the purpose of establishing the facts:

    (a) Source of the arms traffic;

    (b) Persons involved;

    (c) Type of armaments, munitions, equipment and other military supplies;

    (d) Extraregional means of transport;

    (e) Extraregional transport routes;

A/39/562
S/16775
English
Page 20

(f) Storage bases for arms, munitions, equipment and other military supplies;

(g) Areas and routes in the intraregional traffic;

(h) International means of transport;

(i) Receiving unit.

Section 6. COMMITMENTS WITH REGARD TO THE PROHIBITION OF SUPPORT
            FOR IRREGULAR FORCES

32. To refrain from giving any political, military, financial or other support to
     individuals, groups, irregular forces or armed bands advocating the overthrow
     or destabilization of other Governments, and to prevent, by all means at their
     disposal, the use of their territory for attacks on another State or for the
     organization of attacks, acts of sabotage, kidnappings or criminal activities
     in the territory of another State.

33. To exercise strict control over their respective borders, with a view to
     preventing their own territory from being used to carry out any military
     action against a neighbouring State.

34. To disarm and remove from the border area any group or irregular force
     identified as being responsible for acts against a neighboring state.

35. To dismantle, and deny the use of, installations, equipment and facilities
     providing logistical support or serving operational functions in their
     territory, if the latter is used for acts against neighbouring Governments.

Section 7. COMMITMENTS WITH REGARD TO TERRORISM, SUBVERSION OR SABOTAGE

36. To refrain from giving political, military, financial or any other support for
     acts of subversion, terrorism or sabotage intended to destabilize Governments
     of the region.

37. To refrain from organizing, instigating or participating in acts of terrorism,
     subversion or sabotage in another State, or acquiescing in organized
     activities within their territory directed towards the commission of such acts.

38. To abide by the following treaties and international agreements:

     (a) The Hague Convention for the Suppression of Unlawful Seizure of Aircraft;

     (b) The Convention to prevent and punish the acts of terrorism taking the
          form of crimes against persons and related extortion that are of
          international significance;

     (c) The Convention for the Suppression of Unlawful Acts against the Safety of
          Civil Aviation;

A/39/562
S/16775
English
Page 21

(d) The Convention on the Prevention and Punishment of Crimes against Internationally Protected Persons, including Diplomatic Agents;

(e) The International Convention against the Taking of Hostages.

39. To initiate constitutional procedures so as to be in a position to sign, ratify or accede to the treaties and international agreements referred to in the preceding paragraph, if they have not already done so.

40. To respect the commitments referred to in this section, without prejudice to compliance with treaties and other international agreements relating to diplomatic and territorial asylum.

41. To prevent in their respective territories participation in criminal acts committed by individuals belonging to foreign terrorist groups or organizations. To that end, they shall strengthen co operation between the competent migration offices and police departments and between the corresponding civilian authorities.

Section 8. COMMITMENTS WITH REGARD TO DIRECT COMMUNICATIONS SYSTEMS

42. To establish a regional communications system which guarantees immediate and timely liaison between the competent government and military authorities with a view to preventing incidents.

43. To establish Joint Security Commissions in order to prevent and settle conflicts between neighbouring States.

CHAPTER IV

COMMITMENTS WITH REGARD TO ECONOMIC AND SOCIAL AFFAIRS

Section 1. COMMITMENTS WITH REGARD TO ECONOMIC AND SOCIAL MATTERS

With a view to intensifying the process of Central American economic integration and strengthening the institutions representing and supporting it, the PARTIES undertake:

44. To reactivate, perfect and restructure the process of Central American economic integration, harmonizing it with the various forms of political, economic and social organization of the countries of the region.

45. To ratify resolution 1/84, adopted at the thirtieth Meeting of Ministers responsible for Central American Economic Integration held on 27 July 1984, which is designed to re-establish the institutional basis of the Central American economic integration process.

A/39/562
S/16775
English
Page 22

46. To support and promote the conclusion of agreements designed to intensify trade between Central American countries within the legal framework and in the spirit of integration.

47. Not to adopt or support any coercive or discriminatory measures detrimental to the economy of any of the Central American countries.

48. To adopt measures designed to strengthen the financial agencies in the area, including the Central American Bank for Economic Integration, supporting their efforts to obtain resources and diversify their operations, while safeguarding their decision-making powers and the interests of all the Central American countries.

49. To strengthen the multilateral payments machinery within the Central American Common Market Fund and to reactivate the machinery already in operation through the Central American Clearing House. In order to attain these objectives, recourse may be had to available international financial assistance.

50. To undertake sectoral co-operation projects in the area, such as those pertaining to the power production and distribution system, the regional food security system, the Plan for Priority Health Needs in Central America and Panama and others which would contribute to Central American economic integration.

51. To examine jointly the problem of the Central American external debt through an evaluation taking into account the domestic circumstances of each country, its payments capacity, the critical economic situation in the area and the flow of additional resources necessary for its economic and social development.

52. To support the elaboration and subsequent application of a new Central American tariff and customs régime.

53. To adopt joint measures to protect and promote their exports, integrating as far as possible the processing, marketing and transport of their products.

54. To adopt the necessary measures to confer legal status on the Central American Monetary Council.

55. To support, at the highest level, the efforts CADESCA is making, in co-ordination with subregional agencies, to obtain from the international community the financial resources needed to revitalize the Central American economy.

56. To implement the international norms governing labour and, with the co-operation of ILO, to adapt their domestic laws to these norms, particularly those which are conducive to the reconstruction of Central American societies and economies. In addition, to carry out, with the co-operation of the aforesaid agency, programmes to create jobs and provide vocational training and instruction and also for the application of appropriate technologies designed to make greater use of the manpower and natural resources of each country.

A/39/562
S/16775
English
Page 23

57. To request the support of the Pan-American Health Organization and UNICEF, and of other development agencies and the international financial community, to finance the Plan for Priority Health Needs in Central America and Panama, adopted by the Ministers of Health of the Central American Isthmus at San José on 16 March 1984.

Section 2.   COMMITMENTS WITH REGARD TO REFUGEES

THE PARTIES undertake to make the necessary efforts:

58. To carry out, if they have not yet done so, the constitutional procedures for accession to the 1951 Convention relating to the Status of Refugees and the 1967 Protocol relating to the Status of Refugees.

59. To adopt the terminology established in the Convention and Protocol referred to in the foregoing paragraph with a view to distinguishing refugees from other categories of migrants.

60. To establish the internal machinery necessary for the implementation, upon accession, of the provisions of the Convention and Protocol referred to in paragraph 58.

61. To ensure that machinery is established for consultation between the Central American countries and representatives of the government offices responsible for dealing with the problem of refugees in each State.

62. To support the work performed by the United Nations High Commissioner for Refugees (UNHCR) in Central America and to establish direct co-ordination machinery to facilitate the fulfilment of his mandate.

63. To ensure that any repatriation of refugees is voluntary, and is declared to be so on an individual basis, and is carried out with the co-operation of UNHCR.

64. To ensure the establishment of tripartite commissions, composed of representatives of the State of origin, of the receiving State and of UNHCR, with a view to facilitating the repatriation of refugees.

65. To reinforce programmes for protection of and assistance to refugees, particularly in the areas of health, education, labour and safety.

66. To ensure that programmes and projects are set up with a view to ensuring the self-sufficiency of refugees.

67. To train the officials responsible in each State for protection of and assistance to refugees, with the co-operation of UNHCR and other international agencies.

68. To request immediate assistance from the international community for Central American refugees, to be provided either directly, through bilateral or multilateral agreements, or through UNHCR and other organizations and agencies.

A/39/562
S/16775
English
Page 24

69. To identify, with the co-operation of UNHCR, other countries which might receive Central American refugees. In no case shall a refugee be transferred to a third country against his will.

70. To ensure that the Governments of the area make the necessary efforts to eradicate the causes of the refugee problem.

71. To ensure that, once agreement has been reached on the bases for voluntary and individual repatriation, with full guarantees for the refugees, the receiving countries permit official delegations of the country of origin, accompanied by representatives of UNHCR and the receiving country, to visit the refugee camps.

72. To ensure that the receiving countries facilitate, in co-ordination with UNHCR, the departure procedure for refugees in instances of voluntary and individual repatriation.

73. To institute appropriate measures in the receiving countries to prevent the participation of refugees in activities directed against the country of origin, while at all times respecting the human rights of the refugees.

PART II

COMMITMENTS WITH REGARD TO EXECUTION AND FOLLOW-UP

The PARTIES decide to establish the following mechanisms for the purpose of executing and following up the commitments contained in this Act:

1. Ad Hoc Committee for Evaluation and Follow-up of Commitments concerning Political and Refugee Matters

    (a) Composition

         The Committee shall be composed of five (5) persons of recognized competence and impartiality, proposed by the States members of the Contadora Group and accepted by common agreement by the Parties. The members of the Committee must be of a nationality different from those of the Parties.

    (b) Functions

         The Committee shall receive and evaluate the reports which the Parties undertake to submit on the ways in which they have proceeded to implement commitments with regard to national reconciliation, human rights, electoral processes and refugees.

         In addition, the Committee shall be open to any communications on these subjects, transmitted for their information by organizations or individuals, which might contribute useful data for evaluation.

A/39/562
S/16775
English
Page 25

On the basis of the aforesaid data, the Committee shall prepare a periodic report which, in addition to the evaluation, shall contain proposals and recommendations for improving implementation of the commitments. This report shall be submitted to the Parties and to the Governments of the Contadora Group.

(c) Rules of procedures

The Committee shall draw up its own rules of procedure, which it shall make known to the Parties.

2. Verification and Control Commission for Security Matters

(a) Composition

The Commission shall be composed of:

- Four Commissioners, representing States of recognized impartiality and having a genuine interest in contributing to the solution of the Central American crisis, proposed by the Contadora Group and accepted by the PARTIES, with the right to participate in decisions of the Commission. Co-ordination of the work of the Commission shall be by rotation.

- A Latin American Executive Secretary appointed by the Contadora Group by common agreement with the PARTIES, with the right to participate in the decisions of the Commission, who shall be responsible for its ongoing operation.

- A representative of the Secretary-General of the United Nations and a representative of the Secretary-General of the Organization of American States, as observers.

(b) Establishment

The Commission shall be established not more than thirty (30) days after the signing of this Act.

(c) Functions

- To receive current inventories of armaments, installations and troops under arms of the PARTIES, prepared in accordance with the provisions of the Annex.

- To carry out technical studies to be used to establish maximum limits for the military development of the PARTIES in the region in accordance with the basic criteria established in commitment 22 of this Act.

- To verify that no new weapons are introduced which would qualitatively and quantitatively alter current inventories, and to verify the non-use of weapons prohibited in this Act.

A/39/562
S/16775
English
Page 26

- To establish a register of all commercial transfers of weapons carried out by the PARTIES, including donations and other transactions carried out in the framework of military assistance agreements with other Governments.

- To verify the dismantling of foreign military installations, in accordance with the provisions of this Act.

- To receive the census of foreign military advisers and to verify their withdrawal in accordance with the agreed timetable.

- To verify compliance with this Act in respect of traffic in arms and to consider any reports of non-compliance. For that purpose, the following criteria shall be taken into account:

(1) Origin of the arms traffic: this criterion calls for determination of the port or airport of embarkation of the arms, munitions, equipment or other military supplies intended for the Central American region.

(2) Personnel involved: persons, groups or organizations participating in the organization and conduct of the traffic in arms, including the participation of Governments or their representatives.

(3) Type of weapon, munitions, equipment or other military supplies: describing, under this heading, the category of weapons, their calibre and the country of manufacture, if the country of origin is not the same as the country of manufacture, and the quantities of each type of weapon, munitions, equipment or other military supplies.

(4) Means of transport: listing the means of land, maritime or air transport, including the nationality.

(5) Extraregional transport routes: indicating the traffic routes used before arrival in Central American territory, including stops or intermediate destinations.

(6) Bases for the storage of weapons, munitions, equipment and other military supplies.

(7) Intraregional traffic areas and routes: describing the areas and routes and participation or consent by Governments or governmental or political sectors, for the conduct of the traffic in arms, including frequency of use of these areas and routes.

(8) International means of transport: specifying the means of transport used, the ownership of the vehicles and the facilities provided by Governments or governmental or political sectors, indicating whether war matériel is being unloaded by clandestine flights, whether packages are being dropped by parachute or whether small launches, loaded on the high seas, are being used.

A/39/562
S/16775
English
Page 27

(9) Receiving unit: determining the identity of the persons, groups or
organizations receiving the weapons.

- To verify compliance with this Act with regard to irregular forces and
the non-use of their own territory in destabilizing actions against
another State, and to consider any reports in that connection.

- To verify compliance with the procedures for notification of national or
joint military manoeuvres provided for in this Act.

(d) Rules and procedures

- The Commission shall receive any duly substantiated report concerning
violations of the security commitments assumed under this Act, shall
communicate it to the PARTIES involved and shall initiate such
investigations as it deems appropriate.

- The Commission shall carry out its investigations by making on-site
inspections, gathering testimony and using any other procedure which it
deems necessary for the performance of its functions.

- In the event of any reports of violations or of non-compliance with the
security commitments of this Act, the Commission shall prepare a report
containing recommendations addressed to the Parties involved.

- The Commission shall transmit all its reports to the Central American
Ministers for Foreign Affairs.

- The Commission shall be accorded every facility and prompt and full
co-operation by the PARTIES for the appropriate performance of its
functions. It shall also ensure the confidentiality of all information
elicited or received in the course of its investigations.

(e) Rules of procedure

After the Commission is established it shall draw up its own rules of
procedure and shall make them known to the PARTIES.

3. Ad Hoc Committee for Evaluation and Follow-up of Commitments concerning
Economic and Social Matters

(a) Composition

- For the purposes of this Act, the Meeting of Ministers responsible for
Central American Economic Integration shall constitute the Ad Hoc
Committee for Evaluation and Follow-up of Commitments concerning Economic
and Social Matters.

A/39/562
S/16775
English
Page 28

(b) Functions

- The Committee shall receive the reports of the PARTIES concerning progress in complying with commitments concerning economic and social matters.

- The Committee shall make periodic evaluations of progress made in complying with commitments with regard to economic and social matters, using for that purpose the information produced by the PARTIES and by the competent international and regional organizations.

- The Committee shall present, in its periodic reports, proposals for strengthening regional co-operation and promoting development plans, with particular emphasis on the aspects mentioned in the commitments contained in this Act.

PART III

FINAL PROVISIONS

1. The commitments made by the PARTIES in this Act are of a legal nature and are therefore binding.

2. This Act shall be ratified in accordance with the constitutional procedures established in each of the Central American States. The instruments of ratification shall be deposited with the Governments of the States members of the Contadora Group.

3. This Act shall enter into force when the five Central American signatory States have deposited their instruments of ratification.

4. The PARTIES, as from the date of signature, shall refrain from any acts which would serve to frustrate the object and purpose of this Act.

5. Thirty (30) days after the date of signature of this Act, the machinery referred to in Part II shall enter into operation on a provisional basis. The Parties shall take the necessary measures, before the end of that period, to ensure such provisional operation.

6. Any dispute concerning the interpretation or application of this Act which cannot be settled through the machinery provided for in Part II of this Act, shall be referred to the Ministers for Foreign Affairs of the PARTIES for consideration and a decision, requiring a unanimous vote in favour.

7. Should the dispute continue, it shall be referred to the Ministers for Foreign Affairs of the Contadora Group, who shall meet at the request of any of the PARTIES.

A/39/562
S/16775
English
Page 29

8.   The Ministers for Foreign Affairs of the States forming the Contadora Group shall use their good offices to enable the parties concerned to resolve the specific situation brought to their attention. After this venue has been tried, they may suggest another peaceful means of settlement of the dispute, in accordance with Article 33 of the Charter of the United Nations, and article 24 of the Charter of the Organization of American States.

9.   This Act shall not be subject to reservation.

10.   This Act shall be registered by the Parties with the Secretary-General of the United Nations and with the Secretary-General of the Organization of American States in accordance with Article 102 of the Charter of the United Nations, and article 118 of the Charter of the Organization of American States. DONE in the Spanish language, in nine original copies, at ..., on ... 1984.

A/39/562
S/16775
English
Page 30

ANNEX

THE PARTIES hereby agree on the following definitions of military terms:

1.   Register: Numerical or graphical data on military, paramilitary and security forces and military installations.

2.   Inventory: Detailed account of nationally- and foreign-owned arms and military equipment, with as many specifications as possible.

3.   Census: Numerical data on foreign military or civilian personnel acting in an advisory capacity on matters of defence and/or security.

4.   Military installation: Establishment or infrastructure including airfields, barracks, forts, camps, air and sea or similar installations under military jurisdiction, and their geographical location.

5.   Organization and equipment chart (OEC): document describing the mission, organization, equipment, capabilities and limitations of a standard military unit at its various levels.

6.   Military equipment: Individual and collective, nationally- or foreign-owned material, not including weapons, used by a military force for its day-to-day living and operations.

7.   Classification of weapons:

    (a) By nature:

        (i) Conventional.

        (ii) Chemical.

        (iii) Biological.

        (iv) Radiological.

    (b) By range:

        (i) Short: individual and collective portable weapons.

        (ii) Medium: non-portable support weapons (mortars, howitzers and cannons).

        (iii) Long: rockets and guided missiles, subdivided into:

            (a) Short-range rockets, with a maximum range of less than twenty (20) kilometres.

A/39/562
S/16775
English
Page 31

    (b) Long-range rockets, with a range of twenty (20) kilometres or more;

    (c) Short-range guided missiles, with a maximum range of one hundred (100) kilometres;

    (d) Medium-range guided missiles, with a range of between one hundred (100) and five hundred (500) kilometres;

    (e) Long-range guided missiles, with a range of five hundred (500) kilometres or more;

(c) By calibre and weight:

    1. Light: one hundred and twenty (120) milimetres or less;

    2. Medium: more than one hundred and twenty (120) and less than one hundred and sixty (160) milimetres;

    3. Heavy: more than one hundred and sixty (160) and less than two hundred and ten (210) milimetres;

    4. Very heavy: more than two hundred and ten (210) milimetres;

(d) By trajectory:

    (i) Weapons with a flat trajectory.

    (ii) Weapons with a curved trajectory.

        (a) Mortars;

        (b) Howitzers;

        (c) Cannons;

        (d) Rockets;

(e) By means of transportation:

    1. On foot;

    2. On horseback;

    3. Towed or drawn;

    4. Self-propelled;

    5. All weapons can be transported by road, rail, sea or air;

A/39/562
S/16775
English
Page 32

    6.   Those transported by air are classified as follows:

        (a) Transported by helicopter;

        (b) Transported by aeroplane.

8.   Characteristics to be considered in different types of aeroplanes and helicopters:

    (a) Model;

    (b) Quantity;

    (c) Crew;

    (d) Manufacture;

    (e) Speed;

    (f) Capacity;

    (g) System of propulsion;

    (h) Whether or not fitted with guns;

    (i) Type of weapons;

    (j) Radius of action;

    (k) Navigation system;

    (l) Communications system;

    (m) Type of mission performed.

9.   Characteristics to be considered in different ships or vessels:

    (a) Type of ship;

    (b) Shipyard and year of manufacture;

    (c) Tonnage;

    (d) Displacement;

    (e) Draught;

    (f) Length;

(g) System of propulsion;

(h) Type of weapons and firing system;

(i) Crew.

10. Services: logistical and administrative bodies providing general support for military, paramilitary and security forces.

11. Military training centres: establishments for the teaching, instruction and training of military personnel at the various levels and in the various areas of specialization.

12. Military base: land, sea or air space which includes military installations, personnel and equipment under a military command. In defining a foreign military base, the following elements should be taken into account:

- Administration and control;

- Sources of financing;

- Percentage ratio of local and foreign personnel;

- Bilateral agreements;

- Geographical location and area;

- Transfer of part of the territory to another State;

- Number of personnel.

13. Foreign military installations: those built for use by foreign units for the purposes of manoeuvres, training or other military objectives, in accordance with bilateral treaties or agreements; these installations may be temporary or permanent.

14. Foreign military advisers: military and security advisers means foreign military or civilian personnel performing technical, training or advisory functions in the following operational areas: tactics, logistics, strategy, organization and security, in the land, sea, air or security forces of Central American States, under agreements concluded with one or more Governments.

15. Arms traffic: arms traffic means any kind of transfer by Governments, individuals or regional or extra-regional groups of weapons intended for groups, irregular forces or armed bands that are seeking to destabilize Governments in the region. It also includes the passage of such traffic through the territory of a third State, with or without its consent, destined for the above-mentioned groups in another State.

16. National military manoeuvres: these are exercises or simulated combat or warfare carried out by troops in peacetime for training purposes. The armed forces

A/39/562
S/16775
English
Page 34

of the country participate on their own territory and may include land, sea and air
units, the object being to increase their operational capability.

17.   International military manoeuvres: these are all operations carried out by
the armed forces - including land, sea and air units - of two or more countries on
the territory of one of their countries or in an international area, with the
object of increasing their operational capability and developing joint
co-ordination measures.

18.   The inventories drawn up in each State, a separate one being made for each of
their armed forces, shall cover the personnel, weapons and munitions, equipment and
installations of the forces mentioned below, in accordance with their own
organizational procedures:

    (a) Security Forces:

        1.   Frontier guards;

        2.   Urban and rural guards;

        3.   Military forces assigned to other posts;

        4.   Public security force;

        5.   Training and instruction centre;

        6.   Other.

    (b) Naval Forces:

        1.   Location;

        2.   Type of base;

        3.   Number of vessels and characteristics of the naval fleet. Type of
             weapons;

        4.   Defence system. Type of weapons;

        5.   Communications systems;

        6.   War matériel services;

        7.   Air or land transport services;

        8.   Health services;

        9.   Maintenance services;

      10.   Administrative services;

A/39/562
S/16775
English
Page 35

11. Recruitment and length of service;

12. Training and instruction centres;

13. Other.

(c) Air Forces:

1. Location;

2. Runway capacity;

3. Number of aircraft and characteristics of the air fleet. Type of weapons;

4. Defence system. Type of weapons;

5. Communications system;

6. War _matériel_ services;

7. Health services;

8. Land transport services;

9. Training and instruction centres;

10. Maintenance services;

11. Administrative services;

12. Recruitment and length of service;

13. Other.

(d) Army Forces:

1. Infantry;

2. Motorized infantry;

3. Airborne infantry;

4. Cavalry;

5. Artillery;

6. Armoured vehicles;

A/39/562
S/16775
English
Page 36

    7.   Signals;

    8.   Engineers;

    9.   Special troops;

   10.   Reconnaissance troops;

   11.   Health services;

   12.   Transport services;

   13.   War *matériel* services;

   14.   Maintenance services;

   15.   Administrative services;

   16.   Military police;

   17.   Training and instruction centre;

   18.   Precise information on system of induction, recruitment and length of service must be given in this document;

   19.   Other.

(e)   Paramilitary forces.

(f)   Information required for airports: existing airfields:

    1.   Detailed location and category;

    2.   Location of installations;

    3.   Dimensions of take-off runways, taxi ways and maintenance strips;

    4.   Facilities: buildings, maintenance installations, fuel supplies, navigational aids, communications systems.

(g)   Information required for terminals and ports:

    1.   Location and general characteristics;

    2.   Entry and approach lanes;

    3.   Piers;

    4.   Capacity of the terminal.

A/39/562
S/16775
English
Page 37

(h) Personnel: Numerical data must be given for troops in active service, in the reserves, in the security forces and in paramilitary organizations. In addition, data on advisory personnel must include their number, immigration status, specialty, nationality and duration of stay in the country, and any relevant agreements or contracts.

(i) Weapons: munitions of all types, explosives, ammunition for portable weapons, artillery, bombs and torpedoes, rockets, hand grenades and rifle grenades, depth charges, land and sea mines, fuses, mortar and howitzer shells, etc., must be included.

(j) Domestic and foreign military installations: military hospitals and first-aid posts, naval bases, airfields and landing strips must be included.

A/39/562
S/16775
English
Page 38

ADDITIONAL PROTOCOL TO THE CONTADORA ACT ON
PEACE AND CO-OPERATION IN CENTRAL AMERICA

THE UNDERSIGNED PLENIPOTENTIARIES, invested with full powers by their respective
Governments:

CONVINCED that the effective co-operation of the international community is
necessary to guarantee the full force, effectiveness and viability of the Contadora
Act on Peace and Co-operation in Central America adopted by the countries of that
region,

Have agreed as follows:

1. To refrain from any acts which would serve to frustrate the object and purpose
    of the Act.

2. To co-operate with the Central American States on the terms they request by
    mutual consent, in order to achieve the object and purpose of the Act.

3. To lend all support to the Verification and Control Commission for Security
    Matters in the performance of its functions, when the Parties so require.

4. This Protocol shall be open to signature by all States desiring to contribute
    to peace and co-operation in Central America. It shall be signed in the
    presence of any of the Depositary Governments of the Act.

5. This Protocol shall enter into force for each signatory State on the date on
    which it has been signed by all of them.

6. This Protocol shall be deposited with the Governments of the States which
    comprise the Contadora Group.

7. This Protocol shall not be subject to reservation.

8. This Protocol shall be registered with the United Nations Secretariat in
    accordance with Article 102 of the United Nations Charter.

DONE in the Spanish language, in four original copies,
at   . . .   on   . . .   , 1984.

_____   _____
For the Government of Colombia   For the Government of Mexico

_____   _____
For the Government of Venezuela   For the Government of Panama

_____   _____
. . .   . . .

INDEX

THE CONTRIBUTORS

Licenciado Adolfo Aguilar Zinser is Coordinator of the Program of Central American Studies, CIDE, Mexico City, Mexico.

Ambassador Dr Alejandro Bendaña is Secretary General of the Ministry of Foreign Affairs, Managua, Nicaragua.

Dr Falk Bomsdorf is a Senior Researcher at the Stiftung Wissenschaft und Politik, Ebenhausen, Munich, West Germany.

Dr Jack Child is Associate Professor of Spanish and Latin American Studies at the American University, Washington DC, USA.

Licenciado Haroldo Dilla Alfonso is a Researcher on the Caribbean, Centro de Estudios sobre America, Havana, Cuba.

Dr Margaret Daly Hayes is Director of the Washington Office, Council of the Americas, Washington DC, USA.

Licenciada Helen McEachrane Dickson is Caribbean Coordinator, Research Institute for the Study of Man, New York City, USA.

Dr Richard Millett is Professor of History, Southern Illinois University, Edwardsville, Illinois, USA.

Dr Francisco Villagrán Kramer is a former Vice-President of Guatemala.

Dr Henry Wiseman is Professor of Political Studies, University of Guelph, Ontario, Canada.